Special Forces Operations
in South-East Asia
1941–1945

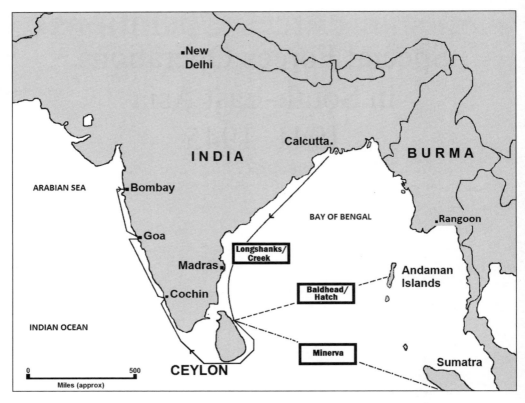

Operations Minerva, Baldhead/Hatch and Longshanks/Creek, 1942–1945

Special Forces Operations in South-East Asia 1941–1945

Minerva, Baldhead and Longshanks/Creek

DAVID MILLER

'Splendid men's deeds often go unnoticed,
Because lesser men fail to record them.'
Boethius, 480–574 AD

Pen & Sword
MILITARY

First published in Great Britain in 2015 by
PEN AND SWORD MILITARY
an imprint of
Pen and Sword Books Ltd
47 Church Street
Barnsley
South Yorkshire S70 2AS

ISBN 978 1 78340 063 8

A CIP record for this book is available from the British Library.

Printed and bound in England by
CPI Group (UK) Ltd, Croydon, CR0 4YY

Typeset in Times by CHIC GRAPHICS

Pen & Sword Books Ltd incorporates the imprints of
Pen & Sword Books Ltd incorporates the imprints of Pen & Sword
Archaeology, Atlas, Aviation, Battleground, Discovery,
Family History, History, Maritime, Military, Naval, Politics,
Railways, Select, Social History, Transport, True Crime,
Claymore Press, Frontline Books, Leo Cooper, Praetorian Press,
Remember When, Seaforth Publishing and Wharncliffe.

For a complete list of Pen and Sword titles please contact
Pen and Sword Books Limited
47 Church Street, Barnsley, South Yorkshire, S70 2AS, England
E-mail: enquiries@pen-and-sword.co.uk
Website: www.pen-and-sword.co.uk

Contents

List of Illustrations viii
List of Tables x
Preface xi
Acknowledgements xiii
Maps xv

Part I: Operation Minerva, Sumatra, 20 December 1942
Chapter 1   Introduction 2
Chapter 2   Sumatra 3
Chapter 3   Operation Minerva, Genesis 11
Chapter 4   The Men..17
Chapter 5   Air Force Participation 25
Chapter 6   The Operation: 20 December 1942.............................28
Chapter 7   Fate 32
Chapter 8   Analysis...36

Part II: Operations Baldhead and Hatch: Andaman Islands.
          1943–1945
Chapter 9   The Andaman Islands 46
Chapter 10   Operation Baldhead 1 55
Chapter 11   Operation Baldhead II 70
Chapter 12   Operation Baldhead III 74
Chapter 13   Operation Baldhead IV 76
Chapter 14   Operation Hatch..82
Chapter 15   Further Operations in the Andamans........................85
Chapter 16   Analysis 88

Part III: Operations Longshanks/Creek: Goa, 8/9 March 1943
Chapter 17   Introduction..92
Chapter 18   The Merchant Ship Situation 103
Chapter 19   Cutting-Out Expeditions 110
Chapter 20   The Situation to 1942...117

Chapter 21 SOE (India) 127
Chapter 22 Operation Hotspur 131
Chapter 23 The Plans 138
Chapter 24 The Units and the Men 144
Chapter 25 Preparations Completed..153
Chapter 26 The Voyage of the *Phoebe* (Hopper Barge Number 5) 155
Chapter 27 The Raid..161
Chapter 28 Aftermath in Goa 169
Chapter 29 Aftermath in London 174
Chapter 30 Analysis 177

Part IV: Envoi 184

Appendix A: Glossary and Abbreviations 185
Appendix B: Dennis Whitehouse 188
Appendix C: Sergeant Lau Teng Kee 193
Notes 201
Select Bibliography...212
Index 215

Dedication

Those who died on these operations are all commemorated on the Commonwealth War Graves Commission roll and named on a war memorial except for one. So, let this be his memorial:

SERGEANT LAU TENG KEE
of the British Army
died on (or shortly after) 20 December 1942
while taking part in Operation Minerva in Sumatra

List of Illustrations

Operation Minerva, Sumatra

Squadron-Leader Basil Russell, RAFVR, who conceived and led Operation Minerva.

Captain Alex Hunter, Royal Engineers, a civil engineer in Sumatra before the war.

Captain Fred Sladen, Bedfordshire and Hertfordshire Regiment.

Sergeant Lau Teng Kee and a group of university graduates after escaping Japanese-occupied Hong Kong in mid-1942.

A Consolidated Catalina of 321 Squadron RAF.

Lieutenant-Commander Gerard Rijnders, RNethN, the pilot on Operation Minerva.

Operation Baldhead, Andaman Islands

Major Terence Croley with his Royal Signals wireless telegraphists and an unknown Indian soldier.

Major Richard Duncan, Garwhal Rifles (left) and Major Terence Croley in their base camp on the Andaman Islands.

Major Terence Croley, Skinner's Horse, commander of Baldhead IV.

Captain Lawrence White, Royal Engineers, the explosives expert on Operations Longshanks (Goa) and Hatch I (Andamans).

Bombing of the Andamans sawmill on Chatham Island in Blair Harbour.

The Japanese formal surrender at Port Blair in October 1945.

Operation Longshanks/Creek, Goa

MV *Ehrenfels*, the target of the British operation.

The Italian SS *Anfora*.

Lieutenant-Colonel Bill Grice, commanding officer of the Calcutta Light Horse.

Captain Robert Hutton Duguid, 36, the leader of the Calcutta Scottish party.

Lieutenant-Colonel Lewis Pugh, Royal Artillery, chief planner for SOE(India).
Lieutenant Cren Sandys-Lumsdaine, Calcutta Light Horse.
Phoebe (Hopper Barge No. 5) in the 1930s.
Phoebe as she was when delivered to Calcutta in 1912.
The three German sailors captured aboard *Ehrenfels*.
The binoculars once owned by the Master of the *Ehrenfels*.

List of Tables

Operation Minerva, Sumatra
Table 1. Known Allied Operations in Sumatra, 1942 – early 1943.   8

Operation Longshanks/Creek, Goa
Table 2. Allied Merchant Ships Sunk in Areas Relevant to India.   101
Table 3: The Four Axis Merchant Ships.   122
Table 4: Armament of *Atlantis* and *Pinguin*.   125
Table 5: Operation Longshanks/Creek, 8/9 March 1943:
  Participants from the Calcutta Light Horse.   150
Table 6: The Voyage of the *Phoebe*.   159
Table 7: Allied Merchant Ship Losses in the Indian Ocean,
  March–December 1943.   178

Preface

This book tells the stories of three exciting and daring special operations in the Second World War, all in South-East Asia. One achieved brief fame in the early 1980s, thanks to a book and a film, while the other two remain virtually unknown. One was a complete success, one achieved a totally unintended success, and the third was a failure. In one the troops deployed by surface ship, in the second by submarine, and in the third by flying boat. All three were carried out by men of great courage and ability, who took great risks, and some of whom gave their lives – they all deserve to be remembered.

Operation Minerva was, most unusually, mounted by a staff branch in General Headquarters India and involved five men landing on Sumatra on 20 December 1942. Their task was to cross that island, whereupon two would go on to Singapore to assess the situation regarding the Allied prisoners-of-war, while the other three would seek to find any Allied personnel still at large in Sumatra. All five disappeared without trace and their fate remains unknown to this day.

Operation Baldhead, later known as Operation Hatch, was a series of landings on the Japanese-occupied Andaman Islands, which took place between January 1943 and May 1945. In these, successive parties of British and Indian troops spent months ashore and carried out daring reconnaissance patrols, gaining very valuable intelligence in the process. They were never once detected by the Japanese, but, had they been, they were grossly outnumbered, there was no prospect of rescue and they would have been annihilated.

Operation Longshanks, also known as Operation Creek, was the attempt on 8/9 March 1943 to capture one of the four Axis merchant ships sheltering in Portuguese Goa. It was a classical cutting-out expedition, with the aim of overpowering the crew and taking the ship to Bombay. This was not achieved, but all four of the Axis captains scuttled their ships, thus playing into British hands by removing the threat of any of them trying to escape. The episode was dramatised in a book – *Boarding Party* – followed by a film – *The Sea Wolves* – both of which were not only highly inaccurate, but also overplayed the amateur status of many of the participants.

To assist the reader, a glossary and list of abbreviations is at Appendix A. In the course of research for this book I have come across two very unusual stories concerning Able Seaman Dennis Whitehouse and Sergeant Lau Teng Kee. Their experiences deserve to be recorded, but since they lie outside the main thrust of the book, they are told in Appendixes B and C, respectively.

I have observed the following conventions:

- Place Names. All place names are as they were in 1942–45. Some names in the (then) Dutch East Indies were spelt in a variety of ways: Dutch, Malay, local usage and British maps. I have standardised on the latter.
- Ranks and Titles. These are as they were at the time of the operations described.
- Lists. Where any names are in a list, this is in alphabetical order of surnames, according to the English spelling and regardless of rank, importance or this author's personal preferences.
- Times. All times are local, unless specified otherwise, and use the 24-hour clock.
- Ship Measurement. Part III mentions merchant ships and their 'tonnage' which can be expressed in various ways. I have standardised on Gross Registered Tonnage (grt) which was in use from 1854 to 1969 and was calculated on the basis of one 'registered' ton equalling 100 cubic feet (2.83 cu m) of enclosed space. i.e., it represented the total internal volume of the vessel. This was the figure used to calculate harbour dues and to report wartime losses. For warships, I have used Full-Load Displacement, which is the weight of water displaced by a ship when fully loaded with fuel, ammunition, crew and stores.
- Abbreviations. Despite my best efforts, a number of abbreviations appear in the text. These are explained on first appearance, but are all also listed in Appendix A.

Acknowledgements

Personal Records

It is surprising how many veterans of the Second World War kept very quiet for many years about their wartime experiences but in later life either wrote it down for their family or made an audio recording for an archive. Most of these documents are unknown outside the family, or, in the case of tapes, listed in an obscure archival catalogue – until some persistent researcher comes along. I would, therefore, like to thank the following most sincerely for allowing me to access and quote from such accounts:

Bickersteth, A.C., privately published diary; book; via Joan MacMaster (daughter of Major Beaton Shearer, 4/10GR).

Bremner, Mrs Anne, unpublished memoir; document; via Mrs Ayeesha Nickol (daughter) and Dr Ian Bremner-Macdonald (son-in-law).

Croley, Major Terence V., Skinner's Horse; *Andaman Sortie*; unpublished memoir; document; via Brian Duncan, Esq (godson).

Davies, Commander B., RN (retd); *Boarding Party* (copy of book marked with extensive MS notes); via Cethin Davies, Esq (son).

Duguid, Lieutenant Robert H., Calcutta Scottish; *Account of Operation Creek*; unpublished memoir; document; via Mary Donald (daughter).

Grice, Lieutenant-Colonel William H., Calcutta Light Horse; *Operation Creek – 13th February to 10th March 1943*; unpublished memoir; document; via Jane Lloyd (daughter).

Pugh, Lieutenant-Colonel Lewis, Royal Artillery; unpublished memoir; document; via his family.

Rijnders, Lieutenant-Commander Gerard F., DFC, Royal Netherlands Naval Air Service; unpublished memoir; document; via Gerardjan Rijnders, Esq (son).

Russell, Squadron-Leader Basil H. S., RAFVR; personal diary; document; via Brian Peek, Esq.

White, Major Lawrence V. S., Royal Engineers; unpublished memoir; document; via Oliver Hunter, Esq. (grandson)

Whitehouse, Able Seaman Dennis, Royal Navy; private interview; tape; via Mrs Pearl Metcalfe.

I also wish to thank the following who were all extremely helpful with information, documents and photographs:

LTC Josepha Altersitz, US Army (retd), Nikki Archer-Waring, C. Burton Stewart, Iris Chan, Professor Peter Cunich, Cethin Davies, John Duguid, Pauline Eismark, Jeff Elson, John Hembry, Chris Hoare, Captain Ho Wing Tho, Oliver Hunter, Brigadier Simon Knapper, the late Alison Krohn, Herry Lawford, Ian MacDonald, James McCarthy, Chris Miller, Ayesha Nickol, Barry Peek, Elizabeth Ride, Cren Sandys-Lumsdaine, Professor Bill Sladen, Ian Standen, Professor Patrick Seow Koon Tan, Linda Willis and Sally Wilson.

Maps

Map 1. Sumatra.
Only places relevant to
this book are shown.

Pulau Weh
Kota Raja
Lhoeksomawa
STRAITS OF
Meulaboh
Medan
MALACCA
MALAYA
Troemon
Permatangsiantar
Trang
Singkil
Lake
Toba
Simaleur
Baroes
Sibolga
Nias
Singapore
Rhio Is
0°
0°
Rengat
Padang
Siberut
SUMATRA
Bangka
INDIAN
Palembang
OCEAN
Bencoolen
0   50   100
Miles
© D. Miller 2014
SUNDA STRAITS
Batavia

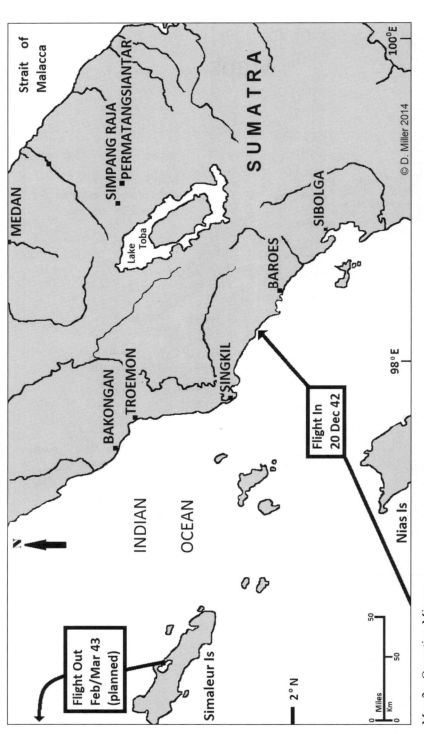

Map 2a. Operation Minerva.
The aircraft flew from Ceylon and passed just to the north of Nias island, where it came under anti-aircraft fire. The landing was between the main beach and a tiny island, Pulau Pandjang, in a deserted area between Baroes and Singkil. The only other firmly known location was their proposed departure point from Dalam Bay on Simaleur Island: how they intended to get there is a mystery.

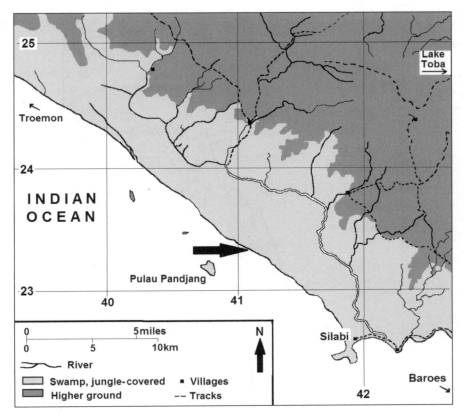

Map 2b. The Minerva Landing.
This is based on a British 1943 map: Rantauparapat GSGS 4550. It shows only a few small, widely separated villages, each with probably no more than 100 inhabitants at most, connected by tracks and footpaths, but no roads. The Dutch Catalina flew in from the south-south-west and then came down on the water in the lee of Pulau Pandjang, an island so small that it is not marked on most maps – the arrow shows the approximate place where Squadron-Leader Russell and his comrades went ashore.

There was a very narrow beach and then a large area of dense, swampy jungle. It is not known exactly where Russell and his party were heading, although Lake Toba seems most probable, but whatever their heading the map shows that they would have to cross a wide area of swamp before reaching the primary jungle at higher level. They were heavily loaded, progress would have been slow and arduous, and they would have had to keep well away from both local Sumatrans and Japanese patrols. But somewhere – quite when and where are not known – their luck ran out.

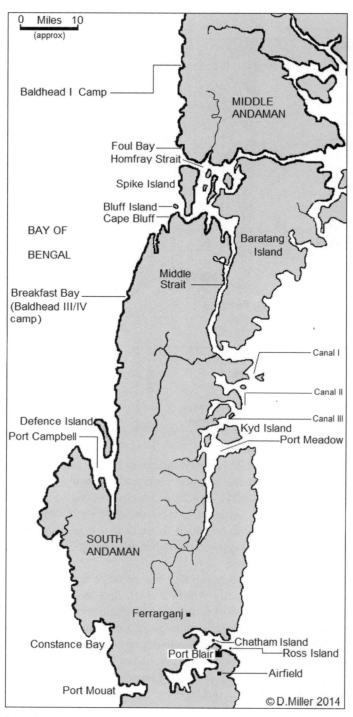

Map 3. Central Andamans.

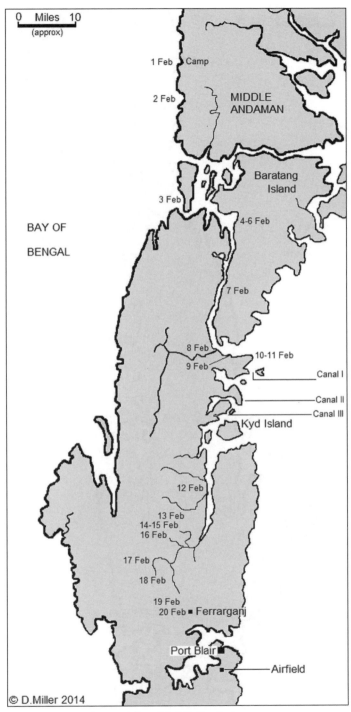

Map 4a. Operation Baldhead I. McCarthy's route out.

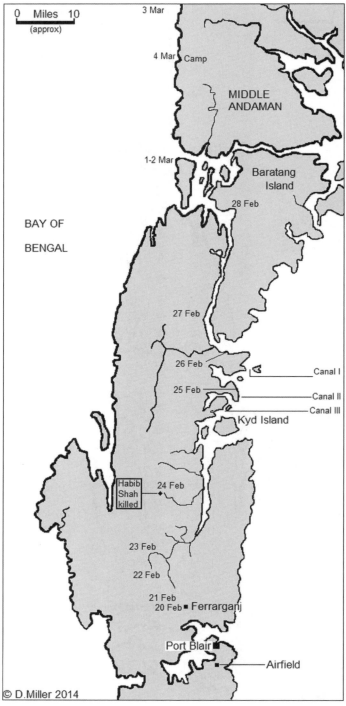

Map 4b. Operation Baldhead I. McCarthy's route back to base.

PART I

Operation Minerva:
Sumatra, 20 December 1942

Chapter 1

Introduction

Tucked away on the shelves of the British National Archives is the final report of an obscure branch of GHQ India which, among many other items, includes four short paragraphs on Operation Minerva, which took place in December 1942. The report states that a Squadron-Leader Russell had 'conceived and executed' a plan whose object was 'to land a party in SUMATRA to contact evaders who had reached SUMATRA after the fall of SINGAPORE, and later to attempt to contact the PW Camps on SINGAPORE ISLAND itself'.[1] In this daring operation a flying boat delivered five men to a beach on the coast of Sumatra and not one of them was ever heard of again. That the operation did not succeed cannot be disputed, but it was a courageous attempt to alleviate the desperate plight of the Allied prisoners-of-war in Singapore and deserves to be better known.

As there were at least three operations with this name, some early clarification is required. The first Operation Minerva concerned the transport of French General Giraud from France to Gibraltar in November 1942, while the last was a planned massive British reinforcement of the Far East in 1945 (which never took place). The second – and the subject here – took place in Sumatra on 20 December 1942 and receives only the briefest mention in a few published histories of the Far East campaign. No records specific to this operation can be found in the National Archives, Imperial War Museum, British Library or RAF Museum. However, the flight logs of the aircraft concerned contain some information and there is some more in the Netherlands Institute of Military History and in the Air Historical Branch. Detailed research makes it clear that five men took part, all of whom disappeared without trace and were later presumed killed by the Japanese: three are commemorated on the Singapore War Memorial, one on the Rangoon War Memorial, and the fifth has no known memorial at all.

Chapter 2

Sumatra

The Japanese invaded north Malaya on 7 December 1941 and swept down the peninsula, crossing to Singapore Island on 8 February 1942 and accepting the British surrender on 15 February. They paused only briefly before continuing their onward rush into Burma, the Dutch East Indies and the British Borneo territories. Many of the British and Allied troops in Malaya and Singapore had no choice but to pass into Japanese prisoner-of-war camps, but a significant number tried to escape, either by crossing the Straits of Malacca to the Dutch East Indies islands of Java and Sumatra, or by attempting to sail direct to India or Ceylon. Many of these were intercepted and either killed or captured by the Japanese, but several thousand got through. However, because the great majority of these escapes were the efforts of small groups or even individuals, the British and Dutch had no idea of the numbers involved, how many had been killed or captured, and how many survived and if so, where they were.

The Japanese attack on Sumatra began at dawn on 12 March 1942 with unopposed landings at Sabang on Pulau Weh Island, just off the northern tip, and on the mainland at Kota Raja (now Banda Atjeh), Idi and Laboehanroekoe. Also on 12 March 1942, Japanese forces reached the important town and airfield at Medan. Dutch forces offered almost no resistance and the conquest of the island was completed on 28 March 1942 when the Dutch commander surrendered with about 2,000 men at Kabanjahe, some 50 miles due south of Medan. This left the formed British units in Sumatra with no option but to surrender as well. In all but a few cases the Indonesians welcomed the Japanese as 'liberators' and many nationalists who had been imprisoned by the Dutch were released, including two of the leaders, Soekarno and Mohammed Hatta. Regardless of events on the ground, however, as far as the British were concerned in 1942–43, the Dutch were the colonial rulers of Sumatra and would be restored to that position at the end of the war.

Following the Japanese occupation of Sumatra, the British and Dutch remained interested in the island for a variety of reasons. Although a considerable distance from Ceylon (1,000 miles) it could be reached by submarines and longer-ranged aircraft, such as the Catalina amphibian. The island included some major resources, the most important of which were the oil fields near Palembang, together with rubber plantations and tea estates. Just off the northern tip of Sumatra was the island of Pulau Weh, whose airfield and harbour at Sabang were of strategic importance as they commanded the northern end of the Straits of Malacca. Although many Australian, British and Dutch servicemen had escaped through Sumatran ports, particularly Padang and Medan, it was believed that there were a number still on the island, who had so far evaded capture, but how many and where they were was not known.

As soon as the Japanese attacked Malaya and the Philippines the Allies established ABDACOM (American-British-Dutch-Australian Command) but after the Japanese had completely overrun Malaya and Indonesia this was disbanded. Responsibility for future operations in Sumatra then came under the British Commander-in-Chief (CinC) India, General Wavell, the only part of the Dutch East Indies (DEI) to do so. The Dutch officer responsible for national interests was Admiral Conrad Helfrich of the Royal Netherlands Navy (RNethN), who had been one of the last to escape from Java. He established his base in Colombo, Ceylon, and in April 1942 was joined by two Dutch Army officers from the UK: Major H. G. C. Pel and Capt J. Scheepens. A number of Dutch submarines, small surface warships and a flying boat squadron had also escaped from the DEI, but while these remained under Dutch administrative control, they were under the operational control of the British.

The Island
Sumatra (see Map 1) is a huge, jungle-covered, sparsely populated island some 1,100 miles in length and 270 at its widest. The Dutch had been in the East Indies since the sixteenth century, but their hold on Sumatra was always disputed and even in areas under their more-or-less 'firm' control their presence was never completely accepted. Under Dutch rule, the island was part of the DEI and was divided by them into a number of administrative regions. The Province of North Sumatra, with a

predominantly Christian population, was reasonably firmly controlled, but the north-western end of the island was the historic Sultanate of Aceh, an Islamic state, which fiercely resisted the Dutch and did not come under their control until the twentieth century. Indeed, even after their 'victory' in the pacification campaign of 1912, Aceh continued to be a thorn in the side of the Dutch rulers, with pockets of resistance surviving until independence in 1945.

When the Japanese invaded Malaya, it was clear that the DEI were under threat, but since the home country – the Netherlands – was occupied by the Germans, there was no question of more than a very few Dutch reinforcements. The British therefore sent increasing numbers of RAF bomber and fighter units, together with some Army units, mostly Royal Artillery armed with anti-aircraft guns. These were concentrated on Sumatra around the oil fields at Palembang, although there were some in the other parts of the DEI.

Apart from these British troops officially stationed in Sumatra, a stream of men started to escape from Malaya and Singapore. Some of these were ordered to make their way back to India, such as Captain Sladen (see below), while others used their initiative to escape during or immediately after the surrender. Anticipating such a possibility, an escape route had been organised by Lt Col Alan Warren, a Royal Marine, of the SOE (Orient Mission), which was known as the River Indraghiri Escape Line. A number of way stations were established with dumps of food, medical supplies and weapons, with directions to the next station. This route led from one island to another in the Rhio Archipelago, which lies to the south of Singapore, up the River Indraghiri and then across the island to the railhead and then onwards to the small port of Padang on the south coast. At Padang a lieutenant-colonel organised a British camp, where the escapers were fed and organised before being called forward to the next available ship. Some 2,600 men were evacuated from Padang between 18 February and 6 March, but many either did not reach Padang, or did so after the last ship had left. Not all escapers followed this route, however, and some headed down to the south-western tip of Sumatra at Oesthaven where they tried to find a ferry to take them across the strait to Java, where they hoped to find other ships which would take them to Australia. Yet others headed across the Straits of Malacca to Medan where they hoped to find ships to take them to Ceylon.

Before turning to Operation Minerva, a number of other operations involving Sumatra need to be mentioned. Operation Mickleham was a plan to smuggle raw rubber out of Malaya to depots in Sumatra and thence to Ceylon; it never actually took place, but featured in Allied planning for many months. Although its planning did not start until after Operation Minerva had taken place and it was never actually launched, Operation Culverin should also be mentioned. This was conceived by Churchill in late 1943 and involved invading north-western Sumatra, which would then be used as a stepping-stone for invasions of Singapore and Malaya, as well as denying the use of the Straits of Malacca to the Japanese navy. Culverin also involved a smaller island, Simaleur, which lay some 100 miles due west of Troemon which was seen as a possible forward air base for the invasion of Sumatra.

As so often in the Second World War, several quite different organisations had an interest in Sumatra. One of these was described to Lieutenant Boris Hembry, when he was summoned to Calcutta in January 1943 for an interview with a Colonel Heath, who explained that:

> . . . he (Heath) was in charge of the Calcutta end of an organisation code-named Inter-Services Liaison Department (ISLD), a branch of the Secret Intelligence Service (MI6), whose headquarters were in Delhi. ISLD was charged with obtaining military and civil intelligence out of Burma, Indo-China, Siam, Malaya and the Dutch East Indies. He, Heath, was busy building up the Calcutta office to manage the various country sections but had not, so far, got anyone for a Malayan section. Would I go to Sumatra? I said that Sumatra was not Malaya. He said that he was well aware of that, but I had worked in Sumatra, and the immediate priority was Sumatra. So, on the basis of the year I had spent in Atjeh, twelve years before, I joined ISLD.

Heath went on to explain that:

> . . .Winston Churchill was strongly in favour of invading Sumatra in order to set up the necessary bases from which to recapture Malaya, Singapore and the Dutch East Indies. The Chiefs of Staff were not in favour of such an enterprise, and certainly not until

they had knowledge of the strength and disposition of Japanese forces in Sumatra. No intelligence of any description had been forthcoming from Sumatra since its capitulation a year earlier.[2]

ISLD was responsible for obtaining intelligence, but prime responsibility for land operations in Sumatra lay with the Anglo-Dutch Country Section of the India Mission of SOE. This was commanded by Lieutenant-Colonel Christopher Hudson of the Royal Army Service Corps, with a Dutch second-in-command, Major F. Mollinger, later succeeded by Major H. G. C. Pel. This Dutch officer was also the commanding officer of the 40-strong *1st Detachment Korps Insulinde*. This unit had been raised and trained in the UK in 1941 and then sailed for the Far East on 7 January 1942, but was still at sea when the Japanese conquered the islands, so it was diverted to Ceylon, arriving in March 1942. Only two of its men had ever been to Sumatra before and none spoke Malay.

Initially, there was some disagreement between the British and Dutch in SOE(India) as to what type of operations were to be conducted in Sumatra. The British wanted to infiltrate agents who would remain for long periods, obtaining information, making contact with local elements prepared to resist the Japanese, and then supplying them with arms and equipment, as was being done in Europe and would be done later in Malaya. Helfrich and the Dutch, on the other hand, favoured commando-style raids of the 'go in, shoot everything in sight, and then go home' variety.

In order to place Operation Minerva in context it is necessary to review all Allied operations which took place in the Sumatra area in 1942–43 – see Table 1.

On 3 May 1942 the Dutch submarine HNethMS *K-XV* sailed from Colombo, carrying First Lieutenant H. E. Wijnmalen to Sumatra, an island he knew well. He landed alone in a rubber dinghy on 12 May at Bonegoebaai near Padang. The submarine then withdrew to patrol off the island of Nias until returning to the rendezvous to re-embark Wijnmalen, but he was not there. After waiting for two days the submarine returned to Ceylon. After the war British and Dutch investigators established that, despite speaking both Malay and Aceh, he had been quickly captured by the Japanese, tortured by the *Kempetei* (secret police) and, when he refused to give any information, tried and

Table 1. Known Allied Operations in Sumatra, 1942–early 1943.

Date	Code-name	By whom	Where	Transport	Landing party
12 May 42	Operation Wijnmalen[3]	Wijnmalen (alone)	Padang	Submarine *K-XV*	Aim was intelligence gathering, but Wijnmalen was captured, tortured, executed
13-16 Dec 42	Operation Troemon	Pel + 11 men; Korps Insulindie	Troemon Meulaboh	Submarine *O-24*	Troemon landing successful; no casualties. Meulaboh landing cancelled
20 Dec 42	Operation Minerva I	5 men (all British)	Pulau Simaleur	Flying boat; 321 Squadron	All missing. See below
13 Feb 43	Not known	Capt Scheepens + 9 Dutch	North coast Sumatra	Submarine *O-24*	No landing due to heavy surf
20, 25 Feb; 23 Mar 43	Operation Minerva II	321 Squadron	Pulau Simaleur	Flying boat 321 Squadron	3 attempts to recover Minerva I party. Nobody at RV
17-19 Apr 43	Operation Valour — Operation Matriarch	Capt Scheepens + 5 Dutch, plus 2 British (Sqn Ldr Brittain, Capt Hembry)	Troemon (17 Apr) Meulaboh (19 Apr) Kuala Trang (20 Apr)	Submarine *O-24*	Two groups with separate code names, but working together

condemned to death as a spy. He died from a pistol shot, although there was some dispute as to whether this was self-administered or performed by his captors. He was buried in Padang cemetery.[4] There were no further known landings until December 1942.

Operation Troemon was an altogether larger, more ambitious undertaking, with a party being transported to Sumatra by the Dutch submarine, HNethMS *O-24*, commanded by Lt Cdr W. J. de Vries, RNethN.[5] *O-24* sailed from Colombo on 6 December 1942 on a patrol scheduled to last for 18 days. After dark the submarine rendezvoused off the Dutch Army's Ceylon base, known as Camp D (Laksapitya) with a launch carrying ten men (five officers, five other ranks) of the *1st Korps Insulindie* commanded by Major Pel. In the early hours of 7 December a landing exercise was conducted to test procedures, practice launch/recovery of folboats (folding canoes), and so on. These rehearsals completed, the submarine sailed for Sumatra.

O-24 arrived off Troemon on 12 December and the party was successfully landed that night and spent two days ashore, returning to the submarine, as planned, in the early hours of 14 December. De Vries then sailed northwards and by 16 December was off Pulau Weh. He stayed in the area for several days conducting observations through the periscope, but apart from seeing a few aircraft he had nothing to report, and then sailed for Colombo on 19 December, arriving right on schedule at 1000 hours on 24 December.

Next in chronological order was Operation Minerva, which is dealt with in detail in the following chapters. In outline, it involved a landing party of five men, who were flown to western Sumatra on 20 December 1942 in a Dutch Catalina aircraft. They are known to have paddled ashore in dinghies, but were never seen again.

Another landing attempt, this time with an unrecorded codename, was made on 13 February 1943. A party of seven Dutchmen, led by Captain Scheepens, was transported by *O-24* with the aim of landing on the northwest coast, near the village of Lhoeksoemawa. This was prevented by a combination of heavy surf and bad weather, and they returned to Ceylon.

Operation Valour/Matriarch was the first to be planned and controlled by Lieutenant-Colonel Hudson and the Anglo-Dutch section of SOE (India). It was commanded by Captain Scheepens, and consisted of six Dutch and two British, Squadron-Leader Leon Brittain, RAFVR, and Captain Boris Hembry, in March 1943. Their mission was described by Hembry as follows:

> We were to contact villagers to obtain as much information regarding the enemy's troop strengths and dispositions as possible, and also to bring back to Colombo two intelligent and well-travelled native Atjehnese for prolonged interrogation. These unfortunates were to accompany us willingly or unwillingly, it mattered not which.[6]

A requirement to bring back two prisoners was to be common to many SOE operations, but this was to be the first time it was issued.

Scheepens and his men (Dutch and British) got ashore and made contact with a number of locals, but these proved lukewarm at best. On its return to the beach, the Anglo-Dutch party was ambushed by the Japanese, who had been alerted by one or more locals, but all managed to make it back to the submarine. The group then tried to make a second landing in a different location but were foiled by the surf, although they did get ashore at a third location where, as instructed, they kidnapped two Achinese farmers and took them back to Colombo, where they were interrogated about conditions under Japanese rule. According to Hembry, these men spent the rest of the war in some comfort at British expense.[7]

These landings, while not particularly successful, show that, despite the defeats by the Japanese in 1941 and early 1942, British and Dutch planners were quick to consider clandestine operations in enemy-held Sumatra, although after the unexplained disappearance of Lieutenant Wijnmalen in May 1942 there was a long gap until December 1942/January 1943, after which a series of operations in Sumatra were undertaken by SOE. These involved infiltration and extraction by Dutch submarines, the first by *K-XV*, but the remainder by *O-24*, whose captain and crew clearly developed considerable expertise in this field and was undoubtedly the reason for the award of the British Distinguished Service Cross (DSC) to the commanding officer, Lt Cdr de Vries, RNethN. Operation Minerva was, however, to be quite different.

Chapter 3

Operation Minerva: Genesis

Military Intelligence Department 9 (MI9) was officially formed in London on 23 December 1939. Its primary tasks were to facilitate and encourage escapes by British and Commonwealth prisoners-of-war (PW) from camps, and instructing those who might find themselves in enemy territory, such as downed bomber crews. MI9 was also responsible for collecting and disseminating information on enemy interrogation methods and treatment of PW, and in maintaining the morale of British and Commonwealth PW in enemy prison camps. In pursuit of these tasks MI9 ran courses and gave lectures on the art of escape and avoiding capture; and in anti-interrogation techniques, as well as devising, manufacturing and distributing escape aids. The majority of its staff were Army, but with strong RAF representation at all levels, and a lesser, but still substantial, RN presence.

In the Army's General Headquarters India a sub-section of the General Staff Intelligence (GSI) branch was established in October 1941 to carry out the MI9 functions in South-East Asia. This was originally part of GSI(d), but in May 1942 it was separated out to become GSI(e) and its head, from 1941 to 1943, was Lieutenant-Colonel W. R. Ridgway, a Territorial Army officer and peacetime master at Winchester College. GSI(e) had subsidiary offices in Calcutta and Ceylon, and was the superior HQ for the British Army Aid Group in China. It also ran the Combined Services Detailed Interrogation Centre (India) (CSDIC(I)) which was located in the Red Fort, Delhi, where it debriefed escapees from prisoner-of-war camps and interrogated the few captured Japanese that came their way. Finally, GSI(e) ran two training camps, one in India, the other in Ceylon.

When the Germans overran Western Europe MI9 in London was able to rapidly build up a picture of the locations of the PW camps they had established and the status of their inmates. This was achieved partly through information provided by the Germans themselves to the International Committee of the Red Cross (ICRC), partly from the ICRC's own resources, and also through PW mail and photographic reconnaissance. There was also a regular trickle of escapees, who could provide first-hand information. But, the situation in South-East Asia was quite different, because when the Japanese invaded Malaya, Burma and the Dutch East Indies their advances were so fast and so unexpected that few networks could be established to feed information back to India. Further, for many months the Japanese would allow virtually no PW mail, while the activities of the ICRC were so restricted by the Japanese as to be useless for GSI(e)'s purposes. Thus, while it was obvious that there were large numbers of prisoners-of-war in Singapore, Malaya and other former British territories, in mid-1942 virtually nothing was known for certain as to the location of the camps and the state of their inmates.

A complicating factor was that some British and Australian units been deployed to the Dutch East Indies, many of them to Sumatra, in the period immediately prior to the Japanese invasion of that island, and it was thought that an unknown number of these men, plus some Dutch, might have avoided capture and be at large somewhere in the Sumatran hinterland. Further, numerous men from Malaya and Singapore were known to have evaded Japanese capture and crossed to Sumatra and then either made their way across the island to ports on its south coast, or crossed the Sunda Straits into Java. Many had found ships to take them to Ceylon or Australia, but it seemed possible that some had not and might be still at large, somewhere in the Sumatran hinterland. One shining example was Corporal Charles McCormac, DCM, who was captured at the fall of Singapore, but escaped from a camp several days later (about 15 February) with sixteen others. The party was gradually depleted, but McCormac and one companion travelled the length of Sumatra and then of Java until being picked up by an Australian flying boat on 16 September.[8] A truly remarkable journey of some 2,000 miles that begged the question: if these two had done it, could there be any more, still trapped in Sumatra?

The one place where GSI(e) did know what was going on was in Hong Kong, which was thanks to a remarkable unit, designated the British

Army Aid Group (BAAG) that had been founded by Lieutenant-Colonel Lindsay Ride. A pre-war professor in the Hong Kong University Medical School, Ride commanded the Defence Corps Field Ambulance at the time of the Japanese invasion and after the short campaign became a prisoner. He then made one of the earliest escapes and on reaching Free China established the BAAG, whose initial mission was to make contact with prisoners and civilians still in Hong Kong who wished to escape and enable them to do so; it also gathered useful military intelligence on Hong Kong and southern China.

GSI(e) in New Delhi became aware of this new organisation in China because the BAAG's mission clearly placed it within the MI9 sphere of responsibility. As a result, Squadron-Leader Basil Russell, RAFVR, who had just arrived in GSI(e) was sent to China to make contact.[9] He arrived in Chungking by air on 22 June 1942, where he had meetings with a variety of high-ranking officials, including the Military Attaché (Brigadier Grimsdale), the Air Attaché, the local representative of the Ministry of Economic Warfare, and the Chinese Minister of War (General Shang Cheung). He then travelled on to Kukong[10] to meet Ride on 7 July, staying there until the 17th, when he returned to Chungking, before flying back to Calcutta on the 25th, from whence he took the train to New Delhi. He immediately wrote a report which so impressed his superiors that General Wavell summoned him to a meeting to discuss it on 1 August – quite an honour for a relatively junior staff officer.

One of the matters Ride had discussed with Russell and which the latter now raised at GHQ was a proposal for a full-scale military operation to rescue a large number of prisoners from Hong Kong. Originally known simply as 'the Ride plan', then as 'the Big Event', this rapidly developed momentum and was then adopted officially and given the name Operation Chopsticks. This would start with a heavy bombing raid by US aircraft on known Japanese military positions on Hong Kong island and the New Territories, and in the resulting confusion a British Indian Army parachute brigade would carry out an assault landing to take over an area in the vicinity of the main PW camp, into which the prisoners would be assembled, prior to being moved overland into Free China. This was an extraordinarily ambitious plan and Russell managed to convince Wavell that it was worth pursuing.

The Chopsticks plan also caused Russell to consider extending it, and his diary records that on 10 August 1942 that: '. . . this morning Sladen[11] and I had a session dealing with the M[alayan] campaign as a result of which I worked out a scheme which I have put up to the D.M.I.'.[12] This would appear to have been the genesis of Operation Minerva, which, from the start, Russell clearly meant to be his own.

Interest in Chopsticks grew rapidly and on 13 August Russell attended a meeting with three British staff officers – General Sir Alan Hartley (Deputy CinC), Lieutenant-General G. N. Molesworth (Deputy Chief of the General Staff at GHQ India), and the Director of Military Intelligence – and two United States commanders – General J. W. Stillwell (commanding US Forces in China, Burma and India) and Major-General C. L. Bissell (Commanding General 10th US Air Force in India and Burma). These were very senior officers, indeed, and Russell, as an acting squadron-leader, was very much the junior, and in his diary he admits that he was rather 'outweighted', but he clearly held his own, and Chopsticks was approved in principle, with Russell being tasked to draft a letter on the subject to the British liaison officer to Generalissimo Chiang Kai-shek.

Meanwhile, Russell was also furthering his own plan and on 25 August he set out for Colombo, arriving there on the 29th. He carried a personal letter of introduction to Admiral Sir Geoffrey Layton (CinC Ceylon), which gained him a face-to-face meeting with the CinC and his chief-of-staff, who agreed his plan in outline. Confident now that his plan would come to fruition, Russell started looking for people. Sladen had already volunteered and, since he worked for Russell and had some, albeit brief, experience of Sumatra, was no problem. Russell was also keen on someone he identified in his diary as 'J', but for an unknown reason he was not included in the final party. Russell also appears to have fallen out with SOE (India) over some unspecified personnel matters, saying that he was '. . . again being double-crossed by MacKenzie'.[13] Whatever the problem was, it was solved by a letter from Russell to the DMI, following which Russell held a meeting with Major Burton Stewart, MacKenzie's deputy.

Russell was back in GHQ on 23 September and on 29 September Colonel Ride arrived from China to discuss a modified form of Chopsticks. Ride stayed until 8 October during which time he and Russell promoted their projects, briefing the DMI on 5 October, who gave his consent to Russell's proposal, albeit with some reluctance. It was also clear that no submarine would be available, so the proposal was recast to include insertion by air and another meeting was held in early October, chaired by DMI, with Air Commodore Darvall, Colonel Hutton and Russell. As DMI explained in a subsequent letter to the Deputy Senior Air Staff Officer (DSASO) they had discussed Operation Chopsticks and then: 'Preliminary reconnaissance for operation to assist British Prisoners-of-War to escape from SINGAPORE. As it will be necessary for a party of four individuals to reconnoitre the area before forming a plan will you please approve of 222 Group dropping a party off the coast of SUMATRA by Catalina.'[14]

Russell immediately set to work and within days was assembling both men and the stores for his operation, recording that he was 'having great fun and games over jungle kits . . . equipment wallahs being obstructive'. Also on the 8th he met a newly-commissioned officer, Alex Hunter, who had worked as a civil engineer in Sumatra for some years, liked what he saw, and recruited him to the team. On 16 October Russell was able to record that his operation had been allocated the name 'Minerva', although once again Brigadier Cawthorn was expressing reservations. Russell also recruited two other men for his operation. He does not describe the process by which he found them, but they were Lance-Bombardier Richard Keyt of the Royal Artillery who, like Sladen, had escaped across Sumatra, and Lau Teng Kee, one of Colonel Ride's agents from the BAAG. Both these men were promoted to the rank of sergeant, to give them some status. On 22 October Russell received confirmation from 222 Group RAF in Ceylon that 'the show is a feasible one. It should come off in about 7 weeks all being well.' He also took the opportunity for himself, Hunter and Sladen to have medical boards, which all passed as 'A1'.

On 26 October official sanction was at last given for Operation Minerva, Russell commenting that 'It has been a long business and I often feel that our greatest obstacle is GHQ'. He worked off his irritation by taking Hunter and Sladen to the range to fire their Sten guns. However, his confidence was clearly recorded in his diary: 'With the new Axis [i.e., Japanese] attitude to P.O.W. I feel that we have taken on a new importance and our show is one that must become a very important one. It is chiefly operationally that we can become of any use, as the instructional part can have little value beyond bucking up morale . . .'

No trace of the operational order can be found, and Minerva is only referred to in passing in a few documents. However, Russell's plan can be reconstructed with a reasonable degree of confidence. Deployment (see Map 2a and 2b) would involve four aircraft, all Catalinas. Three would attack targets in the northern tip of Sumatra to distract Japanese attention, while the fourth, from 321 Squadron, would carry the landing party to a beach on the western coast of Sumatra. On arrival, Russell's party would land using rubber dinghies and then move off in the general direction of Lake Toba. In this phase they would depend upon Captain Hunter's local knowledge of conditions and the people, particularly in the areas of Simpang Raja and Permatangsiantar where he had worked for some years. The party would then establish a base somewhere on the northern coast of Sumatra.

The next phase required men to cross the Strait of Malacca and it is assumed that this would only have been Keyt and Lau, who could merge into the local population, whereas the three Caucasian officers could never do so. They would then make their way to Singapore and once there would assess the general situation, discover the location of the PW camps and attempt to make contact with some of the prisoners. Keyt and Lau would then return to Sumatra, reunite with the others and all five would make their way back across the island to a point on the coast some distance to the north of where they had landed. They would then cross to Simaleur Island. Quite how they intended to cross the 100-odd miles to Simaleur and why it was thought necessary is unclear. The Japanese would almost certainly have had officials at all ports, making it impossible for the three officers to board a ferry, so they would have had to beg, borrow or steal a suitable boat from one of the small fishing ports on the Sumatran coast. They would be recovered from Dalam Bay on Simaleur's north-east coast. A 321 Squadron Catalina would again be used and three dates were agreed: 21 and 22 February, and 21 March. They were thus planning to remain undetected and travel considerable distances in Japanese-occupied territory for between sixty-three and eighty-one days, which seems excessively optimistic. Anyway, that was the outline plan and now it is necessary to take a closer look at the men involved.

Chapter 4

The Men

The men who took part in Operation Minerva were a mixed group: two Englishmen, one Scot, one Malayan Eurasian and one Malayan Chinese; three officers, two sergeants; two regulars, three wartime-only; one married, four not. Although all except one had previous military experience, none had operated behind enemy lines or in a jungle environment before.

Basil Russell

Basil Henry Sackville Russell was named in a 1945 report on the wartime activities of a staff branch in GHQ India, which stated, quite unequivocally, that 'the plan [for Operation Minerva] was conceived and executed by S/Ldr Russell . . .'.[15] Thus, any consideration of this operation must start with this officer. Basil Russell was born in 1904, the second son of a senior official in the Atlantic Cable Company. He spent at least part of his school years at Chateau de Mesnières-en-Bray in Normandy, which accounted for his excellent command of French, and his first jobs were as a representative for various companies, on whose behalf he travelled widely in Africa, Europe and North America. In 1925 he married Barbé Rapinsky, a Parisian of Polish descent, but divorced her in 1934 and the following year married Jocelyn Castleden. The latter couple lived in Portugal from 1936 to 1939, during which time they travelled to the Belgian Congo and French Equatorial Africa.

As soon as war was declared Russell volunteered and in February 1940 was commissioned as a Pilot Officer in the RAF Volunteer Reserve (RAFVR), joining the Administration and Special Duties Branch.[16] This was a non-flying branch, most of whose officers performed staff, administrative and storekeeping tasks, but there were also some employed in less conventional 'special tasks' which was Russell's area. He clearly stood out, being mature, widely travelled, fluent in French and several other languages, and his first posting was as a staff officer/interpreter with General Sir Edward Spears, Prime Minister Churchill's personal representative to General de Gaulle. Russell's first operational experience with the 'Spears Mission' came with Operation Menace, de Gaulle's unsuccessful attempt in September 1940 to rally the Vichy French garrison in Dakar to the Allied cause. Despite that debacle Spears remained with de Gaulle and, still with Russell on his staff, accompanied the Free French leader to Egypt in March 1941.

Russell was with Spears during Operation Exporter, the campaign against the Vichy French in Lebanon and Syria, where he underwent a very curious adventure. It is clear from his diaries that he loathed sitting around doing nothing, so on 19 June 1941, having nothing better to do, he went forward to the Free French front line, as it appeared that Damascus was about to fall and he wanted to be among the first to enter it. Travelling alone, he went too far forward and was captured by a Vichy French outpost. Together with some other British and Indian prisoners he was rapidly moved to the rear area and taken to Aleppo by truck and then flown via Athens to Salonika. After a delay in that city the group was taken by train through Yugoslavia, Austria and Germany into France, ending up in Marseille. In this extraordinary journey the prisoners were directed and guarded by French Vichy troops, but were in constant fear of being seized by the Germans, who were present at every station. Unbeknown to the prisoners, however, the British and Vichy French in Syria had signed an armistice on 14 July,[17] following which their fate had been discovered by the British in Syria and the Vichy French commander was detained until the prisoners were returned to Beirut and freed. As a result, Russell and his comrades, now ex-prisoners, were taken, again by rail to Marseilles, where they boarded a French ship which took them under 'safe passage' back to Beirut, which they reached on 15 August 1941. This was a quite extraordinary journey, but Russell and his fellow prisoners seem to have been returned to Allied hands none the worse for it. Russell was then posted to India, arriving on 3 March 1942, where he was sent to Army General Headquarters (GHQ), to be taken on strength for employment in General Staff Intelligence, sub-branch 'e' (GSI(e)).[18]

Fred Sladen
Hugh Frederick Lambart Sladen, always known as Fred, was born on 14

August 1919. His father, mother, grandfather and grandmother were all senior officers in the Salvation Army, his grandfather having been a close associate of the founder, General William Booth. Sladen attended Christ's Hospital school and then the Royal Military College, Sandhurst from where he was commissioned into the Bedfordshire and Hertfordshire Regiment on 8 June 1939. He joined the regiment's 2nd Battalion on 19 July and after the usual new arrival's indoctrination was sent on a signals course, which was to have an impact on Operation Minerva several years later.[19] He was clearly a very capable young man as he was posted to the regiment's 5th Battalion as adjutant in February 1940 and promoted acting captain in July, just one year after being commissioned. Adjutant was a crucial and extremely busy appointment, requiring excellent organisational and administrative skills, particularly in a recently-mobilised Territorial Army battalion.

He clearly did well and by mid-1941 had been moved to command of C Company as a temporary major. The battalion was part of the ill-fated 18th Infantry Division which sailed from Scotland in October 1941, and after a brief spell in India (30 December 1941 to 17 January 1942) went on to disembark in Singapore on 29 January. They took up defensive positions but the first Japanese troops landed on the island on 8 February and the fate of the island was sealed. Sladen's company was fully engaged in the brief campaign, but on the night of 13 February he was sent for by his Commanding Officer and told that he was one of eleven key men from the battalion who were ordered to escape.[20]

Sladen's group got away in a small boat on 15 February and reached an island in the Rhio Archipelago later that day.[21] After some adventures, but fortunately without interference from the Japanese, they reached Sumatra on 21 February. There they made their way slowly up the River Indraghiri, gathering more individuals and small groups as they went until the party was some 120 strong. They arrived at Rengat on 24 February and after a brief pause to clean up went on by bus to cover some 300 miles to the railhead, and after many delays due to frequent punctures reached it on the 27th.

They boarded the train at 0500 hours the next day and it wound its way, slowly and painfully, down to the port of Padang which was reached that night. There they found some 800 other men, from both the Australian and British armies, as well as numerous civilians, waiting for a ship. After several days of anxious waiting they were taken aboard a British destroyer which carried them 30 miles out to sea where they transferred to the Australian cruiser, HMAS *Hobart*, which took them to Colombo, arriving on 6 March.

Sladen, who had now reverted to his rank of captain, was a young man of considerable potential, which was quickly appreciated and on 30 April he was posted to GSI(e) where his first task was to travel around India lecturing to units on Japanese tactics and battlecraft. His immediate chief was Squadron-Leader Russell, so when the latter started looking for infantry skills, enthusiasm, a knowledge of Sumatra, a second-in-command, and, also, a degree of expertise in communications, he needed to look no further.[22]

Alex Hunter

Alexander Hunter (Alex), the son of an ironmoulder, was born at 25, Howburn Place in Aberdeen on 10 March 1910 and attended Robert Gordon's College, where, despite being 'reticent and unassuming', he was very well thought of and became vice-captain of the cricket team in his final year. He then undertook an engineering apprenticeship with Tawse and Allen, qualifying as a chartered engineer in 1933. In those years of the Depression many young British men had little choice but to seek their fortunes abroad, and Hunter went out to Sumatra in the Dutch East Indies in 1934, where he worked for seven-and-a-half years in two tea estates, being employed as an engineer in the large factories where the tea leaves were processed. The two estates were at Simpang Raja and Permatangsiantar, both a short distance north-east of Lake Toba (see Map 2a). One outcome of this experience was the ability to speak Malay fluently and to have a working knowledge of Dutch.

He appears to have left Sumatra in late 1941 or early 1942 and the next firm evidence about him is when he joined the Officer Cadet Training Unit at Kirkee, a military cantonment on the outskirts of Poona and home to the College of Military Engineering. His course started on 2 March 1942 and he was commissioned into the Royal Engineers on 18 August 1942. He was assessed as 'a quiet, reserved person, who has worked well on the course. Has a good sense of humour.'

Quite how he came to Russell's attention is not known, but he was posted to GSI(e) as an Intelligence Officer on 25 October 1942 and given the acting rank of captain on the same date. Russell described him as '. . . a rather dour Aberdonian and I am hoping to make much use of his knowledge of the country and any contacts he may still have there though these are likely to be few and far between now. He is the only person with any knowledge of Sumatra that I have been able to come across outside the Dutch and they know precious little.'[23]

Richard Keyt[24]

Richard Anthony Keyt was born in Penang, in the Straits Settlements, on 25 January 1914. On leaving school he worked for a time for the Straits Steamship Company and then enlisted in the British Army on 20 November 1939. He joined as a 'local' recruit in the Royal Artillery and was posted to 7th Heavy Regiment (redesignated 9th Coast Regiment in December 1940), one of two regiments manning the heavy coastal guns for the defence of the Singapore naval base. He was stationed on the small island of Blakang Mati just off the southern coast of Singapore.

The Japanese attacked on 8 February and on the 14th Keyt was sent from Blakang Mati to Singapore to look for any of his unit's men. He had no success, but on the afternoon of the 15th fell in with a Sergeant Haid of the Australian Army and the two men determined to escape. That night they stole a sampan, rowed it out to a junk, which, with some others escapers, they sailed to Sumatra. At some point they joined a larger group of Australians led by a Lieutenant King and with them they crossed Sumatra to Padang. Once there, they found berths on SS *Deweert*, a Dutch ship, which took them to Ceylon, arriving on 9 March. Compared with many others who escaped from Singapore, this was a quick and trouble-free journey but Keyt appears to have been unwell on arrival in Ceylon and, because he was with an Australian group, he was admitted to an Australian military hospital on the island before being sent to Australia aboard SS *Katoomba*, arriving in Sydney on 17 May 1942. On making himself known to the British authorities in Australia he was sent back to Ceylon.[25]

As with Hunter, it is not clear how Russell found Keyt, but he had him posted to the Combined Services Detailed Interrogation Centre (India) (CSDIC(I)) which was controlled by GSI(e) and therefore produced no administrative problems. It would also appear that Russell arranged for him to have the local rank of sergeant, since this is the rank stated on all Minerva documents, although not on his records, where he is never shown as higher than Paid Acting Lance-Bombardier.[26] Russell describes Keyt as very willing and helpful, although he seems to have accepted him on trust, since they never met until Keyt arrived in Colombo in November.

Lau Teng Kee
Lau Teng Kee came from Batu Pahat in the State of Johor.[27] He appears to have attended local schools and then gone to Hong Kong, to become a student in the famous Medical School at the University. He had just completed the third year of his four-year course when the Japanese invaded in December 1941. He escaped in early 1942 and joined the BAAG in Free China, where he became Agent No 36. He made two clandestine trips into Japanese-occupied Hong Kong, the aim of the first being to recover the Great Seal of the University, an item of considerable symbolic value to the university authorities. He was not successful, so he returned to Hong Kong with a colleague, who succeeded in recovering the seal, while Lau brought out a group of no less than twenty-three university students.[28]

Russell visited Ride at Kukong from 7 to 20 July 1942 at a time when Lau was in Hong Kong. Thus, they could not have met, but presumably Ride recommended Lau highly, as a result of which Russell decided to take him on the Minerva operation, although obviously subject to Lau's agreement. Lau offered proven courage and integrity as well as first-hand experience of penetrating and surviving in Japanese-controlled territory. Further, as a fourth-year medical student he had more than sufficient training to serve as the medic on Operation Minerva, when required. Finally, as a Malayan Chinese he would have spoken at least some Malay and also been able to blend into the crowds in Singapore. Lau left China in November 1942 and is known to have been in Chungking on 10 November awaiting an onward flight to Calcutta on 14 November.[29] Quite when he joined the others in Ceylon is not known, but appears to have been later in the month.

Lau is referred to in the various Operation Minerva reports and the Catalina flight log as *Sergeant* Lau. During his time with the BAAG Lau was a civilian auxiliary and designated 'Agent 36' but it seems clear that he would not have been allowed to take part in Operation Minerva unless he had proper military status, partly in order to give him prisoner-of-war status if captured (a vain hope where the Japanese were concerned). Extensive searches in UK archives and wide consultation have failed to discover any documentary evidence (e.g., attestation papers) and it may be that Russell made some arrangement in Ceylon in early December 1942, but it appears that this was not followed through and was forgotten when the team failed to return.

The Team
In summary, the team that took part in Operation Minerva comprised:

Squadron-Leader Basil Russell, aged 38, a wartime officer in the RAFVR, in command. He was a staff officer at GHQ, but had some combat experience as a liaison officer at Dakar and in Syria, and had also been a prisoner-of-war for a short period. He spoke fluent French and several other languages, although it seems doubtful that these would have included any of those spoken in Sumatra.

Captain Fred Sladen, aged 23, worked for Russell in GSI(e) and was the next senior in the group. He was a regular infantry officer with combat experience against the Japanese in Singapore, and had crossed Sumatra during his escape from that island. He was designated second-in-command, and as he had attended a one-month signals instructors' course in 1939 he was made responsible for communications.

Captain Alex Hunter, aged 32, a wartime officer in the Royal Engineers, had been posted to GSI(e) on commissioning. He had worked for nearly eight years in Sumatra on two different tea plantations and it seems safe to assume that he had a reasonable knowledge of the area to the north-east of Lake Toba and would have had at least a working knowledge of one or more of the local languages.

Sergeant Richard Keyt, aged 28, a regular soldier in the Royal Artillery. He had been brought up in Penang and had worked aboard ships of the Straits Steamship Company for several years, which suggests that he had some knowledge of seamanship and local waters. He would have been able to speak at least basic Malay and had a reasonable knowledge of Singapore.

Sergeant Lau Teng Kee, aged 22–23, from Johor, a fourth-year medical student. He had witnessed the Japanese invasion of Hong Kong, but had then escaped and joined the BAAG. He had then gone back twice into Hong Kong, so had first-hand knowledge of the Japanese and their methods. He would have known Singapore, spoken at least some of the languages and dialects, enabling him to merge seamlessly into the Chinese population. His medical knowledge would also have been of great use to the Minerva team.

Chapter 5

Air Force Participation

Because no submarine was available, Russell had to turn to the RAF for assistance, and, in the event, that Service was very successful. The three flying-boat squadrons which participated in Operation Minerva all belonged to No 222 (General Reconnaissance) Group RAF, commanded from 1 December 1942 by Air Vice-Marshal A. Lees. All were equipped with US-supplied Consolidated PBY-5 Catalina flying boats and undertook maritime patrols in the Indian Ocean and Bay of Bengal.[30] It so happened, however, that they were from three different backgrounds: 205 Squadron was an RAF unit which had been formed in Ceylon on 23 July 1942 and was based at Koggala while 321 Squadron was formed in Trincomalee, Ceylon, on 15 August 1942 from Royal Netherlands Naval Air Service crews and aircraft which had escaped from the disaster in the Dutch East Indies. The squadron was under the operational command of the RAF, but was administered by the Dutch. Its main base was at RAF China Bay (Trincomalee) and, like the others, the squadron flew anti-submarine patrols over the Indian Ocean, but also undertook transport duties from time to time. The third unit, 413 Squadron, was different again, being a Canadian-manned unit that had been formed in Scotland and arrived in Ceylon in April 1942, just as the Japanese Navy conducted its only serious surface incursion into the Indian Ocean.[31] After this, the unit settled into a routine of anti-submarine, air-sea rescue and convoy escort work.

There were two flying-boat bases in Ceylon. RAF Koggala took its name from a small town on the coast near the southern tip of the island between Galla and Matara. A large lake was separated from the sea by a narrow strip of land and during the war this was developed into the largest flying-boat base in the Far East. RAF China Bay was adjacent to Trincomalee on the north-east corner of the island; one of the finest natural harbours in the Indian Ocean, this was also the main Royal Navy base on the island.

The Consolidated Catalina was a very successful design, with some 4,000 being produced between 1937 and 1945. Its normal operating crew was nine – pilot, co-pilot, four gunners, flight engineer, navigator and radio operator – although this could be reduced, depending upon the mission. It was normally armed with five machine-guns: two 0.50in in the waist and three 0.30in, a pair in the nose, one in the tail. It could also carry up to 4,000lb of bombs or depth charges. Power was provided by two Pratt and Whitney radial engines, giving it a maximum speed of 196mph and a cruising speed of 125mph. Its most remarkable attribute, however, was its range of 2,520 miles, which could be increased by carrying extra tanks, reducing payload, leaving one or more members of the crew behind – or a combination of all three. The RAF purchased some 700 Catalinas, while the RNethNAS bought forty-eight direct from the United States for use in the East Indies.

During the Second World War all RAF squadrons were obliged by Air Ministry regulation to maintain an Operational Report Book (ORB) (RAF Form 541), which was a daily record of missions flown, losses, and major events. Most of these are available today in The National Archives (TNA).[32] Studying the relevant ORBs makes it clear that four aircraft from these three squadrons were airborne over northern Sumatra on 20 December 1942: two from 205 Squadron, and one each from 321 and 413 Squadrons.

The pilot who flew the Minerva party to Sumatra was Lieutenant-Commander Gerard Frederick Rijnders of Royal Netherlands Naval Air Service (RNethNAS).[33] He was born in 1913 and served in the Dutch East Indies before the war and then flew to Ceylon where he joined 321 Squadron RAF. On 22 November 1942 Rijnders was summoned to the Dutch headquarters in Colombo where he was introduced to Russell, who explained that he was a staff officer, working for General Wavell at General Headquarters in New Delhi, and was to lead a group of five men to Sumatra, landing on the west coast, a few miles north of Sibolga. The group would normally have travelled in a submarine, but as none was available they were to go by air and Russell said that he understood that Rijnders was the designated pilot. In the discussion which followed, the Dutchman noted that Russell was careful only to speak about the landing and recovery, and never once gave any indication of what he and his men intended to do once they were in Sumatra.

Rijnders and Russell covered the practical arrangements. They agreed on a date – 20 December, which would be a full moon – but Rijnders would not agree to Russell's request for a night landing, as the aircraft would be heavily overloaded with additional fuel and the five passengers, plus their weapons, ammunition, two rubber dinghies, radio set, rations and other stores. Rijnders also realised that he would have to strip out the aircraft's own protective steel armour, as well as the armament and ammunition. So they agreed that the landing would be at 1800 hours local time, enabling Rijnders to land at last light, while the take-off after dark would be much less of a problem.

They also agreed on arrangements for the recovery. The place was to be Dalam Bay on Simaleur Island, with initially two dates in February, with a back-up date of 21 March 1943, if required.[34] For these recovery flights Rijnders was happy to agree to a midnight landing, as his aircraft would be far less heavily loaded. They also agreed on a system of light signals, so that the pilot could be confident that he was not landing into a trap.

Finally, they agreed on a date for a full-scale rehearsal on a beach on the east coast of Ceylon and this was carried out a few days before departure with complete success. All now being agreed, Russell and Rijnders adjourned to the Officers' Mess, where they enjoyed a traditional Dutch Rijkstafel, washed down by a plentiful supply of Bols gin.

Chapter 6

The Operation:
20 December 1942

The last month before the operation found Russell and his team very busy. Russell insisted on taking Hunter and Keyt for long-distance runs, and Sladen joined them when he returned on 3 December from various missions to New Delhi. Russell does not report Lau's arrival, but mentions him as being present on a train journey on 22 November. On 23 November the Dutch Navy allowed them to test two types of dinghy and they selected the larger US type, which proved easier for them to control. Brigadier Cawthorn, the DMI back in New Delhi, continued to be concerned about the project and requested a more detailed plan, which Russell found a 'ridiculous demand' but reported in his diary that he supposed that he 'would produce some fairy story in the end to keep him quiet'. On 4 December Russell was still writing his plan but admitted that Cawthorn has 'got to make as certain as he humanly can that we are covered in case any questions are asked afterwards in the event of anything going wrong'.[35]

There seems to have been some trouble over obtaining a radio. Sladen had arrived in Colombo on 14 November to report that a Major Jones in Delhi had 'forgotten' the wireless, so Russell immediately sent him back to sort it out. There were no airseats, so the unfortunate Sladen had to travel by train, which was desperately slow, and did not return to Colombo until 3 December, apparently with the wireless, although Russell said that it was still not satisfactory and told his diary that '. . . I rather fear that we may have to do without it altogether'.[36] Nevertheless, Sladen could have been more profitably employed, rather than spending twelve days sitting in trains so close to the departure date.

The operational deployment took place on 20 December 1942 and involved four Catalina aircraft which, although taking part in the same operation and following a coordinated plan, flew and acted independently. These were: FV-O[37] and FV-T from 205 Squadron at Koggala; Y-57 from 321 Squadron, China Bay; and QL-H from 413 Squadron, also based at China Bay (replaced by FV-K).[38]

Catalina FV-O of 205 Squadron, flown by Flight-Lieutenant Maxwell-Hudson, had an uneventful flight to Pulau Weh. On arrival, the pilot dropped to 40 feet for his attack run across Sabang harbour, where, despite his unexpected arrival, he was met by intense light flak. The aircraft was hit in numerous places, and, in taking evasive action, Maxwell-Hudson hit the sea and bounced off again, but regained control remarkably quickly and then set course for Ceylon, Astonishingly, not one member of the crew had been hit but the hull was badly holed and the port engine not functioning correctly, causing excessive vibration. So, Maxwell-Hudson feathered the damaged engine and flew in this way for over seven hours on just one engine. He transmitted a brief SOS shortly after starting the return flight to indicate that his aircraft was damaged, but then maintained wireless silence until shortly after dawn on 21 December. His squadron immediately requested that a 321 Squadron Catalina be sent out to find FV-O and to escort it home or stand by it in case the pilot was forced to come down in the sea. An air-sea rescue launch was also despatched. In the event, Maxwell-Hudson made it back to base and landed safely at 0720 hours, after 23 hours flying. It was a remarkable achievement for which he was awarded the DFC.

Catalina FV-T, also of 205 Squadron, was flown by Flight-Lieutenant Lane, but with Squadron-Leader Stacey aboard. It took off at 0915 hours and had an uneventful flight to Sabang. The aircraft carried out a thorough reconnaissance of the harbour, dropped its bombs and then returned to Ceylon, arriving at 0340 hours. Despite meeting flak over Sabang harbour, FV-T was not hit and the crew unhurt, and they appear to have been unaware of the damage caused to FV-O.

Catalina QL-H of 413 Squadron was flown by that unit's commanding officer, Wing-Commander J. C. Scott, RCAF. He took off on this raid at 0857 hours, but had not long been airborne when the aircraft developed engine trouble, forcing him to divert to China Bay. Scott had signalled ahead, so that a replacement aircraft, FV-K of 205 Squadron, was waiting for him and his crew, and they were on their way again at 1107 hours. On arrival over Kota Raja Scott carried out a thorough reconnaissance, dropped six high-explosive bombs and a number of incendiaries, and then returned uneventfully to base, coming down on the water at 0439 hours on 21 December. The crew were praised for their 'superb navigation' and Wing Commander Scott received the DSO.[39]

The aircraft mentioned above were a diversion for the main purpose of Operation Minerva, which was undertaken by PBY-5 Catalina Y-57 of No 321 Squadron. The entire crew was from the Royal Netherlands Naval Air Service, with Lieutenant-Commander G. F. Rijnders in command. Other members of the crew were Sergeant de Jäger (co-pilot), Lieutenant Polderman (observer), Sergeant de Vos (mechanic/fitter), Aircraftsman Heijligers (fitter), and Corporal De Bruin (radio operator). Rijnders' log book clearly states that the passengers carried were Squadron-Leader Russell, Captain Sladen, Captain Hunter, Sergeant Keith (*sic*), and Sergeant Lau Ten (*sic*) Kee.[40]

They took off at 0400 hours, the time being dictated by the need to arrive off Sumatra at last light (1800 hours Sumatra time), and taking into account a two-hour time difference and eleven hours' flying time. Rijnders needed as long a run as possible to get his heavily overloaded aircraft into the air and over the trees facing him, a process made more difficult by the multitude of small fishing boats setting out for their daily catch, which were cleared by the station motorboat. The take-off went well, however and with fair weather, clear sky and good visibility the flight passed without incident. Rijnders flew at medium altitude until he was about 20 miles west of the island of Nias when he descended to about 30 feet for the run into the Sumatran coast (see Map 2a). This took him past the north shore of the island of Nias and to his surprise he saw little white puffs of smoke near the aircraft, meaning that they had been detected and were under anti-aircraft fire.

Rijnders pressed on and put his aircraft down on the sea off a beach on the mainland opposite Pulau Pandjang ('Long Island'), on time, exactly as planned.[41] The aircraft anchored some 30 yards (30m) off the beach and the passengers and their stores were transferred to the two Goodyear inflatable dinghies. The larger dinghy carried three men and the heavy stores, such as Sten guns and rations, but the smaller was delayed as it had a leak which had to be topped-up from the carbon dioxide bottle in the aircraft; the remaining two men then boarded and paddled ashore. As the aircraft prepared to take-off one of the crew saw that the larger dinghy was already on the beach and the second nearly there. All appeared well, so at about 1830 hours the crew shouted 'Good luck, see you later' to the men on shore, then closed the waist blister, started the engines and took off for the long flight home. Rijnders recorded that, 'I have to admit that having a last look at our British colleagues was difficult. My fellow crew members had similar emotions. Would we ever see them again? I did not have much hope. Crossing the jungle of Sumatra with a rather unfriendly population seemed to us a tricky operation.' With such mixed thoughts, the Catalina droned on over the Indian Ocean, again without incident, arriving at China Bay and landing 21 hours 30 minutes after leaving it.[42]

Not a single radio transmission was heard from the shore party, so the next phase from the Ceylon end was Operation Minerva II, the planned recovery, which was due to take place from Dalam Bay, some 30 miles up the north-eastern coast of Pulau Simaleur from the main village, Sinabang. The first attempt was on 20 February, when Lieutenant Hamers left Ceylon at 0805 hours in Y-25 and flew to the RV, but as there were no signals from the ground, he returned to Ceylon, arriving at 0630 hours. Then, on 25 February 1943, Lieutenant-Commander Rijnders (Y-57), the pilot on the initial mission, took off at 0620 hours, but despite flying around Simaleur for some time there were no recognition signals from the ground, so he, too, returned to Ceylon at 0620 hours on 26 February, after a full 24 hours in the air. Finally, Rijnders returned for one last time on 21 March, but once more no signals were seen and with that, and, in accordance with the prearranged plan, no further attempts were made to recover the Minerva party.

Chapter 7

Fate

No radio transmissions were detected from the very start of the operation, which caused increasing concern in Army and RAF circles. Despite this, as described in the previous chapter, abortive attempts to recover the party according to the plan were made on 20 and 25 February and 21 March. However, the first official response did not come until the last of these attempts had failed, as a result of which the five men were declared to be 'missing on 21 March 1943'. This information was passed to the next-of-kin of the officers, initially by telegram, although at this stage the families were told for security reasons that their relative had been in Burma, since there were large numbers of British fighting there at the time, as opposed to Sumatra where there virtually none. The next-of-kin of Sergeants Keyt and Lau could not, of course, be told because they were in Japanese-occupied Malaya.

The telegrams were sent on 12 July 1943 and confirmed by official letter on 27 July 1943. These were careful to say that the term 'missing' did not necessarily mean the men were dead, but that they might be in Japanese hands. This caused some confusion where Russell was concerned, since the Army had a category of 'Missing, believed prisoner-of-war' whereas the RAF simply recorded a man as 'missing' until there was firm evidence as to his fate; i.e., a prisoner-of-war or killed.

One of the major concerns within the chain-of-command in India must have been that any of the five who survived the initial contact with the Japanese could be tortured into revealing either the aim of Minerva to reach Singapore, or, in the case of Russell, even wider plans, such as that to liberate prisoners in Hong Kong (Operation Chopsticks). It can, however, be stated with a high degree of confidence that this did not happen. The reason for this is Captain David Nelson, MiD, of the Singapore Volunteer Corps, a prisoner-of-war who ran the Bureau of Record and Enquiry (BRE) within the Changi camp. This remarkable man and his helpers maintained, as best they could, records of all Allied personnel who were killed, captured or died in Malaya and Singapore, and in order to achieve this they established a reasonable, but strictly correct, working relationship with their Japanese captors. Nelson later published an account of those years, with 'the aim of presenting an unbiased account of events as they occurred, of camp conditions and maintenance of discipline, together with other facets of prisoner-of-war life'.[43] There can be no doubt that had the Japanese had got wind of the plans for either Chopsticks or Minerva they would have reacted very severely, but there is not the slightest hint in Nelson's account of any Japanese reaction or worsening of relations between December 1942 and the end of 1943. Nor, indeed, does Nelson give any indication that he knew of Minerva from any other source.

After the war the Allies faced a huge task in finding and releasing the surviving prisoners-of-war and sending them home, in locating and identifying the graves of those who had died, and in seeking to account for those who were 'missing.' A 'Searcher Organisation Clearing House' was established at HQ Allied Land Forces South East Asia in Singapore, with teams scattered across the whole area. The 26th Indian Division occupied Sumatra from October 1945 to November 1946 and included Numbers 4 and 7 War Crimes Investigation Teams. Although they tried their best, these teams' efforts were hampered, and in many cases actively prevented, by Indonesian nationalist guerrillas in what rapidly developed into a full-scale civil war between them and the returning Dutch. As a result, no grave which might have been one of those on Operation Minerva was ever found.

The branch which had initiated Minerva, GSI(e) had been expanded and upgraded to E Group in 1944 and pressed hard for some word on the fate of its five men. There was a report that Russell might have been temporarily detained in a prison in Fort de Kock (now Bukittinggi), and another that the name 'Russell, Liut [*sic*] RAF' had been found inscribed on a wall in Number 8 St Joseph's School, Medan, both known locations for the Japanese *Kempetei* (secret police). Another report was that Russell and at least one other, possibly Keyt, had been held in Outram Road Gaol in Singapore in early 1943.[44] There is also some evidence that one or more of those captured claimed to the Japanese that they had been crewmembers of a flying boat that had been shot down off the Sumatran coast. Such a story was clearly intended to disguise the intention of Operation Minerva, but it would have had an unfortunate effect in that the Japanese regarded downed bomber crews as 'war criminals' who were almost always executed.

In a letter to Russell's widow on 20 February 1946, Colonel Raymond Jackman, who had taken over as Head of GSI(e)/E Group from Ridgway in mid-1943, wrote to her that: 'From a report I have just received there seems little doubt that he [i.e., Basil Russell] and one other of his party were held in a jail on Singapore Island as late as May 1943, after which date it is assumed that they were removed to Japan.' These reports that Russell and one or more others might have been sent by ship to Japan were also investigated in 1946 and have been re-investigated by this author. It is known that in 1943 sailings from Singapore took place on 2 April (1,003 prisoners), 25 April (1,500), 15 May (900), 20 September (507), and 21 October (1,155), but whether Russell or any of his comrades were among those 5,065 souls cannot be established.[45] Similarly, no records of any member of the Minerva group were ever found in Japan.

Russell's widow, Jocelyn, was adamant that her husband had survived and for many years continued to lay a place for him at her dining table. She also published an entry in *The Times* 'In Memoriam' column on 20 December 1946 (the fourth anniversary of his disappearance): 'RUSSELL.- In proud and loving remembrance of my husband, S/Ldr BASIL H.S. RUSSELL, RAFVR, missing from a special operation in Sumatra. Dec 20. 1942.' The wording carefully avoided any suggestion that he might be dead. The Air Historical Branch states that 'The exact fate of the team has not been established but there is some evidence that three of them were captured by the Japanese.' There is, however, no indication as to which three of the five this applies, although it is possible that it might have been the officers, since it was normal practice for the Japanese, on capturing clandestine groups, to execute all non-commissioned ranks on the spot.

It is presumed that Keyt's mother was sent a letter after the war; no trace of her or any other descendants can now be found, but it is known that she received his medals in 1947. Hunter's mother and Sladen's father received a telegram and letter in 1943 stating that their sons were missing, but in February 1946 both received a final letter telling them that '. . . the Department has reluctantly, and with deep regret, reached the conclusion that there can no longer be any hope of his survival'.[46] In addition, Fred Sladen's father, a senior officer in the Salvation Army, sent a private letter, via the War Office, to the next-of-kin of the others; the covering letter to Mrs Hunter survives but no copy of the actual letter, which presumably expressed condolences and Christian comfort, can be found.[47] Thus, the names of Hunter, Russell and Sladen are on the Commonwealth War Graves Commission memorial at Kranji, in Singapore, with their dates of death given as 20 December 1942 and the place as Sumatra. Keyt's name is on the Rangoon Memorial, with the date given as 21 March 1943 in Burma.[48] Lau Teng Kee's name appears on no memorial and despite extensive searches no trace of his family can be found, as described in Appendix C.

Chapter 8

Analysis

Despite the very small numbers involved, Operation Minerva was an exceptionally ambitious undertaking, its mission being to discover whether there were any further Allied servicemen still evading capture in Sumatra, while also infiltrating into Singapore to make contact with the prisoners-of-war there. It involved insertion by air, at a range of some 1,000 miles, of a party of five, into a territory with a population largely hostile to the Dutch and occupied by the Japanese who were known to deal with utmost harshness to anyone helping their enemies. Having landed, the party had to travel some 200 miles across Sumatra, following which at least two members would cross the Straits of Malacca, spend some days in Japanese-occupied Singapore, and then return to Sumatra. The whole party then intended to re-cross Sumatra, navigate across 100 miles of open ocean to an offshore island – also Japanese-occupied – before being recovered by air. They intended to spend at least two, possibly three months in enemy-held territory, with no prospect of resupply and little hope of help if anything went wrong.

The air contribution was relatively straightforward. Minerva I, the insertion of the Russell party by one aircraft, went smoothly as did the attacks on Sabang (two aircraft) and Kota Raja (one aircraft). These were intended to create noisy diversions, with each aircraft dropping bombs and then conducting a low-level pass with all guns blazing, and the only aircraft hit by enemy fire managed to return to base. Minerva II, the recovery phase in February/March, consisted of three flights, all of which reached the assigned rendezvous, but there was nobody there to collect.

It is also quite clear that Operation Minerva did not involve SOE(India) in any way. Lieutenant-Colonel Christopher Hudson reported to the SOE Indian Mission headquarters in Meerut in January 1943 and then travelled to Ceylon, where he formed the Anglo-Dutch Country Section. He arrived just in time to meet McCarthy (see Part II, Chapter

10) before the latter left for the Andaman Islands, but too late to influence the conduct of that operation which was 'almost on the point of sailing', which it did on 14 January 1943. Thus he could have had nothing at all to do with the organisation and planning, nor even the deployment of Operation Minerva on 20 December 1942, although he may have taken an interest in the attempted recoveries of the group in February and March 1943.

So, it is clear that Operation Minerva was devised and conducted entirely by GSI(e) of GHQ India. It was the brainchild of Squadron Leader Russell, who did virtually all the planning, selected the personnel and led the actual operation in the field. However, he could only have done so with the approval of his superiors, who must shoulder much of the blame for the debacle.

Control

It would have been standard military practice for Operation Minerva to have established some form of a rear headquarters in either Ceylon or India which would have been required to serve as a focal point for all dealings between the group in the field and the command, administrative and logistic elements in the base. The most important single function would have been to provide one or more terminals for the wireless link to the Minerva party. This would have enabled the rear party to accept reports from the Minerva party and disseminate them to superior HQs; forward orders, instructions, requests or information from superior HQ to the Minerva party; respond to any requests for assistance or guidance; and to vary the recovery arrangements, if requested to do so. Absolutely no trace of any such HQ or arrangement has been found. There is evidence in a letter written by a staff officer in Ceylon that the 'naval HQ' in Ceylon kept a listening watch for any Minerva transmissions at prearranged times but heard nothing.[49] Other than that they seem to have had no involvement. Logic suggests that following the failure of the mission a post-mortem would have been held in an effort to identify what had gone wrong and to learn lessons for the future. No trace of any such report has been found.

Communications

The Minerva party took a wireless set with them. Russell mentions problems in obtaining a set in his diary, but Rijnders, in his memoir, is certain that a set was taken ashore, although of what type is not recorded. It would have been standard practice for there to have been a written signals plan which would have set out frequencies, callsigns, codewords and schedules, with copies issued to the Minerva party and to the base stations in India and Ceylon; no trace of such a document can be found.

The power supply for the radio would have been a major issue. Dry batteries were heavy and had short lives in the tropics, while wet cells were not only also heavy but depended upon a charging engine, which also required fuel; i.e., yet more weight. They may have hoped to obtain recharging facilities, or even mains supply for the set, from friendly Sumatrans, but this could by no means be guaranteed. Another possibility was a hand- or foot-cranked charger, but these were very heavy, typically some 36lbs.

Whichever set they took, it would have been operating in the High Frequency band (HF) (i.e., 3 to 30 Megaherz) which was notoriously challenging in the tropics, particularly at night, and would have required Morse operation and not voice. This required training and practice, and while Sladen had attended a regimental signallers' instructors' course in England in 1939, thereafter he had been so busy that he does not seem to have had any opportunity to put that experience into practice, nor is there any record of him attending a refresher course in India or Ceylon prior to Minerva. In contrast, as described in Part II, the parties which went to the Andaman Islands, which were a similar distance from Ceylon, took at least one Royal Signals sergeant operator and were never out of communication, although, unlike Minerva, they did operate from a static base camp rather than on the move.

There are several possible reasons for the failure to communicate. First, the wireless could have been immersed in water, either during the transfer ashore or in a subsequent river-crossing. Secondly, it could have developed some technical fault which was beyond the expertise of the party to correct. Thirdly, it is possible that Sladen's inexperience in operating the set in such challenging conditions, over such long distances, and, in particular, the need to use Morse, was such that he was unable to communicate before being overcome by the Japanese. Another possibility is that there could have been a procedural problem such as the use of incorrect frequencies, which was by no means unknown in the

Second World War. Finally, the party could have been captured by the Japanese so suddenly, and so soon after landing, that they never had time to set up the wireless and communicate with base, anyway.

Participants

The party, all of whom were volunteers, included a broad range of experience. Russell was a dynamic leader, energetic, optimistic, persuasive, able to get on with people, at ease with his superiors, and had been a prisoner-of-war, albeit for only a short period. Sladen, a professional infantryman, was very highly regarded in his regiment, had some experience of fighting the Japanese, had spent a week in Sumatra during his escape, and was very enthusiastic about the operation. Hunter was not quite such an extrovert as the other two officers and had very little military experience, but knew Sumatra and its people and spoke Malay. Keyt spoke Malay, knew Singapore and had some knowledge of seamanship in local waters. Lau would also have spoken at least some Malay, but more importantly, knew the Japanese occupiers better than the other four from his two infiltrations into Hong Kong, had good medical knowledge, and may have had friends or relations in Singapore.

Against this was the military inexperience of all five, particularly in protracted patrols in enemy-dominated jungle terrain. Sladen and Keyt had crossed Sumatra but had done so relatively quickly and almost entirely by boat, train or motor vehicle. Hunter lived in Sumatra for many years, but even if he had spent part of that time in the jungle it was not in a Japanese-dominated environment.

However, the most glaring factor was that nothing could hide the Caucasian ethnicity of Hunter, Russell and Sladen, and no matter what they did their facial features and height would have made them stand out from the indigenous population. Allied to that was the fact that to most Sumatrans, all Europeans were Dutch and were very unpopular.

Forewarning from Nias

Rijnders' log states that his aircraft came under anti-aircraft gun fire while flying off the north coast of the island of Nias. This clearly meant that the Japanese had spotted his aircraft, identified it as an enemy, and knew that it was flying in the general direction of the mainland, although they would not have known its mission. Presumably they would have had some means, either radio or telephone, to pass this information to their superior headquarters on the mainland.

Were They Betrayed?

One of the strongest possibilities is that the local Japanese garrison was informed of the presence of this party by someone from the Indonesian community. In the early part of the war there were numerous examples in both Malaya and the Dutch East Indies of local inhabitants informing the Japanese of the presence of British or Dutch clandestine parties. For such people, particularly those in the villages (kampongs), those two European colonial powers had been very recently defeated in a disgraceful manner and in 1942–43 there must have seemed little prospect of them returning in the foreseeable future. In contrast, the Japanese were ever-present, and if the villagers did help any Europeans the latter would not be around to protect them when the Japanese caught up with them. When they did so, the Japanese were absolutely ruthless and thought nothing of murdering large numbers, both as punishment and as an example to others.

Boris Hembry, a former rubber planter in Malaya and Sumatra, took part in Operation Matriarch/Valour, the SOE Anglo-Dutch landing on the coast of Sumatra in March 1943. His group's presence was quickly reported to the local Japanese and the raiders had to conduct a fighting withdrawal back to their canoes. Despite this, and having earlier in the war lost several good friends in Malaya in this way, Hembry bore no rancour, writing that '. . . The kampong dwellers who "betrayed" them (his friends) cannot be blamed. They knew that the Japs would have rounded up and shot the entire village if they had not reported the escapers' presence.'[50]

Weapons

Each man carried a Sten gun, then a very new weapon. It was light, easy to carry and had a high rate of fire, but on the other hand it had a short effective range – about 50 yards – and as will be seen only too clearly in Operation Baldhead I (Chapter 10), the early models could be as dangerous to their users as to the enemy. A group of five men, armed with such weapons, would have stood little chance against ten or more Japanese infantry, particularly as the latter would have been armed with their standard rifles, and could simply have stayed out of Sten range and picked off the British party one by one. Further, they would have been unable to carry more than about 100 rounds each, and there was no question of resupply.

Proper Unit

One of the more unusual aspects of Minerva is that it was directly organised by a staff branch at GHQ India, which also provided three out of the five participants. Most special forces operations of this kind are conducted by trained men in dedicated units, who have been carefully selected and undertaken rigorous training before the operation. Contemporary examples were the commandoes in the UK and the Special Air Service, Long-Range Desert Group and Popski's Private Army in the Middle East. In this case, Russell was self-appointed; Sladen shared an office with Russell; Hunter was selected on the basis of a single interview; Lau on the recommendation of Ride; and it is not known how Keyt was recruited.

Had the team been part of a proper unit, the leader would have had support and advice from a commanding officer, signals officer, quartermaster and other specialists. Such men would have taken the administrative and coordinating load off the operational team's shoulders, organised travel, collected stores, prepared and conducted training exercises and the like. As it was, it is clear from Russell's diary that in the last six weeks before deployment all five were rushing around doing all these tasks themselves.

Security

Another unusual aspect of Minerva was that Russell was allowed to go on it at all. This is not to challenge either his personal commitment to the project or his courage, but the fact was that he was a staff officer in the intelligence branch in GHQ with access, albeit intermittently, to the CinC and other senior officers. He would thus have been privy to many more secrets than just Minerva – he certainly knew all about the BAAG and Operation Chopsticks, for example – and it seems ill-advised, to say the least, that his superiors should have allowed him to be in a position where he might be captured by the Japanese and interrogated under torture. However, as discussed in the previous chapter, there is no evidence that either he or any of his colleagues gave any information of any value to the Japanese.

Superiors
It seems extraordinary that nobody further up the chain-of-command cancelled this entire operation. The Director of Military Intelligence, Brigadier Cawthorn, clearly had major reservations and Russell complains in his diary about the brigadier's repeated last minute requests for more elaboration on the plan, a problem exacerbated by the distance between GHQ in New Delhi and Russell on the ground in Ceylon. However, Russell appears to have produced something which satisfied the brigadier or else the latter considered that it was too late to cancel the operation and allowed it to go ahead by default.

Assessment
With hindsight it can be seen that Minerva was hopelessly optimistic. That a party of five men – three of them Europeans – could travel some 200 miles across Sumatra, following which at least some of them would cross to Singapore, and then all return to the west coast seems foolhardy. But, to then plan to cross some 100 miles of open ocean to Simaleur, and for no known purpose, seems preposterous.

They could have carried no more than seven days' rations when they set out and since there was no question of resupply, it must be presumed that they intended to rely on Hunter's local knowledge to enable them to obtain food from the villages. Nor could they have hoped for medical support if one or more of the group had been wounded or taken seriously ill. Lau was almost a qualified doctor but he could have taken little more than a satchel of the most rudimentary medical supplies and instruments.

The Dutch participated to the extent that they supplied the aircraft to lift the land party to Sumatra, but it seems surprising that there was not a single Dutchman in the land group.

Why Has Operation Minerva Been Forgotten?
Until this author made contact with the Netherlands Institute for Military History there has never been a public acknowledgement of Operation Minerva in the UK. There are three known books in which military operations in Sumatra are described, but they all concern operations by

SOE(India) and thus jump from Operation Troemon to Operation Matriarch.[51] In addition, Boris Hembry makes no mention of it in his memoirs. Diligent research in the National Archives, Imperial War Museum, Ministry of Defence, and British Library has failed to unearth any files dedicated to Operation Minerva; that is not to say that they are not there, but only that, if they are, they have yet to be found. The only mention of Operation Minerva at all is in the entries in the RAF squadron Operational Report Books for 20 December 1942, 20 and 25 February 1943 and 21 March 1943, which might reasonably be described as 'obscure', and a brief entry in GSI(e)'s post-war report.

There would appear to be several possible reasons. First, following the total absence of wireless communications and after the ground party had three times failed to keep their rendezvous with the Catalina it would have been patently clear to those responsible for Minerva that something had gone badly wrong. The superior HQs would have had no means of knowing what had happened, but they had perforce to assume the worst case, which was that the five men had been captured and were still being held and interrogated by the Japanese. Thus, it is probable that no public announcement was made in case it prejudiced their situation vis-à-vis the Japanese.

Secondly, Operation Minerva was classified MOST SECRET and knowledge of it confined to the smallest possible number of people on a 'NEED-TO-KNOW' basis. This probably included the planning staff at Intelligence Branches in GHQ and Air HQ India; a very few staff officers in Ceylon; e.g., at HQ 222 Group; and the crews of the Dutch flying boats of 413 Squadron which conducted the flights on 20 December 1942 and in February and March 1943, who would have known that they were carrying a clandestine group but not what they were intending to do.

By 1946, when it was determined that none of the five men were among those surviving in former Japanese prisoner-of-war camps, apart from generating the three known obituaries it was simply forgotten. There was good reason to suppress information on Minerva during the war, but, while it cannot be proved, it appears likely that Operation Minerva has been lost to history through oversight, rather than deliberate intention.

It is inevitable that some missions in war will fail although the reasons will differ. In Operation Flipper, for example, the attack on Rommel's supposed HQ in Cyrenaica on 17/19 November 1941, one man was killed, three escaped and made it back to the British lines, but the remainder were captured – and Rommel was not even there. The raid on Dieppe on 19 August 1942, carefully planned and heroically executed, was a total failure, with heavy loss of life. More recently, US missions such as Operation Ivory Coast, the attempted rescue of US PoWs from Son Tay in North Vietnam (21 November 1970) and Operation Eagle Claw, the attempt to rescue the hostages in the US Embassy in Iran (24 April 1980) have also been spectacular failures.

In comparison, Operation Minerva was a very small undertaking – just five men – but with hindsight should never have been allowed to proceed. However, the men who carried it out were courageous, their attempts to help the prisoners-of-war in Singapore and the evaders still at large in Sumatra were very honourable, and they deserve to be remembered.

PART II

Operations Baldhead and Hatch:
Andaman Islands, 1943–1945

Chapter 9

The Andaman Islands

The Andaman Islands (see Map 3), part of British India, were occupied by the Japanese without any resistance on 23 March 1942. The Japanese then maintained a large garrison on the islands until the end of the war, despite which SOE(India) placed five groups ashore, each of which spent many weeks conducting frequent patrols deep into Japanese-dominated territory, without once being detected. It was a substantial, but little-known, British success.

The Japanese aim in the Andaman Islands was to maintain a strategic outpost on the eastern edge of the Indian Ocean, which could be used as a naval and seaplane base. They also subsequently sought to obtain a propaganda advantage by declaring the islands to be liberated Indian territory, which was, at least in theory, garrisoned by the Indian National Army (INA).

The British, on the other hand, also saw the islands as having possible strategic value, as they might be used to launch air raids and subsequently invasions against Japanese-occupied Burma and Malaya. This led them to maintain a close interest in the islands and there were several naval attacks, by both surface ships and carrier aircraft, an invasion was twice simulated to draw Japanese attention away from US attacks in the Pacific, and a real invasion was planned which, in the event, did not take place, but only after a great deal of planning had been done. Part of this planning was to send ground parties into the Andamans for protracted periods; all went by submarine and, despite the Japanese presence, were never once discovered and attacked; indeed, the only fatality was one man who shot himself accidentally with his own Sten gun. These ground patrols were extremely successful, gathered a considerable amount of information, but since they never became involved in combat and the Japanese eventually surrendered the islands as meekly in 1945 as the British had in 1942, they have been forgotten, but deserve to be remembered.

Background

The Andaman Islands – and the Nicobar Islands to the south – are part of a chain running in an approximately north-south line along the eastern side of the Bay of Bengal, and together form the peaks of a submarine mountain range. The Andamans are actually closer to Burma and Thailand than to India, but were annexed by the British in the nineteenth century and thereafter were administered as part of the British Indian Empire.

The 240 islands and islets in the Andaman group stretch over an area 220 miles from north to south by 32 miles wide, the great majority of them totally uninhabited. Most are covered in particularly dense primary jungle, with no rivers worthy of the name, although a few streams flow into the sea. The main concentration is known as the Great Andaman and consists of the five largest islands – North, Middle and South Andaman, Baratang and Rutland – which are separated from each other by very narrow straits.

When the British arrived in the 1860s there were three main indigenous tribal groups. The Ongis lived on Little Andaman, while some ten individual tribes were grouped together under the term the Great Andamanese. All were seriously depleted as a result of contact with 'civilisation', particularly by measles, and by the early 1940s the Andamanese had mostly been assimilated, while there were only some 100 Ongis remaining. That left the Jarawa, the largest single indigenous group, whose main habitat was on the west coast of South and Middle Andaman islands. They subsisted in remote areas and were so skilled at keeping away from interlopers that even by the Second World War their numbers could only be estimated, very vaguely, as 'some 4,000'. There were no known government contacts with them, nor had there been any private contacts, either, so that there was no knowledge of their language or customs. They appeared to live in small family groups and the only real contact had been in the mid-1930s when a group was surprised while fording a river and fled, leaving a heavily-pregnant woman and a child behind. These were taken to Port Blair, but little headway was made in learning the language and the woman, now plus two children, were returned to their people. There were occasional contacts between Jarawa and forestry groups, particularly small parties of the latter hunting animals. The one activity that was known to provoke the Jarawa was the occasional interference with their women and they had been known to attack forestry camps and kill one or more men in retaliation.

The British patrols that went into the Andamans during the War found the Jarawa a significant factor, as the latter were able to move unseen and unheard through the jungle. Thus, there always seemed to be a possibility that they might take action against small parties or isolated individuals, whom they undoubtedly saw as interlopers. The Jarawa had no firearms but did possess very powerful bows. Major Croley, the leader on Operation Baldhead IV, made positive efforts to appear friendly and unthreatening to the Jarawa. They invariably fled when he encountered one of their camps, but he made it a practice to leave small and useful presents such as pieces of cloth, fishhooks, cords and nails, and sometimes he would return to find small gifts in return, including, on one occasion, a bow. There are no records of the Japanese making any similar efforts to contact the Jarawa.

None of these indigenous people could read or write, so there are few historical records. Marco Polo certainly knew of the islands and wrote about them, but whether he actually visited them is uncertain. A Maratha admiral named Kanhoji Angre had his base there in the early eighteenth century, from where he attacked passing ships and in 1713 even captured the yacht of the British Governor of Bombay. Despite many efforts by European navies, both individually and collectively, Kanhoji Angre was never defeated and died at home in 1729.

The islands were left alone until the British established their first colony in 1789, although this was abandoned only seven years later. The British finally annexed the islands in the mid-nineteenth century adding them to their growing empire and in 1858 established a penal colony in Port Blair for Indians convicted for taking part in the Mutiny. The islands achieved considerable notoriety in 1872 when the Earl of Mayo, Viceroy of India and a noted reformer, was assassinated by a convict while on a tour of inspection. In 1908 the infamous Cellular Goal, a large prison complex, was completed, where newly-arrived convicts were housed in solitary confinement for their first six months on the island, but longer if they failed to behave. The harbour and the prison were at Port Blair, but the capital and main administrative facilities were on Ross Island, just over a mile to the east of Port Blair. These remained on the island until mid-1940 when an earthquake struck the island and the colony's administrative facilities were moved to Port Blair, which was where they were when the Japanese arrived.

The Japanese Invasion

By early 1942 the islands had a population of some 40,000, of whom between 3,000 and 5,000 (but nobody knew for sure) were the indigenous people. There were several hundred Europeans, involved in government, administration and management, with some engaged in forestry and a very few in coconut plantations. The remainder were Indians, who were employed by the government or by the Forestry Department. A significant number of the Indians were former prisoners or their families and descendants, who had been sentenced to exile for sedition and who were banned from returning to India when released at the end of their sentence. There was also a substantial group from the Ranchi area in the state of Orissa, who provided most of the labour force in the forestry camps.

The peacetime garrison comprised a company rotated from British infantry units in the Calcutta area, together with the resident Andaman and Nicobar Military Police Battalion (300 Sikhs with twenty-three British officers). This paramilitary force maintained security in Port Blair and at the forestry camps, where its main task was to prevent labourers molesting Jarawa women and the resulting retaliatory attacks by Jarawa men. There was also a small civil police force responsible for crime and criminals.

C Company, North Staffordshire Regiment had arrived in early December but when the Japanese attacked Malaya on 8 December 1941 the defence of the Andamans was rapidly reassessed. As a result, 4th Battalion 10th Gurkha Rifles (4/10GR) arrived in Port Blair as reinforcements in early January 1942. RAF presence on the islands was limited to two Lysander army cooperation aircraft and a large fuel dump. The Japanese conducted intermittent bombing raids and frequent reconnaissance flights but the ground forces had no defence against either.

The sole naval presence was a Royal Indian Navy auxiliary minesweeper, HMIS *Sophie Marie*, which had been deployed to Port Blair on 27 February 1942. On 1 March she was lying alongside at Port Blair when she was suddenly ordered to sea to avoid an expected bombing raid. The captain took his ship to the southern end of South Andaman and having received the 'all clear' was returning through the

Macpherson Strait when the ship struck a mine and sank within a few minutes. Fortunately, it was only just over a mile from the shore and only one of her crew was lost.

The overwhelming Japanese successes in Malaya and Singapore led to a rapid reappraisal of the defence of the Andamans, which concluded that the islands were indefensible. As a result, on 10 March Indian Hindu priests were evacuated, together with all British women and children except for the Deakes family who remained behind as the father had suffered a stroke and was unable to travel. The Army units – North Staffordshires and 4/10 GR – were withdrawn aboard the troopship SS *Neuralia*, reaching Madras on 20 March.

For their part, having secured Malaya and Singapore, the main reason for the Japanese to invade the Andamans was that they needed to deny them to the British who might use them as a naval and air base to attack the maritime supply route between Singapore and Rangoon. Secondly, they wanted to establish a seaplane base from which to patrol the Bay of Bengal. Accordingly, they mounted Operation D and dispatched a remarkably strong invasion force from Penang, consisting of nine transports carrying an infantry battalion of the 18th Infantry Division and the 12th Special Base Force, with an escort of warships, which arrived in Port Blair on 23 March. Overall commander was Captain Kawasaki Harumi, IJN.

The invaders carried out a surprise landing on Ross Island at 0630 hours, followed by a second on Port Blair shortly afterwards. Detachments were also sent to other known populated areas such as Port Cornwallis at the northern end of North Andaman. There was no armed resistance to the invaders, one of whose first acts was to release some 400 prisoners from the jail. However, for no discernible reason, the Japanese occupation of the Andaman Islands was particularly savage, even though there had been no resistance whatsoever to their arrival. At the same time that the prisoners were being released from the jail, eight senior officials who had remained in their posts in Port Blair were arrested and then forced to dig pits in which they then had to stand with only their heads, shoulders and chest exposed. They were then bayoneted and finally shot. In another incident, Mr Bird, the Chief Commissioner's secretary and an Englishman, was publicly beheaded for having communicated with one his clerks after he had been arrested. Despite this, other British officials and the officers of the erstwhile police force were simply detained and then shipped to Singapore, where they spent the rest of the war in Changi or Sime Road jails. This was accompanied by major looting, rape and compulsory enlistment of numerous local women as 'comfort girls'– a shocking prelude to a consistently cruel campaign against the civil population, which lasted until August 1945 and in which many as many as 30,000, out of a population of 40,000, were killed.

The Japanese Occupation
As soon as the position had stabilised the Japanese set up a seaplane base at Port Blair, with some eighteen flying boats (long-range H6K1 'Mavis' and H8K1 'Emily' types), which were employed to patrol deep into the Indian Ocean. The existing airfield, located some miles south of Port Blair was very small and unsuitable for fighters, which had to be based at Mingalon in Burma, although the airfield was developed enabling it to take a small number of fighters from early 1943.[52] Port Blair was an excellent natural harbour, and became a base for destroyers and cruisers, but never submarines, which were based at Penang and Singapore.

The land forces were concentrated around Port Blair and Ross Island and there were only very minor Japanese outposts in the rest of the Andamans. Patrols were carried out in small motorboats, but these were often noisy and clearly anticipated meeting no enemies. Aircraft also carried out regular reconnaissance flights over the islands, but seem never to have spotted any enemy activity.

The Japanese sought to make political capital out of their occupation by appearing to transfer the administration of the Andaman Islands to the Indian independence movement, Azad Hind. This was purely a façade as they retained all power, even though the Indian leader, Subhas Chandra Bhose, was allowed to visit Port Blair in late 1943 and the islands were given a Bhose-appointed governor and new Hindi names. During his visit Bhose was kept well away from the islanders and even during his brief time in Port Blair the Japanese were arresting and torturing members of the Azad Hind movement. Furthermore, shortly after Bhose had left, on 30 January 1944, forty-four Indians, the majority of them members of the Indian Independence League, were accused of spying and shot by the Japanese in what was known as the Homfreyganj massacre. In reality, the Japanese Navy never handed over any authority to Azad Hind and remained in total control until the capitulation in August 1945.

The worst atrocities were saved for the very last, because as food became increasingly scarce the Japanese decided to get rid of the old and unemployable. So, on 13 August 1945 300 Indians were loaded aboard three boats and taken to an uninhabited island. When several hundred yards off the beach they were forced to jump into the sea; one-third drowned and the remainder who reached the shore were simply left to starve – just eleven were alive when British rescuers arrived six weeks later. In a different event, on 14 August 800 civilians were taken to another uninhabited island where they were dumped on the beach. Shortly afterwards nineteen Japanese troops came ashore and shot or bayoneted every last one of the unarmed civilians. The following day more troops arrived to burn and bury all the bodies.

In contrast, was the curious story of the arrival in early June 1942 of six exhausted survivors of the MV *Woolgar*, which had been sunk on 7 March 1942. The five Norwegian officers and one British Royal Navy gunner, Able Seaman Dennis Whitehouse, had been in the lifeboat for eighty-six days. They were held in custody, where they were not too badly treated, but in December the four surviving Norwegians (one had died shortly after landing) were transferred by ship to Singapore, where they were held in Changi Jail, but Whitehouse was kept behind. The Japanese seem to have had great difficulty with their officers' staff cars and for inexplicable reasons, Whitehouse was taken on as the chauffeur/mechanic and remained on the island for the remainder of the war. He was the only Caucasian in Port Blair and had no means of escape, so his absence would have been noticed within minutes (this story is told in Appendix B).

The Allied Sea and Air Campaign
The Japanese always saw the Andamans as primarily a naval responsibility so the first commander was Rear-Admiral Shigeru Ishikawa, who was succeeded by Rear-Admiral Teizo Hara in 1944, who remained for the rest of the war. Having achieved its mission, the bulk of the Japanese invasion fleet departed on 27 March, leaving 3rd Destroyer Flotilla comprising 11th and 19th Destroyer Divisions, each of one cruiser and three destroyers. The first Allied counter-attack on the

Andamans came on 2 April 1942, only ten days after the Japanese arrival, which was carried out by five B-17 Flying Fortress bombers of the India-based United States' 7th Bombardment Group, led by the group commander, Major-General Brereton, in person. The five bombers overflew Port Blair at 1,000 feet intending to bomb the invasion fleet, which was expected to be still in the harbour, but most had already left and although there were several hits, no significant damage was done.

The first British attacks came on 14 and 18 April 1942, when two Hudson light bombers flew from their base in India, refuelled at Akyab in Burma and then attacked the flying boats at anchor in Port Blair. One British aircraft was damaged in the first raid and one was shot down in the second.

The first operation of any size was Operation Stab, a simulated amphibious landing on the Andamans, undertaken by the British to divert Japanese attention from the US attack on Guadalcanal, which started on 7 August 1942. Force A sailed from Colombo on 30 July, comprising two aircraft carriers, one battleship, three cruisers and five destroyers – all British except for one cruiser and one destroyer, which were Dutch. As these warships came round the north of Ceylon three convoys sailed from Trincomalee, Vizagapatam and Madras, all giving the impression of heading for the Andamans. The warships were sighted at 1040 hours by an enemy reconnaissance aircraft, but as this was precisely what was required, no action was taken.

That night a communications diversion was created, which started with one of the troopships reporting that it had been damaged in a collision with another ship and was unable to proceed. The supposed victim used plain language and the flagship promptly issued a rebuke, also in plain language, for making an operational report in plain language! A further exchange of signals led to the fleet commander announcing that he had decided to cancel the operation and ordered all ships to return to base. The following morning a Japanese H6K1 'Mavis' flying boat was found shadowing the warships, and was promptly shot down by two British fighters. The warships entered Trincomalee harbour just before dark that night. It was certainly an elaborate charade, but whether it misled the Japanese or not is not known.

From then on there were frequent attacks and photographic flights on the Andamans, although virtually all concentrated on Port Blair and the surrounding area, particularly the flying boat anchorage, the dock facilities, the Chatham Island sawmill and the new airfield being built three miles south of Port Blair; there were no significant targets elsewhere. The Japanese anti-aircraft defences were reasonably effective and shot down or damaged a number of aircraft. The US Army Air Force carried out numerous raids, including on 30 November 1942, 7 January 1943, and 15 April 1944. The RAF raided with increasing frequency as the war progressed, including minelaying on Port Blair harbour and its approaches, examples being on 28–29 August 1944 by eleven Liberators (one lost) and 17 May 1945 by twelve Liberators (one lost).

Operation Pedal

The Allied navies carried out several major raids on the Andamans. The first, Operation Pedal, was in June 1944 and carried out by Task Force 60, comprising one carrier, one battleship, one battlecruiser and three cruisers, with eight destroyers providing the screen. The air strike was carried out by fifteen Barracudas escorted by twenty-three Corsairs, which attacked Port Blair at 0530 hours on 21 June; one Barracuda was lost. TF60 returned to Trincomalee on 22 June. There were also numerous bombardments by warships as the British reasserted their grip on the Indian Ocean. On 26 October submarine HMS *Shalimar* surfaced to bombard Port Blair and Ross Island and on 19 March 1945 three destroyers did the same. Between 8 and 18 April 1945 the British undertook Operation Sunfish in which a large task force attacked the Nicobar Islands but two carriers diverted to launch an air attack on Port Blair on 11 April.

In May the British detected a Japanese plan to send the cruiser *Haguro* and destroyer *Kamikaze* to Port Blair to redeploy some of the garrison to mainland Malaya, but the two ships were intercepted and the cruiser sunk.

While all this sea and air activity was taking place, there was also a great deal of action taking place on the ground and not only were British troops ashore in the Andaman Islands for most of the war but their presence, although suspected, was never positively identified by the Japanese.

Chapter 10

Operation Baldhead I

These air and sea attacks, both real and feint, showed that the Allies had not forgotten the Andamans, forcing the Japanese to maintain a sizeable garrison there up to the end of the war. Apparently unknown to them, however, there were repeated ground incursions in which small parties of British and Indian troops landed on the islands and spent protracted periods there, without once being positively detected, let alone attacked by the Japanese or their allies, the Indian National Army (INA) and the Andaman Police Force.

The first problem for the British was that not even the most minimal preparations had been made for stay-behind parties or to leave wirelesses with trusted inhabitants, so from the day the Japanese arrived there was total silence from the Andamans. As described in the previous chapter, the Allies carried out frequent air raids, and there were also photographic reconnaissance flights, but there was no information whatsoever on the actual situation on the ground.

The Japanese carried out several air raids in the Madras area and in the mouth of the Hooghly River in April 1942, leading British Army intelligence staff to suspect that the Andaman Islands were being used as a base for submarines and bombers. In addition, the British were very aware of the possible value of the Andamans as a springboard for their own operations to recapture the lost territories in South-East Asia.

A further factor, according to Lieutenant-Colonel Beyts of SOE, was that General Wavell, the Commander-in-Chief, was bringing pressure to bear on the SOE (India) Mission to justify its existence by quick results.[53] So, two plans were quickly concocted and put into operation. One was Operation Longshanks, a commando-style raid on the Axis merchant ships interned in the harbour at Portuguese Goa, as will be described in Part III. The other was to send a reconnaissance party to the Andaman

Islands, which was initially named Operation Bunkum, but later changed to Baldhead.

SOE(India) conceived a five-stage plan, based on their experiences in Europe:[54]

- Phase 1. Introduction of a seven-man party into the Andamans to carry out a reconnaissance and to establish a radio station and a base camp.
- Phase 2. After the party had been two months ashore to send stores, rations, and two extra men, thus enabling the party to remain for seven months. Also send arms and ammunition to be issued to armed resistance parties.
- Phase 3. Contact, train and equip resistance groups.
- Phase 4. Initiate minor sabotage acts over a large area and at irregular intervals.
- Phase 5. Carry out major acts of sabotage as directed by GHQ India.

All this was intended to lead into an eventual invasion of the Andamans for which the military parties would have reconnoitred the beaches and routes, and once the invaders were ashore, provide guides, while the armed resistance parties would carry out coordinated acts of sabotage and ambushes to distract the Japanese.

Operation Bunkum/Baldhead I

The first incursion was originally designated Operation Bunkum, which was scarcely very inspiring for those involved, but was subsequently compromised, the records do not state how or when, and changed to the less uninspiring Baldhead.[55]

The man selected to lead it was Denis Arthur McKaura McCarthy, who had been serving in the Indian Police for some years before being appointed Superintendent of Police in the Andamans in 1937, a post combined with Commanding Officer of the 300-strong Military Police Battalion. He had travelled widely in his new domain and appears to have been more aware than most of the Japanese threat and from 1940 onwards he had conducted personal reconnaissance of beaches, roads and tracks. He also talked to a few people, such as village headmen and elders, who might be possible contacts should war come to the islands.

Like the majority of British officials, he was ordered to leave the islands in March 1942 and he successfully navigated a small boat across the Indian Ocean to Ceylon. In October of that year he was in Raebareli in India when he was approached by the former District Commissioner of the Nicobar Islands to ask whether he would volunteer to lead a party back to the Andamans to assess the situation, gauge the impact of the Japanese occupation and, if possible, to rescue any remaining Europeans still being held there. McCarthy was eager to volunteer, since not only did he have five years' experience of living in the Andamans, but he had also discussed in very general terms the possibility of collaboration with the headman of Ferrarganj, a village on the outskirts of Port Blair.

The operation order was issued on 9 December 1942[56] and called for a party of six, with McCarthy being allowed to pick his own team. His second-in-command was Jemadar (Lieutenant) Habib Shah, formerly of the Andaman Police Battalion, but now a Viceroy's Commissioned Officer (VCO) in the Indian Army's General Service Corps (IAGSC). Third was Havildar (Corporal) Gyan Singh, also a former Andaman policeman, but now also in the IAGSC, who was the emergency wireless operator. Fourth was Sergeant Dickens of the Royal Signals, the wireless operator. Finally, came two havildars, Joseph Bakla and Peter Bakla, who were cousins and formerly Ranchi workers in the Andaman Forestry Service.

Their tasks, as laid out in the operation order, were to:

- Discover Japanese Naval, Air and Military dispositions.
- Obtain information of assistance to any future combined operations against these islands.
- Raise an organisation to synchronise with any future invading force by means of Fifth Column activities and Sabotage Operations. If no future invasion is envisaged, then such sabotage operations will be carried out on orders from H.Q., whenever the organisation has been reported as ready for action.
- Install a wireless station which would be of essential value to an invading force, but, before the arrival of which could only be used in emergency.

The planned duration of the mission was, to say the least, ambitious. Baldhead I would involve arriving on the island about 20–23 January 1943, establishing a base camp, carrying out a reconnaissance to Port Blair and making contact with locals. Baldhead II would then consist of the return of the submarine on 20–23 March carrying two reinforcements, plus a quantity of additional stores, which would enable the shore party, now eight strong, to remain for a further eight months, a period, it should be pointed out, which would have included the entire south-west Monsoon period. There was, however, an option that if McCarthy considered withdrawing for health reasons, then the stores would still be landed, but all men then taken off to return to Colombo.

The responsibility for the choice of landing place was spelt out in the orders and remained unchanged for all subsequent operations.

The final decision as to the site at which a landing will take place rests with the Commander H.M. Submarine. He will be responsible to the safety of the S/M and will have discretion to cancel the Operation should it appear to him to be attended by undue risk to the S/M. The leader of the party is responsible for the party once they have left the S/M. He has discretion to cancel the Operation should it appear to him to be attended by undue risk. Should the primary landing place prove to be impracticable every endeavour will be made to carry out the Operation at an alternative place.

The six men assembled at the newly-established 'Guerrilla Training Unit' at Kharaksavala near Poona, which was conveniently sited next to Lake Fife, where the canoe training was carried out.[57] Having completed their training, they arrived in Ceylon on 23 December to undergo a further period of briefings and training at the SOE's Advanced Operations School, near Trincomalee. They sailed aboard the Dutch submarine HNethMS *O-24*, commanded by Lt Cdr Wopke Johan de Vries, RNethN, on 14 January 1943. Apart from the six men, *O-24* carried some 4,000lb (1.8 tons) of stores including three two-man collapsible canoes (folboats), wireless equipment, rations, and cooking equipment, as well as a Sten gun for each man.

Communications
At sea the submarine had the usual ship-shore communications link, but only when surfaced. Once ashore, McCarthy's party had wireless communications to the SOE base stations in Calcutta and Ceylon. There was no direct link between the shore party and the submarine, although messages could have been sent from the Andamans to Calcutta or Ceylon, where they would have been passed to the Royal Navy for onward transmission to the submarine via the normal naval fleet communications systems. There was no question at this stage of the war of forward communications between the base-camp and the patrols.

Sergeant Dickins' wireless set was a Mark III, one of the early variations of the 'suitcase sets' developed for use by SOE agents. It was powered by secondary (i.e., rechargeable) batteries and the loading list included a petrol-fuelled charging set and eight gallons of petrol. The operation order stipulated that '. . . the party will not use their W/T once communications have been established except in emergency or to report the party ready to be re-embarked'. At the other end, however, the Andaman frequencies would have been monitored regularly.

The communications team carried codes and cyphers, although their exact nature is not known. Codewords were used, both for security purposes and to minimise transmission times; thus, for example, Dickens sent the codeword '*Jazey*' at 0030 hours on 30 January, indicating that they were safely ashore and had established their base-camp in the Andamans.

The Operation
The submarine reached Middle Andaman on 19 January making the landfall, as planned, on the west coast, some four miles south of Flat Island and 70 miles from Port Blair. After dark the men and all their equipment went ashore and the six men set up their first campsite some distance from the shore and near a stream. McCarthy and his men then spent a week in getting themselves sorted out, setting up a 'bolt-hole' about 800 yards away, learning how to get food from the jungle, and generally adjusting to their new environment.

Their first disappointment was the rations. The situation had been helped by McCarthy's agreement (and, presumably, that of Sergeant Dickens as well) to eat vegetarian rations. McCarthy had been assured before leaving that the rations had been carefully selected, but once ashore, they discovered that the major items were a large supply of dried pumpkin, with plenty of ghee and some rice; there was also some dried potato, but only sufficient for eight meals. The sole luxury was a small amount of chocolate. It was therefore fortunate that McCarthy had had the foresight to include a fishing net and a silenced .22 rifle among their stores. A further problem was that the can labelled 'rifle oil' contained linseed oil, which caused the weapons to jam, but then they found that the ghee, of which there was a plentiful supply, worked much better.

McCarthy's Month-Long Trek (see Maps 4A, 4B)

1 February. McCarthy, Habib Shah and Joseph Bakla set off for Port Blair at 1940 hours on 1 February, leaving Sergeant Dickens, Gyan Singh and Peter Bakla behind in the base-camp. McCarthy and Habib Shah were in the leading folboat, towing Joseph Bakla in the second. Each man had his personal kit with him, and there was one case of rations in the leading boat, and two cases in the second. In order to minimise weight, they took only one groundsheet, one mosquito net and one blanket between the three of them. There was also a watertight parcel contained the camera, film, maps and a notebook. They paddled out to sea until about a mile offshore and then turned south, parallel to the shore. Progress was slow, partly due to their inexperience, but also because the tidal set was against them.

2 February. At about 0130 hours, after some six hours of continuous paddling, McCarthy decided that they had had enough for the first night; they were tired, the canoes were filling with water and he had no idea where they were. On reaching the shore they hid the stores and folboats in the jungle edge and then, cold, wet and weary, tried to get some rest. When it became light McCarthy discovered that had not reached Spike Island, as he had thought, but had only got as far as Foul Bay. They were undisturbed throughout the day and after dusk they set off again.

3 February. Although they felt that once again they were making little progress, they did, in fact, reach Spike Island in the early hours of 3 February, where they made camp. This island lay across the western end of Middle Strait, a very narrow waterway which separated Middle and South Andaman. Even though the three men had only been going for three days, conditions were already bad. Afloat they were constantly wet and cold, and when they were ashore sleep was difficult, and one man always had to be on guard. Fresh water was proving difficult to find and as the waterholes were few and far between there was always the danger that they might bump into a hostile patrol on a similar quest. They were, therefore, frequently reduced to obtaining water from bamboo, although the quantities were small and it took time. Finally, the ever-present ticks were proving to be a particularly annoying factor in their lives.

McCarthy's original idea was to paddle as far south as possible down the western shore of South Andaman, before hiding the folboats and continuing on foot to Port Blair. But he now decided that the worsening weather, coupled with his lack of knowledge of the western side of South Andaman, indicated that it would be better to go through Middle Strait and then down the east side of South Andaman instead. So, having hidden two food containers for their return journey, they started into the Middle Strait at 2130 hours.

4 February. The men arrived off Flat Bay at 0130 hours 4 February, but were unable to reach the shore until just after dawn. Once again they were soaked through and very cold, and McCarthy began to feel ill, a state which was to continue for the rest of this remarkable expedition. They did not move that day, and McCarthy's illness quickly developed into fever, vomiting and shivering fits.

5–6 February. That night McCarthy became so ill and cold that he woke the others at 0400 hours and lit a fire, huddling together to try and get warm. In the morning (5 February) McCarthy felt too ill to travel and sent his two companions off to reconnoitre on their own. They left at 0900 hours on 5 February and returned at 1600 hours the following day, which meant that McCarthy underwent a period of over 30 hours entirely alone and very ill – not a pleasant experience. When the two men returned they told him that they had found traces of Jarawa, although they had not actually met any. They had come across several foresters' campsites, but those, too, were deserted and they had also seen some wild cattle. One fortunate find was a bottle of engine oil, which they had brought back and all three then used it on their weapons in place of ghee.

7 February. After a night's rest and a quiet day they set off again in their folboats at 1900 hours on 7 February. Their aim was to land near

Entrance Hill at the southern end of the Middle Strait to see if a known campsite was occupied.

8 February. The night was very dark and it was, as usual, raining, with occasional flashes of lightning, one of which fortunately enabled them to spot a boat of some sort anchored off Entrance Hill. All three had seen the boat but differed in their interpretation of its size, so McCarthy changed his plan and turned back to a site he knew at Belle Island. When they reached it, however, they found some signs of recent habitation but could not find the well, so they crossed the strait again and went ashore on Baratang Island. The landing was difficult but the campsite was pleasant and had a water source. At one point they heard a boat's diesel engines in the distance, but were not otherwise disturbed and were ready to move off again after dark, but had to wait for the tide.

9 February. They had to wait so long for slack water that they were only able to move a short distance before approaching daylight forced them to head for the shore. It rained for most of the day. They observed two columns of smoke, which they presumed to be Jarawa campsites and also heard diesel engines, but again saw no boats.

10 February. At this point McCarthy was searching for a route through the mangrove swamps, known as 'Canal I', but could not find it. The terrible conditions, their tiredness and their apparently slow progress were beginning to tell, and Joseph Bakla, in particular, became very depressed, although McCarthy, despite his own continuing sickness, tried his best to keep up their spirits.

11 February. McCarthy went out on his own and found the entrance to the canal, which had been marked incorrectly on the map. These canals were narrow channels which had been cleared by the foresters through the otherwise impenetrable mangrove swamps. The channels were just wide enough to allow the passage of a timber-laden barge, propelled by oars. McCarthy and his men also hid yet another cache of food for the return journey. Their campsite had signs of previous occupation by Jarawa and they also found an opium stick which could not have come from the Jarawa and was most likely to have been left behind by someone running away from the Japanese in the town.

12 February. After two days in the same camp, they left just after dark on 12 February and made good progress through Canal I. Fortunately, they did not meet anyone coming in the opposite direction as there would have been little room in which to turn and escape, but luck was with them and they had just left the southern end of the canal and were once again in open water when a timber boat passed them at a range of only 100–200 yards. The raiders clearly heard the sound of voices and laughter, but were unable to identify the language; it was certainly not Bengali, Hindustani or Punjabi, and the two Indian soldiers thought it might be Burmese.

They pushed on and successfully passed through Canal II followed by Canal III and then passed inshore of Kyd Island. It was a clear night and the moonlight enabled them to paddle on close to the edge of the mangrove. As dawn approached they were exhausted – they had covered some 20 miles and were too tired to make the effort to find a campsite, so they tied the two canoes together and stayed afloat. They tried to sleep, but all three were soaked through and cold, while McCarthy continued to suffer from his fever.

13 February. Despite the evidence of other marine traffic, and after just a few hours rest, they pushed on after dawn, but found a landing place in the late morning and went ashore. They rested for the remainder of the day and then after dark paddled a short distance to a camp known as Baratagajig, which Joseph Bakla had known some seven years previously when working for the Forestry Department.

14–15 February. This was the end of the canoeing phase of their journey and they underwent what even the indomitable McCarthy could only describe as 'two miserable days' as they dragged the canoes and heavy gear up a steep slope and camouflaged them.

16 February. From now on they moved on foot and by day, and after so many days sitting in a canoe and paddling, walking and carrying a heavy load must have been very hard work. McCarthy continued to be ill and found increasing difficulty in carrying his share of the load, but he persevered. McCarthy described this as 'another miserable day' but without further elaboration, except to comment that he was 'very sick all night'.

17 February. They started the next morning by building a raft to ferry their stores across a minor river and then continued on their way, but with great care as they encountered increasing signs of human activity. They stumbled on empty boats, saw the instantly recognisable prints of Japanese footwear, and even heard a patrol singing around its campfire.

They also found traces of the Jarawa, but never met them either, although that is not to say that the Jarawa were not aware of them. There was also an increasing danger of meeting foresters, as Joseph was convinced that he saw evidence of new logging tracks.

18–19 February. Two further rough days followed as they neared their objective, but with ever increasing dangers as they not only came across increasing human activity, but also encountered traces of elephants, which were widely used in the Forestry Department's logging operations. Fortunately, Joseph Bakla was very familiar with them and was able to identify tracks of elephants pulling logs, elephants ridden by mahouts, sick animals and even rogue elephants.

Still McCarthy and his two companions pressed on, walking through the dense jungle without cutting in order to avoid leaving a recognisable track. This slowed them even further and they continued to suffer from the attention of the ever-present leaches, and from the many thorn bushes which engaged in their clothing. They eventually stumbled on the main road and, recognising the spot, McCarthy realised that they were just half-a-mile away from their destination, Ferrarganj, a village some 10 miles due north of Port Blair, where he wanted to meet the headman, whom he had known in pre-war days.

20 February. They were able to approach the village without being detected during daylight, but then waited in the jungle until after dark when McCarthy and Habib Shah entered the village to find the headman, while Joseph stayed behind to prepare a meal. The headman was astonished to see them, but very courageously took them to a storeroom in his house, where he briefed them at length on the horrors of Japanese occupation.

McCarthy heard for the first time details of the Japanese arrival, of the execution of Mr Bird, secretary to the Chief Commissioner, and of the subsequent random killings, assaults and rapes. He was also told that the surviving colonial officials had been taken away by ship, but seems not to have been told about the lone Able Seaman Whitehouse.[58] Their conversation was interrupted by the arrival of Japanese and a local interpreter. The Headman invited them into the central room of his house, so that McCarthy and Habib Shah were able to hear clearly all that was discussed, which involved the headman in giving the names of all inhabitants of the village, and ended with the Japanese stressing the need to obey the curfew. At no point did the headman give any indication of his other visitors in the adjacent storeroom.

When McCarthy and Habib Shah left the headman's house they nearly bumped into two Japanese soldiers standing less than ten yards away on the side of the main road. The two men managed to change course and stroll as innocently as possible back into the jungle, taking particular care not to fall into the soldiers' trap of keeping in step with each other. They apparently aroused no suspicions and were very relieved when they slipped into the jungle without having been challenged.

The following night McCarthy and Habib Shah returned for a second rendezvous with the headman in the jungle fringe, where the latter told them that there was a large number of Japanese in the village police post. This shortened the second meeting, although the headman was still able to give them a lot of detailed information on Japanese dispositions in and around Port Blair. The two soldiers then withdrew back to their jungle camp where Joseph was waiting for them.

21 February – see Map 4b. McCarthy and his companions left at 1500 hours on 21 February with the intention of returning in about two weeks' time. They headed for the camp where they had left their foldboats, but McCarthy was finding it increasingly difficult; he was sick, weakened both by illness and malnutrition, and simply exhausted, but he had no alternative but to keep going.

24 February. On this day there occurred the most distressing incident of the entire operation. All six men in the Baldhead I party were armed with Sten guns, which were light, easy to carry and effective at short ranges, but these weapons were very new and suffered from some serious design faults. In the early afternoon the three men were working their way through some very dense jungle, when Habib Shah spotted a way through and called to the others. At this point he stumbled on some undergrowth and fell headlong into a dry stream bed, but as he fell his Sten swung forward and hit the ground, butt first, the shock causing the bolt to travel back sufficiently far to engage a round from the magazine, whereupon it was pressed forward by the return spring. That the weapon would fire was now inevitable, but most unfortunately it did so straight into Habib Shah's chest, passing through his body and exiting from his back just below the liver. He died within two minutes, leaving McCarthy and Joseph stunned by the tragedy and its suddenness. They scraped a shallow grave with their mess tins, laid the body in it and then covered it with stones. They moved away a short distance to spend a lonely and miserable night.

25 February. At first light the two men returned to the grave to remove anything which might identify the body, if found by the Japanese, and then, after a final farewell to their fallen comrade, moved on. They chanced upon a drag-path used by elephants to haul timber, which enabled them to reach the camp at Jirkatang at 1000 hours, where they found that someone had visited the site in their absence, but fortunately had not discovered the folboats. They found a packet of Japanese cigarettes, although this had not necessarily been dropped by a Japanese soldier as they frequently used cigarettes to pay locals for labouring tasks. They recovered the folboats and now with one man to each, departed at 1730 hours. They passed an abandoned dugout canoe. By this stage Joseph was very tired, so that McCarthy, ill as he was, had to take him in tow.

26 February. The two men staggered ashore at about 0500 hours, whereupon Joseph managed to light a fire and brew some tea to try to help McCarthy recover. They then moved to one of their former campsites, where they found that it had been visited by the Jarawa but the cache of stores was untouched.

27 February–3 March. The two men carried on paddling by night and resting ashore by day, and reached Spike Island on 1 March. They were both now very weak and water was again becoming a major problem, so once again they had to cut bamboo. By 3 March they were well on their way, and abreast of Flat Island, but the surf was so strong that they were forced to spend the night at sea, the first time they had done this.

4 March. At dawn McCarthy discovered they were 2–3 miles too far to the north, so they paddled back southwards and then landed at 0730 hours, whereupon Joseph went inland to make contact with base-camp while McCarthy sat on the stores and changed into dry clothing.

Together Again
On joining forces once again and having told the three at base camp the sad news of Habib Shah's death Sergeant Dickens reported that he, Gyan Singh and Patrick Bakla had had a quiet time apart from a brief brush

with some Jarawa who attacked with bows and arrows but were repelled. Wireless communications with Colombo were in good order, so McCarthy sent a brief report on his travels, plus a request to be picked up.

They had to wait for some three weeks before the submarine arrived, but the monotony was broken when they saw three B-17 Flying Fortresses fly overhead and then bomb what McCarthy presumed to have been targets identified by him in his radio report.

On the morning of 21 March McCarthy and his companions erected the two canvas squares on the beach and that night HNethMS *O-24*, the same boat that had brought them arrived to relieve McCarthy and his remaining four companions. What happened next is related in the next chapter. McCarthy and his men had been sixty-two days on an island totally in the hands of the enemy. The Jarawa obviously knew the location of the base camp and probably saw the moving party frequently as well, but as they had neither the means nor the desire to communicate with the Japanese, this had no effect on the British mission.

McCarthy and his group had spent thirty-three days on a patrol in which he and Joseph covered some 200 miles, repeatedly encountering evidence of the Japanese presence. They found Japanese boats moored on various islands, saw prints of *tabi* shoes in the mud and were even close enough on several occasions to hear Japanese talking, singing, and even, on one memorable occasion, snoring. But never once did the Japanese spot them. They also came close to various groups of foresters and villagers, but, again, avoided detection. The only person they did make contact with, the headman at Ferrarganj, welcomed them and clearly did not subsequently report them to the Japanese or the police.

McCarthy and the four Indians had previous knowledge of the Andamans and their people, which was of immense help, although even they had no knowledge of the language spoken by the Jarawas.

Intelligence Report
The intelligence summary resulting from Baldhead I was the first hard news the British high command had received from the Andamans since the arrival of the Japanese. Considering the meagre resources at McCarthy's disposal, it was very detailed and of high value. Its main conclusions were:

- **Enemy Forces.** Some 13,000 Japanese troops had taken part in the invasion. This number had slowly fallen to about 2,000 by November, but was then increased by a further 5,000 later in the same month. Ross Island had been cleared of all local residents and the garrison commander, an admiral, had his HQ in the former governor's residence. McCarthy also gave locations of main Japanese barracks, strongpoints and gun positions, both coastal and anti-aircraft.
- **Naval.** McCarthy saw only light naval forces, but heard occasional naval gunfire, which he thought was on a firing range. One cargo ship made a monthly voyage to the mainland and another smaller vessel visited the outlying garrison at Stewart Sound, also on a monthly basis, calling at coastal villages *en route*. Both ships spent two weeks in every month alongside at Port Blair.
- **Air.** Port Blair was serving as a seaplane base, and some seaplanes had been damaged in a USAAF raid. The airfield at Port Blair was being extended and it was reported that another was being built elsewhere. There was little evidence of enemy air activity.
- **Enemy Ground Activity.** Enemy troops appeared to spend most of their time in their cantonments, but with occasional visits to outlying villages in either trucks or motor launches.
- **Civilian Population.** There were numerous prohibited areas and nobody was allowed to leave their village without a pass, which was regularly checked by Japanese sentries. All domestic wirelesses had been seized and use of the telephone was banned. The Japanese ruled through fear and drastic punishments, and there was an increasing number of 'runaways' living in the jungle.
- **Industry.** Some forestry work continued but all the timber had to be placed at the disposal of the Japanese. Rubber growing had ceased. The Japanese also forced villages to produce working parties.
- **Commerce.** Food had to be bought from a central store, but no new clothing of any sort was available. Japanese currency had been introduced and Indian money handed in, although silver rupees were being hoarded.
- **Potential for Special Operations.** It was considered that there was potential in the Andamans to raise a subversive organisation.

- **Map.** McCarthy's intelligence report was accompanied by a detailed trace of his route and a carefully annotated map of the Port Blair area showing all the enemy facilities he had detected.

One factor which should not be overlooked is the extreme vulnerability of this group. Even when they were together, six men armed only with Sten guns and pistols would have stood no chance against a determined attack by the Japanese. This was particularly so in the jungle where the enemy could have approached very close without being detected. This vulnerability was increased when they split into two and even more when Habib Shah was killed. In many respects, McCarthy and Joseph were very fortunate to get back alive.

Another weakness was the lack of medical support and it was fortunate that McCarthy had an extremely steely character which enabled him to continue with the operation despite having a high fever. If any of the party had developed a really serious illness, been seriously wounded by the enemy or badly injured in an accident they would have struggled to cope.

One aspect which clearly worked well was the communications. There seem to have been no major problems, despite the very long distance, the inadequacies of the equipment which was designed for use in Europe, and the known (and many) problems of high-frequency working in the tropics. Sergeant Dickens would have been responsible not only for operating the set but also for charging the batteries, the maintenance of the equipment and the repair of any faults. That there were no adverse comments about the communications speaks volumes – they worked.

The only really serious setback was the death of Habib Shah, but the early models of the Sten gun were designed and produced in a great rush and this was by no means the only death or injury to the shooter. There were cases of soldiers jumping from the backs of lorries and the shock of impact alone being sufficient to fire the weapon. It was, perhaps, fortunate for McCarthy and Joseph that Habib Shah died so quickly, as coping with a wounded man would have been very difficult; they would have had no treatment for him, and for two men to carry him any distance would have been impossible.

But, this was the first major incursion by the British Army into enemy territory and there were many lessons to be learnt – and they were, as will now be seen.

Chapter 11

Operation Baldhead II

Baldhead II was led by Acting Major Monty Rodulfo[59] with Captain Francis Manford[60] as his second-in-command, both SOE officers, heading a small party of British and Indian soldiers. Their task was to resupply the Baldhead I party with rations, weapons and stores, leave behind two of their number as reinforcements and then return to Ceylon, which would enable McCarthy and his Baldhead I party to survive for another three months until the southwest monsoon had run its course. They sailed aboard HNethMS *O-24* (Lt Cdr de Vries), but with two further passengers. One was Lieutenant-Colonel Billy Beyts, chief-of-staff at headquarters of SOE (India), who wanted to see for himself what was going on in the field.[61] The other was Captain Rappaport, a Royal Army Medical Corps doctor, who sailed in response to a signal sent by McCarthy on 4 March saying that he was sick, and while he wanted to stay on, he was in need of a 'medical overhaul'.[62] There were also some four tons of rations, supplies and equipment.

O-24 arrived on 21 March 1943, saw the recognition signal and surfaced off the rendezvous at 2050 hours where they were greeted by McCarthy, who had paddled out with Joseph Baxla. McCarthy was in very poor physical shape and could scarcely walk, while his news of the death of his second-in-command came as a serious blow and meant that there would be nobody of sufficient rank and experience to take charge should his sickness worsen, or he be wounded or die. In addition to that, McCarthy said that he suspected that their wireless transmissions had been intercepted and possibly identified by direction-finding (DF) by the Japanese, as a reconnaissance plane had been seen overhead some days earlier; he was, therefore, concerned that the stores should not be landed here as planned.

An anxious conference was held aboard the submarine between McCarthy, Beyts, Rodulfo and de Vries. Rodulfo was in no doubt that he was in command and that Beyts, although senior in rank, was present as an observer, but nevertheless the latter's opinion had to be taken into account. The meeting concluded that Rodulfo should take his men ashore to eliminate all traces of McCarthy's camp and return to the submarine the following night. Accordingly, all the men of Baldhead II, led by Joseph Baxla, paddled ashore in five folboats, towing three recce boats, and leaving McCarthy and Beyts aboard the submarine. The canoes were hidden some 30 yards inside the jungle and Rodolfo's men settled into the camp for a restless night. They expected Beyts to paddle ashore later to join them and he did set out, but landed too far up the beach, could not find them in the dark, and returned to the submarine.

As soon as it was light the remaining Baldhead I stores were carefully buried and all traces of occupation carefully eliminated. During the day they saw fresh footprints in the sand, suggesting that Jarawa were nearby and when one of his men saw two figures some 70 yards away in the jungle edge Rodulfo fired at them with his Sten gun, which, with hindsight, seems somewhat impetuous, as they do not seem to have posed any threat, not least because their only weapons were bows and arrows.

At about 2000 hours seven folboats and four recce boats, all heavily loaded, put to sea to rejoin the submarine, but when passing through the gap in the coral reef they met Beyts and McCarthy paddling for the shore. Beyts told Rodulfo that the plan had been changed and the supplies aboard the submarine were to be landed here after all. Not surprisingly, Rodulfo was somewhat put out by this and there was a brief hiatus as the nine folboats, five of them towing recce boats, milled around in the darkness while the officers worked out what to do. Rodulfo explained that the camp had been totally dismantled and the stores buried, while there was no doubt that the area was under surveillance by the Jarawa. He won the day, and all the canoes were then paddled on to the submarine where they and their stores were taken aboard.[63]

The submarine then moved to the new site, but meanwhile the doctor had completed his examination of all the Baldhead I party and advised that McCarthy and three of his four men were not fit enough for another stint on the island. This, combined with the loss of McCarthy's second-in-command, led Beyts to decide to cancel Baldhead II, but to put the remaining stores ashore at a place they designated Landing Place B, except for the wireless equipment, which would be taken back to Ceylon.

So, at 1930 hours that evening (23 March) they were preparing to launch the folboats when someone spotted three bright lights near the proposed landing place, and, unsure whether these were Japanese or Jarawas, it was decided not to land. This was followed by a further lengthy conference, the outcome of which was a decision to take the stores to yet another new spot, which was designated Landing Place D.

The submarine arrived off D in the early afternoon and after a lengthy periscope reconnaissance, waited until dark and then surfaced at 2005 hours. It was a very dark, moonless night and Rodulfo led two folboats to look for a way through the reef. They did not find a gap but managed to cross the reef and then disembarked to push their canoes through the very shallow water to the beach, which was a mere eight feet wide and bordered by dark, dense jungle. Although not ideal, Rodulfo decided to go ahead, so the two canoes returned to the submarine.

Ferrying the stores ashore was a long and arduous task, involving five canoes and three recce boats shuttling between the submarine and the beach, paddled by Colonel Beyts and five soldiers. Captain Manford acted as beachmaster, and with the assistance of two soldiers, helped unload and stack the stores, while Rodulfo and three soldiers acted as the covering force in case of attack. The stores had to be carried ashore, which was unpleasant work as the bottom was mostly sharp coral, but with hidden potholes, which could cause a twisted ankle and sometimes were also home to stingrays. The work was completed with a dawn stand-to, collecting stores which had been dropped in the night, and then a period of relaxation until 0900 hours. The ever-precise Rodulfo recorded that they had landed ninety-seven food packs (5,293lb); five packs of explosives (253lb) and a quantity of arms and equipment (464lb), for a total of 6,010lb (2.7 long tons).

The next task was to seek a more permanent hiding-place for the stores and Rodulfo found a suitable thicket where they cleared a space in the middle, laid a base of loose stones, and then soaked it in kerosene in a (probably vain) effort to keep insects at bay. The stores were then neatly piled on the stone foundation and then covered with tarpaulins. Finally, a wall was built around the dump to keep out wild pigs and the whole thing disguised with canes, vines and foliage. In a strange twist, Rodulfo left six primed grenades attached to the wall of the dump to serve as a deterrent to any inquisitive Jarawa, although it seems highly unlikely that they would have had the slightest idea what they were.

Rodulfo then led a small patrol on a search for water, leaving the beach at 1030 hours and returning at 1230 hours. No water was found, although they did discover traces of the Jarawa. That done, the afternoon was spent in tidying up and removing all traces of their presence. The canoes were carried down to the water's edge after dark and, after several adventures in which one canoe was lost, they were all aboard the submarine by 1955 hours and the boat set off for Ceylon, arriving on 29 March.

McCarthy was immediately admitted to hospital where it was found that he had lost three stone in weight and that his blood count was 1.25 million, compared with a normal reading of 4.5–6.5 million. McCarthy was awarded an MBE and Jemedar Habib Shah was Mentioned in Despatches[64] while de Vries was awarded the British DSC. McCarthy prepared a very detailed report and map of Japanese deployments, and wanted to return to the Andamans, but his health was so poor that he was returned to the UK where he was invalided out of the Army.[65]

Chapter 12

Operation Baldhead III

The aims of the next incursion into the Andamans were the same as before – to assess the situation in the islands, to discover the size and deployment of the Japanese garrison, and to reconnoitre landing beaches. The operation was divided into was into three phases, all involving the British submarine, HMS *Taurus*, commanded by Lt Cdr M. R. G. Wingfield, DSO, DSC, RN:

- Baldhead III. Fourteen men landed on 19 December 1943.
- Baldhead IV. A further twelve men landed on 23/24 January 1944 to join the Baldhead III party.
- Baldhead V. All twenty-six men re-embarked on 27/28 March 1944 and returned safely to Ceylon.

Deployment on the next Andaman operation was conducted in two phases, designated Baldhead III and IV, two voyages being necessary because space inside the submarine was limited and there were too many people and stores to be carried in one lift. Baldhead III was led by Major C. L. Greig,[66] who was fifty-three years old but well used to the outdoor life, with Captain K. J. Falconar[67] as his second-in-command, with two British Royal Signals radio operators, Sergeants A. R. Dickins (who had been on Baldhead I) and F. Allen. There were also two Indian officers and eight Indian NCOs: two Gurkhas, four Malays and two Ranchis. They also had some 8,000lb of stores, rations and equipment.

Taurus arrived off Breakfast Bay in South Andaman on 19 December and first ashore was an advance party of Greig and three soldiers in two folboats. Once these had been launched, the submarine withdrew seaward. Greig found no suspicious signs, so he displayed the agreed signal, a square of yellow canvas with a large black ball in the centre, at 1200–1300 hours and again at 1700–1800 hours. That night the submarine closed the shore again, but there was a series of problems. None of the agreed light signals from the shore could be seen, so Falconar was sent ashore in a folboat, but landed in the wrong place. Eventually the shore party was contacted and the submarine's captain having been assured that all was safe, landing the stores commenced, which took two nights and thirty-one round trips.

The procedure was for the submarine crew to bring four recce boats up to the submarine casing, where they were inflated using the submarine's air supply. They were then loaded and the stores firmly tied in place, and the boats linked using ropes. The folboat then came alongside and the towrope from the first recce boat secured to its sternpost. The folboat crew then paddled slowly ahead, while the submarine crew lowered each recce boat into the water in turn. The miniature convoy was then towed in line astern through the breakers to the shore, where the waiting shore party pulled the recce boats into the beach and unloaded them. The recce boats were then relaunched for return to the submarine for the next load.

Once sorted out and the base camp established, the party undertook two reconnaissance patrols. Falconar led a six-man patrol which left in three folboats on the evening of 26 December to investigate the Port Campbell area. They did much useful work, although they were hampered by very inaccurate maps and heavy rain, which made foot patrols particularly hard work. No contact was made with Japanese, although they saw many traces of Jarawa, and one of the Indian soldiers met an INA patrol, but the latter had failed to realise that he was an interloper before he disappeared into the darkness. Major Greig, meanwhile, patrolled in the Breakfast Bay area.

All men were back in the base by mid-January and on the 23rd the Baldhead IV party arrived, also aboard HMS *Taurus* and Baldhead III people were absorbed into Baldhead IV.

Chapter 13

Operation Baldhead IV

Taurus returned to Trincomalee and immediately embarked the Baldhead IV party, comprising Major T. V. Croley,[68] Major R. G. H. Duncan,[69] Sergeants D. Thomas and R. H. Wooldridge, both Royal Signals' wireless telegraphists, one Viceroy's Commissioned Officer, Subedar Bakshish Singh, always addressed as the 'Subedar Sahib', and seven Indian soldiers. Also loaded was a considerable quantity of stores. *Taurus* safely reached the same beach as before on the night of 23/24 January, with contact being made with the Baldhead III party at 2300 hours. Major Greig and Captain Falconar paddled out to the submarine, where they were fed scrambled eggs and beer. The stores were offloaded: one hundred and sixty packages requiring forty-two 'recce boat' trips. The distance from the submarine to the shore was only some 250 yards, but the heavily-loaded boats had to be taken over the reef and then the stores carried several hundred yards up a steep jungle slope to the camp. The whole night was needed and by daybreak all were thoroughly exhausted.

The directive[70] issued to Croley instructed him to:

- Collect all possible information about the enemy.
- Look for suitable hidden bases for naval motor-launches.
- Secure information helpful to invasion on beaches, reefs, roads and tracks.
- Report on possibilities of sabotage of important facilities, such as the radar, direction-finding and telecommunications sites; and enemy aircraft on the ground.
- Suggest methods of preventing the enemy from destroying facilities needed by an invasion force.
- Suggest methods of attacking enemy shipping.

Boats

The small boats were absolutely essential to this and many other missions, and since Croley left a particularly detailed account, they are described here. The 'folboats' were made of hickory frames and struts with a covering of proofed canvas. They were 18 feet long and 2 feet wide, and when loaded drew only about 4 inches of water; they could be assembled by two men in seven minutes or less. There were flotation bags fore and aft and inflatable tubes along the sides just above the unloaded water level, which prevented the boat from tipping over too far. The onboard load was carried in canvas containers, measuring some 3 feet x 2 feet x 1 foot, which could carry between 100 and 150lb depending on the space required, with up to three per boat in addition to the two-man crew. The containers were fitted with shoulder straps for carrying ashore. Croley exercised strict military discipline during the voyages. They rested for ten minutes every hour, which gave them a normal speed of advance when fully loaded of four miles in the hour, although on one occasion, with a following wind, they covered 18 miles in three hours. With such a load the folboats were often paddled up to 30 miles at a stretch during the hours of darkness.

Also used were 'recce boats', smaller versions of the well-known RAF inflatable dinghies, almost circular in shape, and capable of carrying four containers, or up to about 600lb of stores. The normal practice was to tow two behind a folboat although their skittish behaviour added greatly to the labours of the paddlers. The recce boats carried no way and if the paddlers stopped, the folboat and its charges simply stopped, too. They were normally on a short tow attached to the folboat's carrying handle, although most paddlers let them out to the full length of the tow rope when going through surf.

Base Camp

Croley, now in overall command of the combined Baldhead III and IV parties, had been told that he and his men would be on the Andamans for at least four months and he planned that they would spend an average of twenty-five days a month on patrol. So, one of his first instructions was that, within the requirements of security and sustainability, the base camp should be as comfortable as possible. They certainly had plenty of stores with them, so that by the time Baldhead III and IV had joined up they had some 25,000lb (10–11 tons). This included: weapons and spares; ammunition; boats; rations; four wireless sets, a charging engine and batteries; and survival equipment, such as cooking utensils, axes, fishing tackle, clothing, medicines, nails, rope and so on. The tinned and dried rations were supplemented wherever possible with fresh fish, prawns, oysters, mussels and the very occasional wild pig, although with the latter there was a danger that the sound of the shot might be heard by an enemy. One of the Royal Signals sergeants was placed in charge of the stores and rations in addition to his communications duties.

The first base camp was on a bluff, surrounded on three sides by mangrove swamp and on the fourth, landward side, by steep-sided, jungle-covered ravines. There was a regular freshwater supply, and they dug out pools for drinking, cooking and washing. There was even a steam-house to wash their clothes, which was very necessary as their clothes were constantly sweat-soaked and smelt badly. The site, however, proved too small for the twenty-six now present, so that, despite making themselves so comfortable Croley found it necessary to move after a month to a new site some two-and-a-half miles down the coast. This involved carrying all the stores back down to the shore, loading them into the folboats and recce boats, paddling to the new site and unloading it all – a back-breaking task.

Patrols Phase 1. 6–25 February
Once they had settled in, the combined parties undertook a rigorous programme of patrols, leaving only a small group in the base camp, comprising the four signallers and a few sick men. Croley issued his orders on 6 February, instructing that one party (Greig) would cross Andaman Island to the east coast, the second (Falconar) would go north along the west coast, and the third, which he would lead, would go south. These initial patrols were to be completed by 25 February.

Falconar's patrol consisted of two signallers, Sergeants Dickens and Austin, and one Indian soldier. They left on 8 February in two folboats and worked their way northwards, taking particular care to assess beaches for landing and, when ashore, for discovering sources of fresh water, which often proved a problem. They established a food store as far north as possible and then returned to base camp on 15 February.

Greig set out at 0300 hours on 10 February, accompanied by four

Indian soldiers, in two folboats, a dismantled recce boat and patrol rations. They reached a forward base that night and having buried the folboats and recce boat he left two soldiers to guard this base and set off himself with two soldiers, with a week's rations. They were back in this camp on the 13th and set out again on the 17th, this time accompanied by one of the signallers, Wooldridge, who had now joined them, and four Indians, and with strict orders not to take any risks of being seen. Greig established a patrol base and then, leaving Wooldridge and three Indians, he set off with just one companion on the 19th. The two soon heard a large group of men who were shouting and singing, and, having hidden themselves for the night, saw some men in a boat wearing 'fore-and-aft' caps, suggesting that they were soldiers, probably of the INA. Greig went forward alone for a close reconnaissance and then returned to his comrade when two men, probably Japanese, paddled past, only five yards away and oblivious to the enemy presence. Greig then returned to his patrol base, collected the remainder of his party and was back in the base camp on the 23rd.

Croley set off on 6 February and having established an advanced base, left Duncan in charge and then left in a folboat with an Indian soldier as sole company. Two days later he was thrilled to see a group of fourteen Jarawa and when they moved on he investigated their camp which he found to be clean and neat, so he left a red bandanna and four large fish hooks as presents. On the 11th he spent most of day in a mangrove swamp and on the 13th they searched Defence Island and found no trace of Japanese but did see some Jarawa. They returned to the advance base at 2300 hours on 14 February where they were welcomed by Duncan with a mug of tea heavily laced with rum.

Patrols Phase 2. Late February – Mid-March
After the break a large party, led by Croley, left the base camp on 29 February carrying a heavy load of stores to establish a forward base, which also included a wireless station coded 'M'. A party of ten then pushed on for a further three days. On 4 March Croley and the Subedar Sahib then went on, travelling light, leaving Duncan, who was again suffering from fever, in charge. Three days later Croley and the Subedar Sahib returned and then set off again, but this time accompanied by Duncan, who had now recovered, and one of the Gurkha soldiers. They

crossed a ridge of hills and by 9 March were within a mile of the village of Ferrarganj, which they entered after dark, but were spotted and chased, so Croley decided to withdraw.

Greig, Falconar and two Indian soldiers left the main camp on 4 March in two folboats, heading north to Cape Bluff. They spent the first night at Breakfast Bay, but heavy seas caused them to stay another night and they did not leave again until 1900 hours on 6 March. On 8 March they approached Bluff Island and saw lights on the shore at southern end. They closed to within some 200 yards using single paddles and saw a motor launch, a canoe and several men. They returned to their camp and the following day Greig and Falconar approached the enemy camp on foot and, as their subsequent report stated, observed:

BLUFF ISLE. Launch anchored, one canoe ditto, one canoe beached. Three men on launch, four on shore by a sort of earthwork or concrete revetment, four more on shore, about ¼ mile West of launch, walking eastwards, at same time two high prowed canoes, each with two paddlers inside reef in [Grid Square] 5756 going towards BLUFF ISLE. Two more men on mainland near canoes, making seventeen in all. No signs of intention to leave, so concluded BLUFF ISLE was garrisoned as also FOUL BAY, and in view all men being in clothing (uniform), and having a motor launch, that they were JAPANESE soldiers and not I.N.A., and that it was unsafe to proceed so returned to camp and arrived at Main Camp 13/3/44.

Baldhead V

Baldhead V was originally to have been the delivery of large amounts of stores in February to enable the Baldhead III/IV party to stay longer. However, this was cancelled and Baldhead V became the name for the extraction of the combined Baldhead III and IV parties by HMS *Taurus* on the night of 27/28 March 1944. The shore party had suffered no casualties, but left behind large caches of stores and equipment, although a tentative plan for the signallers to remain as a relay station for SOE stations further afield (e.g., in Malaya and French Indochina) was abandoned and they, too, returned to Ceylon.

Withdrawal

By mid-March everyone was looking forward to departure, which was initially scheduled for 25 March, but spirits were first dashed when this was postponed by twenty-four hours and then raised when that date was brought forward by two days. They were all tired, felt permanently filthy, were totally fed-up with being endlessly bitten by ticks, their clothes were rotting, and there was the never-to-be-overlooked danger of the Japanese. Most of them had suffered from the nameless fever, and all had bruises, boils and festering cuts. Some were becoming very short-tempered and Croley once found himself hammering at a rock and cursing loudly, regardless whether there might have been an enemy within earshot.

Chapter 14

Operation Hatch

Baldhead VI and VII
The next operation, Baldhead VI, was scheduled for mid-1944, but was cancelled for unknown reasons, which meant that the planned extraction, Baldhead VII, was also cancelled.

Operation Hatch I (ex-Baldhead VIII)
The next major incursion into the Andamans was to have been named Operation Baldhead VIII, but this was changed, for unknown reasons, to Operation Hatch I before they sailed. This involved twenty-eight men, the largest single group ever to be taken there, who landed from the submarine HMS *Clyde* (Lieutenant R. H. Bull, RN) on 21 December 1944 and remained there until 28 March 1945. Bull carried out a careful periscope reconnaissance of the coast before surfacing off Breakfast Bay at 1845 hours on 21 December. Two folboats were assembled and launched, and while their crews conducted a preliminary reconnaissance Bull took his submarine out to sea until receiving the 'all clear', whereupon he closed the shore and unloading commenced. A motorised canoe was supposed to have helped unload the stores, but broke down almost immediately (as had been expected), so the stores had to be towed ashore as before in six recce boats, each towed by a folboat. This was a very slow process and when it was realised that it would not be completed by dawn they stopped the shuttle at 0220 hours and Bull took *Clyde* out to sea to spend the day submerged.

In command ashore was Major Charles Greig, who had been on Baldhead III and IV. This time he was accompanied by Captain Alan Shaw and a Subedar and eight Pathans of the Punjab Regiment; and an unnamed British officer, a Subedar and eight Malayalam-speaking soldiers from southern India. Also in the party was Captain Lawrence White, Royal Engineers, an SOE officer who had earlier taken part as the explosives expert in Operation Longshanks (see Chapter 24). Finally there was a strong party of six wireless telegraphists from the Royal Signals.

There was, however, a sub-plot, because also present on the outward voyage was a lieutenant-colonel from the SOE staff in Trincomalee who had gone along for 'operational experience', much to the amusement of the professional special forces. This visiting staff officer had planned to pay only a brief visit to the shore 'to get the feel for operational conditions' but by agreement between the Army officers and *Clyde*'s captain, as soon as the colonel set foot on the beach the party sent a signal saying the night's work was completed, at which the submarine put to sea immediately, leaving the dismayed staff officer to spend the rest of the night and all of the following day ashore in 'enemy territory'. This was almost certainly the work of Lawrence White whose very active sense of humour got him into frequent scrapes during his military career and nothing gives a front-line soldier greater pleasure than the sight of a discomfited staff officer. *Clyde* returned the following evening and offloading continued from 1940 hours to 2200 hours, at which point Bull collected the now thoroughly experienced colonel and withdrew seawards for several hours, although he returned at 0400 hours to check that all was well ashore, before setting off for Ceylon.

Once the men had settled in, Greig decided to establish a second camp some distance along the coast and instructed that a small party would walk along the shore, while the bulk of the stores would be loaded into Recce Boats and towed by folboats, paddled by Pathans, with White in charge in the lead craft. This proved to be much harder than had been anticipated, with the towed boats difficult to control, especially in an adverse tide, and with many of the Pathans also suffering from seasickness. The little convoy was still at sea at dawn, but for some reason the usual daily Japanese patrol plane did not fly that day and they reached their goal undetected. The lesson was learnt, however, and all future moves of stores were done in short carries over land.

They saw much wildlife, including snakes, wild pigs and a type of monitor lizard known locally as a cobroanga, which proved rather less dangerous than described in their 'Andamans Handbook'.[71] Fortunately, they suffered no problems, although there were some close shaves with cobras, which curiously had never bothered the earlier parties. They were out on patrol for much of the time, but inevitably also spent many hours in camp where, apart from routine administrative tasks, they had a lot of free time. Lawrence White spent much of this reading the *Complete Plays of Shakespeare* and the *Rubaiyat of Omar Khayyam* or listening to *ITMA*, a popular BBC comedy, on the signallers' wireless.

Greig ensured that his men kept up an active programme of patrolling, which included establishing advance bases. These patrols were intended to provide information for intelligence staffs planning major operations in the Andamans and contact with the enemy was to be avoided, but one patrol took two prisoners, who were held at the base camp until being evacuated to Ceylon.[72]

One of the hazards of these operations in the Andamans was that there was no medical support and when White was struck down with what he described as 'sandfly fever' at one of the advanced bases, there was no alternative but for him to take to his hammock and sweat it out, which took a week.[73]

Operation Hatch II

In March Greig received orders to pack up and at 0745 hours on 28 March *Clyde* approached the shore, saw the agreed signal, a large white flag with a black circle in the centre, in the prearranged position and withdrew to return again after dark. Lawrence White was sent out in a folboat to establish contact and so precise was his positioning that *Clyde* surfaced virtually alongside his frail canoe. White then contacted the shore part by 'walkie talkie' wireless and with embarkation completed by 2135 hours the submarine, complete with all the men, plus two prisoners, returned to Trincomalee. They had spent three very active months ashore, had suffered no losses, had gathered much information and had not been discovered by the Japanese. It was, in every respect a most successful operation.[74]

Operation Hatch III

A further SOE party sailed aboard HMS *Clyde* on 9 May 1945 bound for the Andamans, but the submarine developed a serious fault with its hydroplanes and was forced to return to Ceylon. As a result, Hatch III was cancelled and no further British operations in the Andamans took place until the reoccupation in September 1945.

Chapter 15

Further Operations in the Andamans

Operation Buccaneer

Operation Buccaneer never took place but is of interest as the operation towards which the Baldhead/Hatch patrols were working. It was a plan for an amphibious landing on the Andamans, which was originally considered in 1943 and then substantially revised in 1944 for possible implementation in 1945. It was proposed to Chiang Kai-Shek by Roosevelt at the Teheran Conference (28 November to 1 December 1943), who was most enthusiastic as it held the promise of distracting Japanese attention and efforts away from China. However, it had to be postponed when it became clear that the British did not have the resources, particularly landing craft, with which to mount it in combination with already-planned and higher-priority amphibious operations in Europe. Thus, Buccaneer was cancelled in 1943[75] but remained under consideration.

In their 1944 review for an operation in the Andamans in 1945, the British assessed the Japanese Navy would be relatively insignificant, with attacks being limited to interference by submarines and a few torpedo boats. Air forces would be limited to a small number of floatplanes operating out of Port Blair harbour and a few land-based fighters on the only airfield just south of Port Blair. Some bomber raids from the Asian mainland might also be expected. The Japanese land forces were assessed to be 10,000 strong, comprising one infantry brigade of six battalions (7,000 men), one tank company (fifteen tanks, 150 men), some 1,000 anti-aircraft, civil defence and base troops, and 2,000 naval infantry. The great bulk of these (6,000) were in the Port Blair area, with the remained spread in small, isolated detachments across the islands.

The British plan involved a naval task force comprising five carriers, two battleships, fourteen destroyers, eight minesweepers, and a large number of landing and other amphibious craft. The assault was to take place on the East coast of South Andaman, with preliminary bombing of Port Blair and diversionary naval attacks on Car Nicobar Island and Sabang in Sumatra, The actual assault would have involved a reinforced infantry division, with three brigades landing simultaneously alongside each other on a four-mile stretch immediately to the South of Port Blair. There would also have been subsidiary landings by one commando on Ross Island, while on the North shore of the entrance to Port Blair, a second commando would have eliminated the two 5in guns, following which a battalion would have landed in North Bay. There would have been a brigade as an afloat reserve and another brigade as a follow-up force.

Operation Bacon

At a much lower level, Detachment 404 of the US Office of Strategic Services (OSS) in Ceylon conducted a series of operations in the Andamans, codenamed Bacon. At the time, the OSS was considering establishing a base in the northern part of the Andaman archipelago for use in possible future operations elsewhere in the theatre and needed intelligence for the planners to work on. The hard-working British submarine HMS *Clyde* sailed from Ceylon on 18 January 1945 and on 21 January delivered the OSS party to Pocock Island which lies a short distance due East of Cape Price, the northernmost tip of North Andaman Island.[76] The original group was reinforced by a further two men and 2,100lb of supplies on 27 February, but this time delivered by a Catalina of 240 Squadron, RAF, which flew them in from Madras.[77] A second flight on 26 March, also by Catalina, brought in three more men and 1,000lb of supplies.

It was planned to bring all these men back to Ceylon in mid-May aboard HMS *Clyde*, but the submarine suffered repeated faults in her after hydroplanes and once again 240 Squadron came to the rescue. Two Catalinas flew from Madras on 21 May, bringing in two meteorological staff and two assistants, who then remained to run the weather station, while the original men and much of their equipment returned to India. The weather station was reinforced by a further two men on 11 June and yet another two men on 19 June. On the latter occasion the Americans ashore on Pocock Island were alarmed to see a small Japanese patrol craft sail past just before the aircraft was due to arrive, but having been given adequate notice by a 'native' they managed to escape detection. As a result, the next supply delivery on 12 July was made to Landfall Island. Further supply flights on 28 July and 30 August reverted to Pocock Island, but, the war having ended, the entire base and staff were vacated in September.

Operation Balmoral
Having dropped the original Bacon party on 21/22 January, *Clyde* continued eastwards to Pachumba Bay (90° 24'N 97° 49'E) on the west coast of Thailand. There, on the night of 23 January, it dropped off an SOE party (Operation Balmoral IV) and then returned to Trincomalee, arriving on 26 January. *Clyde* sailed on 7 April and conducted Operation Balmoral VII in same area on nights 12/13 and 13/14 April. Balmoral is known to have been an ongoing British operation by Force 136, but no further details can be found.

Unknown Operation
On 25 February *Clyde* embarked an 'SF party' and sailed one hour later. At 1912 hours on 1 March it surfaced and 'carried out special operation' in a bay on the West coast of Sumatra at 02° 50'N 97° 33E, just South of Troemon and due east of Simaleur Island. No further information can be found.

Operation Popcorn
With the general Japanese surrender on 2 September 1945, there was no further need to invade the Andaman Islands and with a vast number of Japanese-occupied areas to be retaken, the reoccupation was given a relatively low priority. The Royal Indian Navy sloop HMIS *Narbada* escorted a convoy of amphibious ships and minesweepers into Port Blair on 27 September and British control was rapidly reasserted.

Chapter 16

Analysis

When British and Indian troops landed at Port Blair in September 1945 the Japanese not only offered no resistance, but proved to be surprisingly cooperative. One facet of this was that the erstwhile commander, Vice-Admiral Teizo, gave a very frank interview to a senior RN officer on 28 September.[78] In a wide-ranging discussion (it did not rate being categorised as an interrogation), he never once mentioned any Allied ground activity in the Andamans over the period of his command (i.e., 1944 to 1945) and it seems that the Japanese simply never knew the men of Operations Baldhead and Hatch were there, a remarkable tribute to the skill, determination and courage of those who had taken part.

Health, both individually and collectively, was an issue for all the parties, and the longer they stayed the more severe it became. McCarthy was one of the first to be laid low, Croley's diary includes frequent comments on a fever, which laid even the fittest low for several days, and even White on Hatch I – an energetic, fit and otherwise healthy young man – was not immune. The cause was not known, although they were regularly covered in ticks and the two may have been interrelated. A few men even suffered more than one attack, in the second of which their temperature went past 102 degrees and they then had to be placed on permanent base duties.

The ticks could not be deterred and neither tobacco nor the issue ointment kept them at bay, so that the men often had to pick them off each other at the end of a day's marching.[79] Mosquitoes were also an ever-present hazard and the issued citronella ointment was not only useless but could also be smelled at a range of over 100 yards, which made it of little value in a combat environment. Other complaints included boils, sores, festering cuts and swollen feet. Drugs included Atabrine, quinine and Aspro, and they also had a plentiful supply of iodine and M&B Powder. Croley also admitted to suffering from blind rages and he described one man as 'off his head'. There were no more serious illnesses, nor, despite many falls, were there any broken bones, although there were frequent sprains. This was very fortunate as they did not have a medical officer, nor even a qualified first-aider.[80] There were also no dental problems worth mentioning.

Water was a constant problem. Natural sources could usually be found, but sometimes they had to resort to obtaining it from bamboos, which was very slow as it required an hour to fill one waterbottle.

All parties saw evidence of the Japanese presence on the west coast, one patrol even encountering several obviously abandoned huts and an abandoned boat. Both McCarthy and Croley penetrated as far as Ferrargandj and on several occasions were within a few yards of Japanese soldiers, but were never detected. Several patrols did, however, see some Indians, who they thought were INA while Greig saw a Japanese detachment on Bluff Isle. In all such cases, however, the enemy were noisy, careless and clearly not in the slightest concerned about a possible hostile presence in the area, let alone actually observing them. On one occasion (18 March) Croley's patrol entered a village and were spotted, but moved off quickly and if there was any attempt at pursuit they were not aware of it. According to a local historian the Japanese were vaguely aware of some British activity and occasionally intercepted wireless transmissions, but did not have a detection-finding capability to accurately locate the transmitter.[81] All parties reported occasionally hearing or even seeing four-engined flying boats overhead but these did not appear to be searching for them.

Unlike the Minerva party, all Baldhead and Hatch parties took proper communications detachments, ranging from just one man on Baldhead I to four on Baldhead III/IV – Sergeants Allen, Dickens, Thomas and Wooldridge, all Royal Signals. The latter had four wireless sets with the associated secondary batteries, but only one charging engine. For all these operations in the Andamans the communications worked well, with Croley recording that: 'So far as I was concerned, no technical hitches took place . . . Whenever I wanted messages sent they went and presumably were received and vice-versa.' The only minor problem was that the communicators worked shifts, so that Croley became concerned about the repetitiveness of their task and instituted a system in which at least one of the four was always away on one of the patrols.

The morale of all the parties remained remarkably high. In large part this was due to the officers, who faced the same dangers, underwent the same hardships and ate the same rations as the men. They also took their turn at night sentry duty, paddled canoes, and carried the same loads as the men, not only when on patrol but also when stores had to be shifted. Thus, in every sense, they led from the front.

All parties encountered numerous animals. There were many wild pigs and a large rat-like animal whose name they did not know, but was easy to catch and made good eating. They regularly heard elephants, which they knew were used to move timber, which meant that there were men, too, so they kept well clear of them.

Croley made particular efforts to make contact with the Jarawa; there was clearly no prospect of befriending them, but at least he sought to minimise any mistrust and ensure there was no animosity. Early one morning in February he sighted a group of fifty, unusually large in his experience, and he and Greig lay for some hours watching the group playing and laughing together, crossing a river with individuals swimming, while several of the men towed a raft. When the two observers were forced to move, however, they were quickly spotted and the Jarawa, as usual, screamed and fled into the jungle. For all that the Jarawa were jungle-wise, the British were clearly able to spend many hours watching them and were only detected if they moved too obviously. The Indian soldiers in the party, particularly those who had lived previously in the Andamans, regarded the Jarawas as savages, describing them very disparagingly as '*haskhis*' (negroes) and were prepared to shoot them for no reason.

The maps were almost entirely based on air survey and were found by all users to be inaccurate.

All these parties lived in the deep jungle, and while they brought plenty of stores and rations with them, they had to support themselves throughout their stay. Their leaders ensured that they pursued a very active patrol programme, and while all had at least some period in the basecamp they were kept busy. The leaders led from the front and all the officers shared fully the hardships and rigours with their men, and also ate exactly the same rations. Had the Japanese found them they would have stood little chance of survival. They were few in number and only lightly armed, and while they might have survived for a few days, perhaps even several weeks, they would almost certainly have been either killed or captured.

PART III

Operations Longshanks/Creek:
Goa, 8/9 March 1943

Chapter 17

Introduction

The British raid on the German merchant ship *Ehrenfels* in Goa in 1943 remained a closely-guarded secret until the publication of the book *Boarding Party* in 1978. Written by James Leasor, a well-known author of the day, this book was in a style known as 'faction' in which the basic story was enhanced by fabricated events and conversations, and with some of the characters being real, some heavily disguised and a few pure inventions. This was followed by the film *The Sea Wolves* in 1980, which also had the genuine story at its heart but added even more fanciful elements, some for dramatic effect and others to satisfy the whims of certain actors. Both book and film gave the impression that the raid was a rather melodramatic affair, mounted by a handful of middle-aged accountants and tea planters, using an antiquated, steam-propelled barge as transport. The aim was depicted as capturing a German ship and taking it out to sea, which proved impossible to achieve, giving the impression that it was a brave, foolish and rather amateurish failure.

There are grains of truth in all of that, but the reality is that it was a warlike operation with a very serious aim. It was carried out with great precision and resulted in five deaths, the destruction of four Axis merchant ships together with several million pounds' worth of cargo and, most important of all, the total elimination of a major potential threat to Allied naval operations in the Indian Ocean.

The situation had arisen because on the outbreak of war in 1939 three German merchant ships sought shelter in Mormugao harbour in the Portuguese enclave of Goa on the west coast of India, joined by an Italian ship in 1940. It is important to appreciate their status. Portugal was neutral in the conflict, a very difficult role to play. At home the Portuguese found themselves the unwilling hosts to the intelligence organisations of both sides. There were also Allied and Axis transport agencies, with the British Overseas Airways Corporation (BOAC) and

Lufthansa both having offices in Lisbon airport from where they operated landplane services to their own countries, while BOAC and PanAm had flying-boat bases on the Tagus River. The capital of Portuguese East Africa, Lourenço Marques (now Maputo in Mozambique), also hosted agencies of both sides.

In 1942 Portugal also acted as the intermediary between the Allies and Japan for two major exchanges of diplomats and civilian internees, both at Lourenço Marques. The first of these, between the United States and Japan, took place on 28–29 July 1942, involving the US-chartered Swedish liner *Gripsholm* on one side and the Japanese-owned *Asama Maru* and Japanese-chartered Italian liner *Conte Verde* on the other. A similar British-Japanese exchange took place, also at Laurenço Marques, between 27 August and 16 September 1942, involving four British and two Japanese liners. All these ships sailed under 'safe passage rules' and completed their voyages unmolested.

Portuguese India comprised three geographically-separate enclaves on the western coast of the sub-continent, two of which were tiny – Daman and Diu – and need not be considered further. The third, and by far the largest, was Goa, situated in the centre of the Malabar coast, some 1,400 square miles in area, virtually the same size as the US state of Rhode Island and the English county of Essex, and in 1940 with a population of just over five million. It had been a Portuguese possession since the sixteenth century and was administered by a governor-general answerable to the government in Lisbon, where Antonio Salazar had been prime minister and virtual dictator since 1932.

The head of government in Portuguese India was Colonel José Ricardo Pereira Cabral (1879–1956), who had trained as a cavalryman, but spent most of his career from 1906 onwards in his country's colonial service. He worked his way upwards and was appointed Governor of Moçambique in 1926, which he held until appointed Governor-General of Portuguese Possessions in India in 1938. A married man, he and his wife had no less than ten daughters.

Cabral knew the British well, having fought alongside them in the East African campaign in the First World War, for which he was appointed an honorary Commander of the Order of St Michael and St George (CMG) in 1919. On 1 June 1940 he was made an honorary Knight of the Order of the British Empire (KBE), a most unusual honour and one which may well have inclined him towards friendship towards the British.[82] The British consul, Bremner, described him as a most charming man who invariably kept his word. 'He is a most meticulous observer of correct official etiquette and procedure, and will not be bounced. Nonetheless, such are our good relations that he has helped me unofficially to accomplish much that he has regretted his inability to approve officially without reference to Lisbon.'[83]

Goa's entire landward frontier was with British India and there were customs posts at all official crossing points. There was also a long coastline, cut in two by a large bay, on the southern lip of which was Mormugao Harbour, one of the finest natural harbours in India and in peacetime a busy port.

The Government of British India was represented in Goa by a Consul, Lieutenant-Colonel (retired) Claude Bremner, MC (1891–1965), who served in the British Army from 1911 to 1914 and then in the Indian Army (1914–19), before transferring into the Foreign and Political Department of the Government of India. A widely travelled and capable man, who spoke no less than seventeen languages, he was appointed British consul to the Portuguese possessions in India in November 1940, for which he was based in Goa, where he lived with his wife, Anne, and three very young children.

By 1942 the position of Goa had become delicate. The colony was a long way from the Portuguese homeland and official relations with the British were, of necessity, correct, although at a personal level reasonably cordial. But, as in the home country, the Portuguese administration turned a blind eye to a certain degree of discrete espionage on both sides. There was, however, a significant complication – the presence in Mormugao Harbour of the four Axis merchant ships which appeared fated to remain there until the war's end, although there was always the possibility that one or more might try to escape.

Legally, these ships were taking shelter, while their crews were visitors rather than internees. This meant that for as long as the ships lay at anchor, paid the appropriate harbour dues and chandlers' bills, and their crews behaved with reasonable discretion, they were left to their own devices. The crews were allowed ashore and permitted to roam anywhere in the colony. Some even had small sailing boats and canoes which they used for recreation and fishing within Goa's territorial waters.

The Portuguese authorities had inspected the ships on arrival and removed wirelesses and aerials, since transmitting from a neutral port was banned under the Hague Convention of 1907.

The Threat

Throughout the Victorian era the Indian Ocean and its northern arms, the Arabian Sea and the Bay of Bengal, was virtually a British lake, but during the First World War there were a number of incursions by German surface warships. *Königsberg*, a light cruiser, shelled Dar-es-Salaam on 20 September 1914 and also sank several ships off the coast of East Africa before being trapped in the Rufiji delta and eventually destroyed in July 1915. Also in 1914, another light cruiser, *Emden*, shelled Madras and Penang before she was sunk at Cocos-Keeling Island on 10 November 1914. In addition to these warships, the Germans also employed converted merchant vessels, two of which, *Wolf* and *Seeadler*,[84] operated with considerable success in the Indian Ocean.

During the early 1930s the *Kriegsmarine* (German Navy) brought three 'pocket battleships' into service, one of which, *Admiral Graf Spee*, was in the central Atlantic when war was declared. It then conducted a raiding cruise which included a brief, albeit not particularly glorious foray into the Indian Ocean, where she sank just one British ship, the small tanker *Africa Shell* on 15 November 1939. *Graf Spee* then returned to the Atlantic, where she fought three British cruisers, took shelter in Montevideo and was then scuttled.

The second of the three 'pocket battleships', *Admiral Scheer*, sailed from Germany in October 1940, transiting through the Denmark Strait, and her first successes were to sink the British armed merchant cruiser HMS *Jervis Bay* and five ships (out of thirty-seven) in Convoy HX-84. *Scheer* went on to capture three ships in the South Atlantic before rounding the Cape of Good Hope and entering the Indian Ocean in February 1941, where she operated as far north as the Seychelles, capturing one ship and sinking three. *Scheer* returned safely to Germany on 1 April 1941 having sailed some 46,000 nautical miles and sunk seventeen merchant ships totalling 113,223 grt.

As in the First World War, the *Kriegsmarine* also set great store by armed merchant cruisers (AMCs). *Orion* was completed in 1931 as the merchant ship *Kurmark* for the Hamburg-Amerika Line (HAPAG), but was converted to an AMC in 1939–40, and renamed *Orion*. She sailed from Germany in April 1940, rounded Scotland and then traversed the length of the Atlantic, reaching Cape Horn in May, having sunk one British merchant ship on the way. *Orion* arrived in New Zealand waters in June and laid mines which sank three large and three small vessels. She then operated in the Pacific and Indian Oceans before returning safely to Bordeaux on 23 August 1941. *Orion* had been at sea for seventeen months, covered some 127,000 nautical miles and sunk ten ships (62,915grt).

Steiermark was also built for HAPAG and was completed in 1938, but acquired by the German navy in 1939, converted to an AMC and renamed *Kormoran*. She sailed on 3 December 1940 and sank eight vessels between 13 January and 8 April 1941 as she sailed down the Atlantic, followed by a further three in the Indian Ocean (June–September 1941). During her time in the Indian Ocean *Kormoran* sailed well into the Bay of Bengal, before heading for Australian waters where she was sunk by HMAS *Sydney* on 19 November 1941, an engagement in which the Australian cruiser was also lost with all hands.

Santa Cruz was completed in 1938 for the Oldenburg-Portuguese Line, but requisitioned in 1939, converted to an AMC, and commissioned as *Thor* in March 1940. Her first raiding voyage lasted from June 1940 to May 1941 and was confined to the Atlantic, during which she sank or captured twelve ships (96,647 tons). *Thor* set sail again in November 1941 and concentrated initially on the Cape of Good Hope area, where five victims were sunk in March–April 1942. The ship then moved into the Indian Ocean where she sank two more ships and captured a further three, which were successfully taken to Japan by prize crews. *Thor* herself then sailed to Japan, arriving on 9 October 1942, where she moored alongside the German tanker *Uckermark* for dockyard work in preparation for a further raiding voyage. However, *Uckermark* blew up in an unexplained explosion on 30 November, destroying both ships.[85]

The Hansa ship *Goldenfels* (a sister-ship of *Ehrenfels*) was completed in 1937 and requisitioned and fitted out as an AMC by the *Kriegsmarine* in 1939. Renamed *Atlantis*, she sailed in March 1940 and in 602 days at sea sank or captured twenty-two ships (144,384 grt) in the Atlantic, Pacific and Indian Oceans. *Atlantis* was sunk by the cruiser HMS *Devonshire* on 22 November 1941.

Pinguin was built for the Hansa Line as *Kendelfels* (also a sister-ship of *Ehrenfels*) and entered service in 1937. In 1939 she was requisitioned by the *Kriegsmarine*, converted to an AMC and renamed *Pinguin*. She sailed from Germany on 15 June 1940, reached the Atlantic via the Denmark Strait, sank one ship during the voyage south and rounded the Cape of Good Hope on 20 August. She captured or sank a further twenty-seven ships and her mines accounted for another four – all in the Indian Ocean or Australasian waters. *Pinguin* was finally sunk by HMS *Devonshire* on 8 May 1941.

The Polish freighter *Beilsko* was requisitioned by the *Kriegsmarine* and converted, first, to a hospital ship and then in 1941 to an AMC. In March 1942, now renamed *Michel*, she set out on a raiding cruise and, unusually, ran the gauntlet of the English Channel, reaching the South Atlantic where she sank her first victim on 19 April. Michel then moved to the Indian Ocean, eventually reaching Japan in March 1943; in 346 days at sea, she sank or captured fifteen Allied ships (99,000 tons grt).

During the inter-war years the *Kriegsmarine* devoted considerable resources to developing a replenishment-at-sea capability, which would enable its surface warships, converted merchant ships and U-boats to undertake sustained operations in distant waters. The five replenishment ships of the *Dithmarschen* class were purpose-built for this role and carried large amounts of fuel, ammunition, food and spare parts, the best known being *Altmark*, which supported the 'pocket battleship' *Graf Spee* in her cruise in the Atlantic and Indian Oceans between August and December 1939.

A class of specialised supply U-boats were also built, designated the Type XIV. Also, in emergencies operational U-boats were frequently used to replenish each other, although this was the most time-consuming and hazardous of all the methods. In addition to the purpose-built ships and U-boats, a number of merchant ships were given limited conversions to enable them to serve in the resupply role and several operated in the Indian Ocean, for example the *Brake* and *Charlotte Schliemann*.

The *Kriegsmarine* replenishment method was much less sophisticated than that developed by the Americans and British. The latter employed ships sailing close alongside each other at a speed of about 12 knots, which required some skill but was rapid and reliable. In the German method, the tanker towed the receiving ship or submarine at about 4 knots, with a floating pipe conveying the fuel, while ammunition, food and spares were transferred by motor boats. This resulted in a time-consuming process during which both vessels were very vulnerable to enemy action, but at least early in the war it achieved its purpose.

In addition to its other measures, the *Kriegsmarine* also positioned a number of civilian supply ships in Spanish harbours. These lay at anchor and the U-boats slipped in under cover of darkness, refuelled and took on other supplies and then left before dawn. There seems little doubt that the Spanish authorities knew about these activities, but they did nothing to stop them.

The Japanese Threat

For the British, the enemy threat in the Indian Ocean increased dramatically when Japan entered the war. On 26 March 1942 a large and powerful Japanese surface task force penetrated deep into the Indian Ocean with the two-fold aim of destroying British naval power and providing implicit encouragement to the Indian independence movement. The attack opened at dawn on 5 April with air raids on Colombo, but the British were ready and the Japanese were not as effective as they had hoped. The Japanese were more successful in other areas, however, and sank two cruisers, *Dorsetshire* and *Cornwall*. The overwhelming Japanese strength forced the British fleet to withdraw, first to Addu Atoll in the Maldives and then to Kalindini in Kenya. Japanese aircraft then attacked Trincomalee, the main British naval base in Ceylon, inflicting considerable damage, following which they sank the carrier *Hermes* and her attendant destroyer, HMAS *Vampire*. Meanwhile, a northern attack between 5 and 9 April spread mayhem in the Bay of Bengal. Many merchant ships were sunk and carrier aircraft also conducted the first air raids on Indian soil. In summary, the Japanese sank some 151,000 tons of merchant shipping and a number of important warships, conducted air raids against Ceylon and India and forced the Eastern Fleet to withdraw to Africa. At this point, and very fortunately for the British, the Japanese naval forces began to run short of supplies and their ships were also in need of repairs, so they withdrew. It had, however, been a humiliating experience for the British, but the IJN now had naval bases in the Andaman Islands, Singapore, Penang and the Dutch East Indies, and remained a very potent threat.

Rumours

Rumours can have great significance in wartime as they tend to gather strength with constant repetition, they are often very plausible, and, all too often, must be investigated before they can be rejected. In the case of U-boats there were persistent reports that they were being clandestinely refuelled by German sympathisers on the western coast of the Irish Republic and on the eastern seaboard of Canada. There were also somewhat less plausible reports that refuelling operations were being conducted in Argentina and Brazil. None of these were correct, but they added to the atmosphere of mistrust and fear.

The Lessons

Up until late 1942 the number of Axis surface raiders in the Indian Ocean was never great – no more than two or three or four simultaneously, often fewer. They operated independently, although some met supply ships and U-boats from time-to-time. By 1940 the great majority of Allied merchant ships carried wireless and there were arrangements for the transmission of simple messages to indicate an attack by surface, submarine or air. The Germans knew this and elimination of the radio room or jamming of transmissions was always a top priority.

The unfortunate fact was that these raiders were very difficult to find. Despite the size of the Royal Navy, and the huge effort devoted to destroying the raiders, the Allied navies had a vast area to cover. Later in the war electronic countermeasures and radar would make a huge difference, but in the early years finding and locating a single raider was often as much a matter of luck as of planning.

Japanese Submarines

The first Axis submarines to operate in the Indian Ocean were those of the Imperial Japanese Navy (IJN), starting with six boats in January 1942. These reached Ceylon and the Bay of Bengal, sinking some twenty merchant ships, with four more damaged, for a loss of one of their own. By March the IJN had established a forward base in Penang and five boats sailed from there on an Indian Ocean patrol on 30 April 1942. A reconnaissance aircraft from one of these spotted British warships in Diego Suarez in French-ruled Madagascar, as a result of which midget submarines were launched. The battleship HMS *Ramillies* was hit and seriously damaged by one torpedo, while a tanker was sunk by another.

The Japanese submarines then cruised along the east coast of Africa, mainly in the Mozambique Channel, with significant success, sinking twenty-two merchant ships. At the same time two Japanese armed merchant cruisers were at large in the central and western Indian Ocean, where they sank one merchant ship and captured two others. Five submarines again sortied out of Penang in August 1942 and returned in November, having sunk twelve cargo vessels, one in the Arabian Sea, four off the African coast, five in the Bay of Bengal and two in the Indian Ocean.

Thus, IJN submarines posed a significant threat to Allied shipping in the Indian Ocean. A large part of their success was due to the fact that Allied shipping sailed almost always without escorts. This was partly due to a shortage of escort vessels, anti-submarine aircraft and modern aids such as the latest radar and sonar, all of which were concentrated in the North Atlantic. But, there was also a vestige of a Royal Navy mind-set against convoys, because they took time and effort to assemble, and proceeded at the speed of the slowest, even though their effectiveness had been shown in the Atlantic. There was, however, an even more ominous development in submarine warfare – the Germans were coming.

German U-boats

Although its major effort was devoted to the Battle of the Atlantic, the German Navy gradually extended its U-boat operations southwards down the west coast of Africa. The first to reach Cape Town was *Gruppe Eisbär* (Polar Bear Group) consisting of four Type VIIC attack boats and one Type XIV tanker, which sailed in August 1942. Three of the attack boats reached Cape Town but to their astonishment the harbour was empty, so Admiral Dönitz authorised the captains to operate at will. Joined by a newly-arrived, long-range Type IXD boat, they proceeded to sink twenty-four ships around southern Africa for a total of 163,100grt during October 1942. The total sunk would have been greater but for heavy storms and poor visibility, which hampered their efforts. Nevertheless, two boats proceeded up the east coast as far as Durban.

Even before *Eisbär* had reached the Cape Dönitz sent another group, this time all of the new long-range Type IXD, which rounded the Cape and worked its way North to the Mozambique Channel, where they sank thirty-six Allied merchantmen between November 1942 and March 1943. Every one of the targets was sailing alone – easy pickings.

Table 2. Allied Merchant Ships Sunk in Areas Relevant to India[86]

Area	October 1942		November 1942			December 1942		January 1943		February 1943		Totals
	Ger	Jap	Ger	Jap	Ita	Ger	Jap	Ger	Jap	Ger	Jap	
Bay of Bengal		2										2
Ceylon		2	1									3
Arabian Sea		1		1			1					3
Indian Ocean	2											2
Mozambique Channel			12			3						15
Southern Africa	18		11		1	1				5		36
TOTALS	20	5	23	2	1	4	1	0	0	5	0	61

These sinkings caused increasing alarm in various Allied headquarters and major efforts were made to find a cause. One possibility seemed to be that Axis submarines were being informed of Allied shipping movements and a rumour soon gained ground that information on sailings from Bombay was being taken by courier to Goa, where it was handed to Robert Koch, a German resident, who then took it to *Ehrenfels*, which had a powerful transmitter which was transmitting nightly to submarines at sea.

Conclusions
There was no question of the presence or nationalities of the four ships in Mormugao Harbour being hidden in any way; they lay at anchor several hundred yards offshore in full public view, flew their national ensigns daily and members of their crews regularly went ashore. Up to February 1942 it was entirely reasonable that the British should have suspected that one or more of the ships might break out and attempt to reach France, where they would be refitted as AMCs. But, once the Japanese had captured Singapore, the Dutch East Indies and the Andaman Islands, there was no longer a need for them to sail around Africa and up through the Atlantic, as they could now sail to a Japanese-occupied port.

Furthermore, once German U-boats were known to be operating in the Indian Ocean, it seemed possible that one or more of them might enter Mormugao Harbour after dark, and either refuel from one of the German ships, land sick crewmen or deliver equipment, as was known to have happened in Spanish ports.

It was, therefore, entirely reasonable for British Intelligence to have viewed these four ships with grave suspicion. Among other measures, an 'Aide Memoire' was presented to the Portuguese government by the British ambassador in Lisbon on 13 March 1942. This stated that the four Axis ships in Mormugao '. . . may receive instructions to attempt to break out of their place of refuge and take an active part in the war, for instance as supply ships to navy vessels'.[87]

Chapter 18

The Merchant Ship Situation

The raid on the ships in Mormugao Harbour did not take place in isolation but was part of a continuing problem which had vexed the British from the earliest days of the war. There were many such Axis ships taking refuge in neutral harbours around the world, and several attacks against them had either been carried out or been planned.

Germany rebuilt her merchant fleet after the First World War and by 1939 had a substantial number of ships at sea, the great majority less than twenty years old. Inevitably, many of these were in foreign waters when war was declared on 3 September 1939, some of them on the high seas but many in port – there were no fewer than thirty-nine in the Spanish port of Vigo, for example.

All German ships' masters carried secret orders to be opened only on receipt of codeword '*Essberger*' by radio, and in this case it was issued on 25 August 1939. This directed them to leave potentially hostile ports as soon as possible, or, if at sea, to divert from the usual shipping lanes. Shortly afterwards a second codeword was broadcast ordering masters to change their ship's name and appearance, communicate only in a new code enclosed with the orders and head for either Germany or a neutral port. Some, which were in British or French ports were interned, some were able to reach Germany, but most headed for the nearest neutral port in order to avoid capture or sinking.

Having reached a neutral port, the German captains were faced with major problems. First, they had to maintain their ships and ensure that engines and other systems remained in working order and supplied with fuel and lubricants. Secondly, they had to look after their crew, making sure that they were fed, paid, given medical treatment and kept occupied. Thirdly, they had to make two sets of plans, the most important being for an escape, while the second was for destruction of the ship, either in port or on the high seas, if threatened with overwhelming enemy force.

For the Allies the German ships, crews and cargoes represented a substantial enemy resource. They also posed military threats since, if they escaped, they could be employed as AMCs or as supply ships, replenishing both surface ships and U-boats. The British were also paranoid about the German ships being used to gather intelligence about British ship movements, particularly sailings, which could then be sent by ship's wireless to patrolling U-boats.

The worst case for the Allies was that, despite all their precautions, the German ships would sail immediately after nightfall and then have many hours before their absence was noticed from the shore the following dawn, by which time the escapers would have disappeared over the horizon. Sometimes the RN could afford to put their own warships on patrol off likely ports and on occasions these succeeded in intercepting the enemy ships.

The Allies were helped by their global network of maritime representatives and contacts. There were naval attachés in most countries, including neutral ones, and many foreigners were well-disposed towards the British and ready to offer information such as German preparations to sail by taking on fuel or rations, or settling harbour dues and requesting clearance to sail, or, in the worst case, that they had actually sailed. The British also leant on local port authorities to ensure that the provisions of international law were followed in such items as making long-range wirelesses unusable, removing weapons, and so on.

Many German naval attachés had two responsibilities, the first being to their ambassador, but the second was as part of the *Marineattaché-gruppe* (Naval Attachés Group), reporting to the *Kriegsmarine* staff in Berlin. Their responsibilities here were primarily as head of the regional section of the *Etappendienst* (supply service) and the naval attaché in Tokyo, for example, was head of *Etappe Ostasien* (Supply Service East Asia), which controlled German-flagged merchant vessels throughout the Pacific and Indian Oceans. This included safeguarding them against Allied seizure, acquisition and loading of cargoes, supply of fuel, and sailing and routing instructions. The disposition of German merchant navy ships in the early months of the war was as follows.

Argentina

The passenger liner *Monte Pascoal* of the Hamburg Sudamerika Line, a veteran of the Germany–Argentina, run was in Buenos Aires on the day war was declared. Her captain acted with great promptness and resolution, had the ship refuelled and painted grey overall, and sailed on 9 September. He managed to avoid the Royal Navy blockade, sailed northabout around the British Isles and arrived in Hamburg on 14 October.

Another passenger liner, SS *Ussukuma*, was off Lourenço Marques on 1 September 1939 when she was requisitioned by the *Kriegsmarine* and ordered to sail immediately to the Argentine port of Bahia Blanca. She was then ordered to move to Montevideo, sailing on 4 December 1939, but her departure was seen and reported to the British warships then off the coast looking for the *Graf Spee*. She was found by British cruisers, but was scuttled before she could be captured.

Brazil

Dresden was in a Chilean port in September 1939, but was later ordered to sail to deliver a quantity of urgently-needed carbonic acid to *Graf Spee*. When, however, the latter failed to keep the rendezvous *Dresden* went into Santos in Brazil on 25 November. After many months there she sailed again on 28 March 1941 and refuelled the AMC *Atlantis* on 18 April. She was then tasked with accepting a large number of PoWs, which were safely delivered to a French port on 20 May.

The liner *Windhuk* sailed from Lourenço Marques on 19 August 1939 but when '*Essberger*' was received she had insufficient fuel and fresh water to reach a German port, so made for Lobito Bay, arriving on 30 August 1939. Five crewmen left in a motor lifeboat on 5 November and reached Las Palmas on 20 January. Meanwhile *Windhuk* left Lobito on 16 November disguised as a Japanese ship and reached Santos in Brazil on 7 December. The ship remained there until 27 January 1941 when she was seized by the Brazilian authorities.

Chile

Some ships made remarkable escapes. The Norrdeutscherlloyd ship *Bogota*, for example, received '*Essberger*' on 25 August whilst loading in Puerto Cristobal at the Pacific entrance to the Panama Canal. She sailed the following day, arriving at Guayaquil, Ecuador, on 1 September, where she joined another German ship, *Quito*. They were still there when war was declared two days later, but *Bogota* did not sail until 3 January 1940 followed by *Quito* a day later, and both reached Coquimbo, Chile on 11 and 12 January 1940, respectively. As instructed from Berlin, both captains tried to sell their ships to the Chilean government, but when this failed they were ordered to break out and sail to Japan. They duly sailed after dark on 18 May 1941 but separated as soon as they were clear of the coast. *Bogota* refuelled in the Marshall Islands from the German supply ship *Elsa Essberger* (6,103 grt) and having been disguised as a Japanese vessel, she sailed again on 18 June 1941, but then intercepted a signal from another German ship, MV *Osorno* (6,951 grt) of the HAPAG line, whose engines had broken down. *Bogota* found the disabled ship and took her in tow and the pair reached Yokohama on 3 July 1941 – a remarkable voyage. *Quito* proceeded independently and arrived without incident in Yokohama on 27 June 1941.

Portland was in Talcuhano, Chile but sailed in January 1941, albeit with minimal fuel oil. She replenished her fuel tanks from the supply oiler *Nordmark* on 11 February 1941 and then rendezvoused with the 'pocket battleship' *Admiral Scheer*, accepted 327 prisoners taken by that ship and then sailed to Bordeaux, arriving safely on 14 March 41.

On 3 September 1939 *Rhakotis* was in Callao, Peru, but sensing that the recently-elected government was sympathetic to the Allies, the captain moved his ship to Antofagasta on 16 May 1940, and, having refuelled proceeded to Japan, arriving on 29 June 1940.

Dutch Possessions

Nineteen German ships were in various ports in the Dutch East Indies on 3 September 1939, three of which had been earmarked for employment by the German Navy. *Wuppertal*, a new (1936) ship with the then-revolutionary diesel-electric drive was in Padang when war broke out and was still there in 10 May 1940 when she was taken over by the Dutch and reflagged as MV *Noessaniwi*. *Rendsburg* was sunk as a blockship by the Dutch on 2 March 1942, but was raised and pressed into service by the Japanese, only to be sunk by a US submarine on 25 December 1944. *Rheinland* was pressed into service by the Dutch as *Berbala* but was sunk by a German U-boat on 23 May 1941.

Four German ships sought shelter in Curaçao in the Netherlands Antilles, but were diverted by the Dutch authorities to Aruba, arriving on 30–31 August 1939. *Antilla* was in Galveston, Texas, on 25 August, when she received '*Essberger*' and her master sailed as soon as possible to shelter in Dutch waters off the island of Aruba. She was still there in May 1940 when the Germans invaded the Netherlands and Dutch Navy vessels surrounded the German ship and ordered the master to surrender. His response was to set explosive charges which were detonated after the crew had safely left the ship, which settled on the bottom.

The master of the *Consul Horn* decided to risk an escape, sailing on 9 January 1940 disguised as a Russian freighter and, successfully avoiding the waiting British, sailed northabout around the British Isles reaching Germany in February 1940. The two other ships were not so fortunate. *Troja* and *Heidelberg* were anchored off Aruba from 31 August 1939 to 29 February 1940, when both sailed just after dark in an effort to reach Germany. Both were found within days by the British, but their crews were able to scuttle both ships to avoid capture.

Italian Somaliland

On the outbreak of war in August 1939 two German ships, *Tannenfels* and *Uckermark*, took refuge in the port of Chisimayo in Italian Somaliland and lay there for some sixteen months. In January 1941 it became known that the British were about to invade, so both attempted to escape. *Tannenfels* broke out on 31 January 1941, met the 'pocket battleship' *Admiral Scheer* at sea, replenished and took on PoWs, and then sailed for Bordeaux which she reached in mid-April. Following *Tannenfels*' successful escape, *Uckermark* sailed on 10 February 1941, but, not surprisingly, the British were waiting for her. She was intercepted by the British cruiser HMS *Hawkins* on 14 February but he crew scuttled the German ship before it could be seized.

Mexico

There were numerous German merchant ships in the Gulf of Mexico in August 1939, only two of which were of any significance. *Emmy Friedrich*, a tanker (4,732 tons), sailed from Tampico to support the *Graf Spee* but was cornered by the British and scuttled on 23 October 1939.

Weser (9,179 tons) was sheltering in Manzanillo on the Mexican

Pacific coast, and sailed on 25 September 1940 to resupply the AMC *Orion* but was caught by the British and sunk the following day.

Peru
Four German ships took shelter in Callao, two of which – *Hermonthis* and *München* – attempted to break out on 1 April 1941, but made the crucial error of failing to obtain clearance from the port authorities. This entitled the Peruvians to track them by air and to inform the patrolling HMCS *Prince Henry*, a Canadian AMC, of their locations. The Canadian ship approached each ship in turn but their German crews scuttled them before they could be sunk or captured. Meanwhile, the other two – *Leipzig* and *Montserrat* – which were still at anchor were scuttled by their crews before the Peruvian Navy could board them.

Japan
At least a dozen German merchant ships were either in Japanese ports on 3 September 1939 or reached one in the following months. Even though it did not join the war until December 1941, Japan, while legally neutral, was well-disposed towards Germany. Thus, most of these German ships were subsequently employed as blockade runners carrying Japanese goods to Germany, although a few of the smaller one were employed under joint German/Japanese control as transports.

Beira
Rufidji, a small coaster, was trapped in Beira in September 1939 and remained there until 1943 when it was seized by Portugal.

Spain
Spain had a somewhat ambivalent relationship with Germany. The Germans had given Franco generous help during the Spanish Civil War, but despite strong pressure from Hitler Spain remained officially neutral, although prepared to turn a blind eye to certain matters, which, at least early in the war, included refuelling U-boats.

In accordance with pre-war plans, six German tankers and supply ships were positioned in Spanish ports and the replenishment drill was the same in each case with the U-boat entering the port immediately after darkness had fallen and leaving before dawn. Wherever possible the

Left. Squadron-Leader Basil Russell, RAFVR, aged 38, who conceived and led Operation Minerva.

Above. Captain Fred Sladen, Bedfordshire and Hertfordshire Regiment, aged 23, a professional soldier who had been ordered to leave Singapore in February 1942.

Left. Captain Alex Hunter, Royal Engineers, aged 32, a civil engineer in Sumatra before the war, who knew parts of that island well.

Below. Sergeant Lau Teng Kee (third from right with trilby) led this group of university graduates to freedom from Japanese-occupied Hong Kong in mid-1942 before taking part in Operation Minerva.

Above. The aircraft which delivered the Minerva party was a Consolidated Catalina (PBY-5 in US and Dutch service) of 321 Squadron RAF, which was manned entirely by officers and men of the Royal Netherlands Naval Air Service.

Right. The pilot on 20 December 1942 was Lieutenant-Commander Gerard Rijnders, RNethN, a man of great courage and ability, who also flew two of the three recovery missions – but there was nobody at the rendezvous. He was awarded the DFC for these missions.

Above. Major Terence Croley with his Royal Signals wireless telegraphists – Sergeants Allen, Dickins, Thomas and Wooldridge – and an unknown Indian soldier. The wireless link to India was rock solid throughout the time in the Andamans and the transmitters were never located by the Japanese.

Below. Major Richard Duncan, Garwhal Rifles (left) and Major Terence Croley in their base camp on the Andaman Islands. Exploits such as theirs proved that the British were not just as good, but actually better, jungle fighters than the Japanese.

Left. Major Terence Croley, Skinner's Horse, commander of Baldhead IV, operated in the Andamans from 23 January to 25 March 1944.

Above. Captain Lawrence White, Royal Engineers, took part in the evacuation from Dunkirk, and the Fall of Malaya and Singapore, was the explosives expert on Operations Longshanks (Goa) and Hatch I (Andamans), and finally received the surrender of Japanese troops in the Malayan State of Perak.

Left. The most important product of the Andamans was timber, brought by sea to the sawmill on Chatham Island in Blair Harbour, which was regularly bombed, this picture showing a spectacular direct hit.

Left. The Japanese formal surrender at Port Blair in October 1945. Despite a large garrison the Japanese never detected the British infiltrations made during Operations Baldhead and Hatch.

Operation Longshanks/Creek, Goa

Above. MV *Ehrenfels,* very modern and a potential commerce raider, was the target of the British operation.

Above. The Italian SS *Anfora,* one of four Axis merchantmen trapped in Marmagao Harbour, was scuttled by her own crew.

Above. Lieutenant-Colonel Bill Grice, commanding officer of the Calcutta Light Horse, took part in the raids on Zeebrugge (22 April 1918) and Marmugao (8/9 March 1943)

Above. Captain Robert Hutton Duguid, 36, the leader of the four-man Calcutta Scottish party, postponed his wedding to take part in Operation Creek.

Above. Lieutenant Cren Sandys-Lumsdaine, Calcutta Light Horse, worked for Williamson Magor tea merchants, but played a very active role in Operation Longshanks/Creek.

Left. Lieutenant-Colonel Lewis Pugh, Royal Artillery (seen here as a captain) was the chief planner for SOE(India) and also took part in the raid.

Above. *Phoebe* (Hopper Barge No. 5) in the 1930s. Although ageing, she did everything that was asked of her.

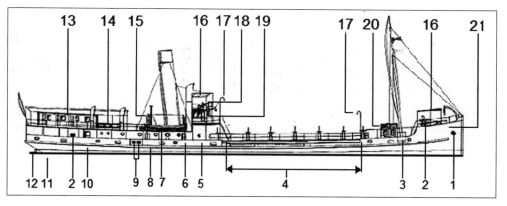

Above. Based on the builder's plans, this shows *Phoebe* as she was when delivered from Clydebank to Calcutta in 1912.

Phoebe	7. Ship's boat (2)	15. Davits
KEY	8. Pump room	16. Awnings
1. Anchor	9. Discharge pipes (2)	17. Lights
2. Steam capstan	10. Engine room	18. Upper bridge
3. Crew's quarters	11. Propellers (2)	19. Wheelhouse
4. Hopper (24,000 cu ft)	12. Rudder	20. Deckhouse
5. Coal bunker	13. Officers' accommodation	21. Forecastle
6. Stokehold	14. Engine room skylight	

Three German sailors were captured aboard *Ehrenfels*, spent the remainder of the war as PoWs in India and in 1946 were sent to England. Heinz Bernardini (**above left**), a steward, was granted British citizenship, changed his name to Shortland, married and settled in Sussex. The fates of deckhands Anton Harms (**above right**) and Hans Borchers (**below right**) are not known.

The binoculars once owned by the Master of the *Ehrenfels*, Captain Röfer, are now in a private collection.

U-boat was secured on the side of the replenishing ship away from the shore, but there can be little doubt that the port authorities knew what was going on. All of these replenishment operations included fuel, but there was also lubricating oil, water, rations, and in some cases also torpedoes. Among the known refuelling operations were *Bessel*, in Vigo, which supplied eight U-boats; *Max Albrecht* in El Ferrol, three; *Thalia* in Cadiz, six; and *Charlotte Schliemann* in Las Palmas, Canary Islands, six. The last of these refuelling operations took place in May 1942.

Italian Ships
Italian ships in foreign waters were given three days' advance notice of Mussolini's declaration of war on 10 June 1940. There were 200-odd Italian ships outside the Mediterranean on that date, of which thirty-three were in British or Commonwealth ports and were immediately interned. Those in neutral ports comprised: USA – twenty-six; South America – fifty-eight; Spain and possessions – thirty-two; Portugal and possessions – three; Iran – four; Far East – nine; and various northern European ports – fourteen. Finally, thirty-three were in East African waters and thus in or near Italian-owned harbours. Twenty-five ships are known to have tried to return to Italy, but only seventeen made it, delivering some 89,000 tons of cargo. Generally speaking, few of these Italian ships and their crews seem to have caused the British as much concern as did the German ones.

Chapter 19

Cutting-Out Expeditions

The British had a tradition of cutting-out expeditions, where enemy warships or merchant ships which thought they were safely protected in harbour were attacked without warning from the sea, their crews overwhelmed, and the ships taken out to sea. They were then either incorporated into the British fleet or sold commercially as 'prizes of war'. Such actions were rare in the Second World War, but there were a few examples.

Operation Countenance: Bandar Shahpur (25 August 1941)
The Persian port of Bandar Shahpur was situated some 30 miles up the Khor Musa deepwater channel at the north-eastern end of the Persian Gulf.[88] The harbour facilities were on the seaward edge of a large mud flat which extended northwards some seven miles to the mainland and offered limited facilities, comprising a jetty and two berths for visiting ships. The nearest town was 10 miles away. In 1941 Bandar Shahpur became strategically important to the Allies because was it was also the southern terminus of the Trans-Persia Railway which ran north, via Teheran, to the port of Bandar Shah on the southern shore of the Caspian Sea. It thus presented an ideal route for Allied supplies to be passed safely and rapidly to the USSR.

The capture of the port was complicated by the presence of eight Axis merchant ships which had taken refuge in the neutral port in 1939–40 and, together with their crews and cargoes, had been unable to leave. The German ships were *Hohenfels*, *Marienfels*, *Sturmfels*, *Weißenfels* and *Wildenfels*, all relatively modern cargo ships belonging to the Hansa Line, while the Italian ships were *Barbara*, *Brontë* and *Caboto*, belonging to Lloyd-Triestino.

The Axis captains considered – correctly, as it transpired – that the main threat to their ships was from a British 'cutting-out' expedition and made preparations accordingly, with all ships being prepared for destruction. The Germans placed explosive charges where they would damage the ships' watertight structure, and also ensured that the Kingston valves were ready to open. As a further measure, explosives were placed in the holds, with long lengths of safety fuze laid to the bridge, where boxes of matches were readily available to the watchkeeper. Setting fire to the cargo involved dousing the holds in kerosene, which would then be ignited by black-powder bombs or short lights. The Italians employed electrically-fired TNT and gelignite charges, coupled with stacks of kerosene drums, interspersed with bombs fitted with varying lengths of fuze.

The British assembled a force to attack Bandar Shahpur. The naval element comprised one AMC, two sloops, a corvette, two tugs, a river gunboat, an armed trawler, a dhow and an RAF launch. Eight boarding parties were assembled from the crews which were trained in secret at a remote anchorage, each party being divided into two groups, one for the upper deck, the other for the engine-room, and were directed that men must always work at least in pairs and complete their tasks as quickly as possible. The army element, which did not take part in the boarding operation, comprised two companies of the British Indian Army's 3/10th Baluch Regiment.

Zero hour was 0410 hours local time on 25 August 1941. Two Iranian gunboats and a floating dock were captured intact without a shot being fired, but the Axis merchant ships were a different matter and as soon as the alarm was raised, fuzes were lit, charges blown, fires started and valves opened. The main activity for the boarders was firefighting and most of the ships were saved from destruction, although it proved impossible to save the *Weißenfels*, which sank the following morning, while *Hohenfels* was beached. *Marienfels* and *Wildenfels* were saved, virtually undamaged, while *Sturmfels* had one cargo hold still smouldering. The fires aboard the Italian ships had been extinguished but there remained a possibility that they might spontaneously reignite.

All the surviving Axis merchant vessels were subsequently taken to Basra and thence to India, reaching Bombay in September 1941, where they were refitted and pressed into service by the British. The crews of all the ships were made prisoners-of-war.

Operation Postmaster (14 January 1942)

Shortly after the outbreak of war two small German vessels took shelter in the harbour of Santa Cristobel on the Spanish island of Fernando Po off the west coast of Africa; a tug, *Likomba* (70 tons) and a smaller barge, *Bibundi*. The latter had been used by the staff of a German-owned plantation in British Cameroons to escape imminent internment. Such small vessels were of little concern to the British, but in June 1940 the Italian liner, *Duchessa d'Aosta* (6,700grt), *en route* from Cape Town to Genoa with a mixed cargo of coffee, copper, copra, animal hides and timber also took shelter there. An SOE officer in 1942 assessed the Italian crew as being debilitated and demoralised, and the only threat was posed by the wireless, which had not been sealed by the Spanish.

The first plan sent to London by the head of the Neutral Colonies (NeuCol) section was to seize the *Likomba*, but only to immobilise the *Duchessa d'Aosta* by destroying her propellers, which was effectively vetoed by the bureaucrats in London. However, in an entirely unrelated development, two small parties from SOE's Small-Scale Raiding Force (SSRF) arrived in Freetown. First to arrive (20 September) were five men who had sailed a converted Brixham trawler, *Maid Honor*, from Poole in exactly six weeks, a major achievement at any time, let alone in war. A further group from the SSRF later arrived aboard a troopship. At first nobody knew quite how to employ these men, so they were sent on a series of reconnaissances into various bays and river mouths seeking a rumoured U-boat resupply facility, but none was found.

However, a new plan was now developed which involved the use of the SSRF team (but not *Maid Honor*) and centred on the seizure of *Duchessa d'Aosta*. This was carried to London in early November, was approved by the Foreign Office on 12 November and allocated the codename Operation Postmaster on 20 November 1941. In Africa the British Consul in Fernando Po gave his approval of the plan, as did the Governor of Nigeria, who also made a tug and a launch available, together with their crews. No SOE path was ever smooth, however, and the local naval and army commanders-in-chief both objected, and it took several weeks to satisfy them as to the practicability of the operation. Then, even when the army C-in-C had very reluctantly agreed to the operation in principle, he still declined to make any troops available. Fortunately, the Governor of Nigeria, Sir Bernard Bourdillon, was more enterprising and authorised the planner of the operation, Major Victor Laversuch, to call for volunteers from the colonial administration. The men nominated by the governor assembled in Lagos on the 9th, were addressed by March-Phillips on the 10th and asked if they would volunteer for a 'job of military character'. To a man they accepted and boarded the ships between 2300 and 2400 hours that night.

The raiding party was commanded by Captain Gustavus March-Phillips and comprised thirty-two men: four from local SOE staff, eleven from the SSRF group associated with *Maid Honor*, and the remaining seventeen from the volunteers from the Nigerian service. They sailed from Lagos at 0530 hours on 11 January 1942 aboard two Nigerian government tugs, *Vulcan*, the larger of the two, and *Nuneaton*, which would be beset by mechanical problems. Training for the members of the party was carried out during the voyage, the folboat canoes were rigged, and briefings and rehearsals conducted.

As planned, the two vessels entered Santa Christobel harbour at 2330 hours on 14 January 1942. Entertainments for eight members of the Italian crew and two Germans from *Likomba* had been organised ashore by local SOE agents, leaving twenty-six Italian men, one Italian woman and one Spaniard aboard *Duchessa d'Aosta*, but only a few African crewmen aboard *Likomba*.

The raiders were organised into groups, each with a specific task: quelling resistance; destroying the wireless; taking control of the forecastle and severing the anchor chain; and securing the two smaller tugs. The Italians aboard *Duchessa d'Aosta* were taken completely by surprise, although one African crewman dived over the side and swam ashore. The anchor chains were then quickly destroyed and *Vulcan* took *D'Aosta* in tow, and with great skill towed her out to sea. Most of the men in the boarding party established proper seagoing watches, while the twenty-nine prisoners were guarded by nine of the civilian volunteers from the Nigerian colonial service, although the prisoners were subsequently employed in cleaning the ship and manning the galley and dining-room.

Nuneaton launched two folboats whose crews successfully boarded the *Likomba*. The two German officers were ashore and the remaining crew were quickly overpowered by the raiders, although two managed to jump into the water and escape. *Bibundi* proved to be unmanned and was quickly taken. All five vessels left the harbour just after 0100 hours, the entire operation having taken just 35 minutes.

Vulcan towed *D'Aosta* slowly towards the rendezvous but *Nuneaton* suffered repeated engine trouble and at one point the tug had to leave *D'Aosta* drifting while it went back to find the smaller vessel. Having been assured that repairs were under way, *Vulcan* transferred fuel and water to *Nuneaton* and then returned to *D'Aosta*. As planned, a Royal Navy corvette, HMS *Violet*, 'chanced upon' *D'Aosta*, although somewhat later than intended, at 1230 hours on Sunday. The three captured vessels reached Lagos at 2000 hours on 22 January. There were no serious injuries on either side.

The outcome of Operation Postmaster was very satisfactory. The plan had been implemented successfully; a sizeable Italian ship and its cargo had been captured intact, while the tug and launch could be employed locally by the Nigerian government.[89] The aim of avoiding any direct evidence of British involvement was also achieved. The Spanish government made a strong protest which was easily rebuffed by the British, while the German captain of *Likomba* made a very strong personal protest to the British consul on the following morning, but was arrested and forced to apologise.[90] The only residual problem was the prisoners, who were unceremoniously dumped on the Nigerian administration, which had done so much to help in the operation itself. The problem was that they could not be put into a conventional PW camp as they would then tell the others about the British involvement in their capture in a neutral port.

Operation Ramification (Planned but not implemented)
The German ships *Wameru* (4,076 grt) and *Wagongo* (3,118 grt) had been lying in Lobito Bay in Portuguese Angola together with their crews and cargo since September 1939. In September 1942 the SOE mission in Lagos produced a plan to remove them on 8 November 1942.

The plan was fairly simple. An assault party of thirty commandoes would be flown out from the UK to Lagos. Two tugs, loaded with the necessary stores, would leave Lagos on 29 October and arrive in Punta Negra (Pointe Noire) in the Belgian Congo on 4 November. There they would refuel and be joined by the assault party who had flown down by flying boat from Lagos.

The assault force would then sail to Lobito Bay, arriving on 8 November. Meanwhile, SOE agents ashore would have bribed certain Portuguese port and customs officials (the harbourmaster was said to be paid regularly by SOE) who would find an excuse on the morning of 8 November to search the two ships. The SOE agents would also ensure that the crews were incapacitated in some way (the documents do not say how) and when all was prepared the agents would send a signal to the waiting tugs at 2300 hours, whereupon the tugs would enter the harbour, the two German ships would be captured, anchor chains dropped, the tugs be secured alongside and the two targets would be towed out to sea.

Once outside the three-mile limit two RN ships, which 'happened to be passing' would 'seize' the ships and tow them to the small port of Banana in the Belgian Congo. After refuelling, the two ex-German ships would proceed under their own steam to Lagos, still under RN escort, where they would be impounded by the British and the crew made prisoners-of-war.

The cover story would be that the German crews, disgruntled and bored with their monotonous life, had put to sea to reach a Vichy port, but had been intercepted at sea by an RN warship, which chanced to be passing by.

The plan was passed to and fro between Lagos and London, various elements being revised in the process, but all came to naught when the situation was unexpectedly resolved by other means. Separate negotiations resulted in the British agreeing that the Portuguese government could take over the German ships lying in Lobito Bay, Lourenço Marques and Beira, and that the German crews would be exchanged for an equal number of British seamen in Axis hands.

Conclusion

There were many Axis ships in neutral harbours around the world: German from September 1939, joined by Italian in May 1940. Many of these ships tried to escape by sea, either to return to Germany, or, after July 1940 to Bordeaux, or to Japan, which required Allied surveillance of ports and anchorages to see whether ships were either preparing to or had actually sailed. This also required a large seaborne surveillance force of warships and AMCs, which could intercept and either capture or sink their quarries. The most immediate threat was that such ships could be used to refuel U-boats, as had been done on various Spanish and Portuguese ports, an operation which could be completed in the hours of darkness of a single night.

For their part, both Germans and Italians had shown that they would always try to escape, if possible, failing which they would scuttle their ships. On the other hand the question of neutrality arose, particularly with Spain and Portugal. These two countries, especially Portugal, were valuable to the Allies and it would not do to upset them too much; thus, if there was to be a cutting-out expedition in Goa it would have to be planned with great care.

Chapter 20

The Situation to 1942

The general naval threat to British India has been described above, but the four Axis merchant ships lying in Mormugao Harbour posed a more immediate problem. They had crews totalling some 200 merchant navy officers and seamen, most of them young and reasonably fit. The Portuguese had removed some weapons – presumably rifles and pistols – when the ships arrived, but it was possible that a few had been retained, in which case, these men might be organised into one or more armed groups for operations in British India, although the chances of groups of armed Caucasians lasting long among an Asian population seemed remote.

Of greater significance was the danger that one or more of the ships might try to slip away on a dark night, and the Commander-in-Chief India and the commanders of the Royal Navy and Royal Indian Navy told the Head of SOE's India Mission that it would be very helpful if the four ships could either be somehow taken into British possession or destroyed where they lay at anchor.[91] However, all these Service commanders were adamant that they would not allow any of their ships or men to take any part in an operation against ships sheltering in a neutral port, nor would they give any active assistance, such as providing a ship to transport a raiding party to and from Goa.

The Schomberg Report

Apart from the four merchant ships, Goa was of little strategic importance to the British, but they kept a close eye on the place and sent regular visitors to assess the situation. One such was Lt Col R. C. F. Schomberg (1880–1958), one of those remarkable people who thrived in the British Empire, in his case as soldier, explorer, writer, diplomat and priest – and was both successful and respected in them all. Early in the war he was appointed Consul-General in the French Establishments and Portuguese Possessions in India and he submitted a report on Goa in September 1940. He found that Goa was essentially a fascist state, with leading elements exchanging fascist salutes and overtly supporting the anti-British Congress Party in India, while ruthlessly suppressing the anti-Portuguese movement in Goa. However, all in Goa anticipated a German entry into Spain, following which Portugal would also be taken over and, with no further support from the motherland, Portuguese Goa would have little choice but to declare for the Allies. In such a case, Schomberg warned, the Germans would immediately scuttle their three ships and flee to British India to avoid being interned by the Portuguese. He described the German sailors as well-behaved but bored, and longing to be back home with their families. The ships, he said, were 'more barnacle-bound than ever; their cargoes more decayed'.

The Goan Transmitter
The British knew that the Portuguese authorities had either removed or disabled the normal commercial radios installed in each of the Axis ships, but they became increasingly concerned that the Germans had retained a hidden transmitter, which could have had two significant uses. The British felt particularly vulnerable to the activities of the various Indian independence movements. There were many supporters at large in India and the Indian National Army had been formed in Singapore in November 1942. Further, one of the leaders, Subhas Chandra Bose, had escaped from India in 1941 and was known to be in Berlin.

A second factor was the arrival in the Indian Ocean of German U-boats, as described in Chapter 17; twelve ships were sunk between 10 and 31 October and another twenty-six in November. The Allies frantically searched for possible explanations and one story that gained credence was that spies were obtaining sailing details from the Bombay port authorities, passing them by courier to Goa, where a hidden transmitter aboard *Ehrenfels* sent the details to waiting U-boats. '*Nous somme trahis*' is always a popular explanation when the enemy appears to be better informed than they should be. The more this was discussed the more likely it seemed to be and before long *Ehrenfels* was credited with a secure radio room in the hold, equipped with the same sets as a 'pocket battleship'.

The Wavell Proposal
The Japanese invaded Malaya on 7 December 1941. Penang was abandoned on 17 December and by the middle of the month the Japanese were approaching Kuala Lumpur. With disaster approaching in Malaya, the CinC India, General Wavell, still found time to consider Goa and on 21 December 1941 sent a signal 'personal for' CIGS, copied to CinC East Indies:[92]

> Goa. Present position is intolerable, as a number of German ships are lying in the harbour and their crews are at large. Wireless station is utilised continuously and there is a grave danger of a leak of information. There have been reports, though not confirmed, that port has recently been used by an enemy submarine. Possible alternatives are to:
> a) Request that wireless station be shut down. This we are entitled to do but previous requests have met with no response.
> b) Put in hand 'cutting out' operations to seize enemy ships. This is the only possible way getting them intact and avoiding danger of clash with Portuguese.
> c) Occupy colony with land forces. These could later be withdrawn subject to conditions which would ensure control over use of wireless and of harbour and also internment of crews of enemy ships. It is unlikely to secure enemy ships intact.
> d) To put pressure on Portuguese to take action themselves or to allow us to do so with their connivance.
> Last named course renders surprise impossible and increases possibility of resistance result of which will be unfortunate. It will also permit of escaping or scuttling of German ships which we wish to avoid. We therefore recommend course (B) (repeat B) and consider that in view of entry of Japan and U.S.A. into war that political effects of such action can now be disregarded.

Reaction was immediate. The naval CinC East Indies, Vice-Admiral Sir Geoffrey Arbuthnot, whose HQ was at Trincomalee in Ceylon, had clearly not been consulted before the proposal was sent to London and even though the two HQs were widely separated an exchange of signals would have been possible. As it was, Arbuthnot disagreed with Wavell's proposal: 'I am unable to agree with conclusion reached in alternative B.' He ended somewhat plaintively 'Has my Chief of Staff been consulted on this appreciation please', making it very clear that he had not. However, even that pales into insignificance compared to the firm rebuff from London: 'Chiefs of Staff consider and Foreign Office concur that we should not (repeat not) attempt anything in Goa at present . . .'[93]

By late 1942 the four ships had been in the harbour for over three years and the crews were becoming bored and fractious. The British Consul-General, Lieutenant-Colonel Bremner, did his best to keep an eye on matters and sent regular reports to New Delhi. The Governor, Colonel Cabral, also did his best. The German and Italian sailors were allowed to go anywhere within the geographical limits of Goa. Bremner was particularly concerned that many of the sailors appeared to be suddenly 'very flush of money' but without any explanation of where the money had come from, although he suspected (but had no proof) that it might have something to do with a recent arrival of anti-British Indian Congress elements. One individual he named in his reports was Robert Koch, a German businessman who had arrived in Goa aboard *Ehrenfels* in 1939 and now lived in Nova Goa.

Escapes

From time-to-time German and Italian sailors attempted to escape from the boredom and unpleasant conditions. Some simply went ashore, rented accommodation, mixed with the local population and stayed there for lengthy periods, without attracting any noticeable reaction from either their ships or the Portuguese authorities. Others travelled the railway line to the border with British India and then returned; presumably because even such a short journey gave the impression that they were actually going somewhere. All of these caused great anxiety to the British consul, who dutifully reported all incidents to his superiors in New Delhi.

On 19 November 1942, for example, Bremner was told unofficially by the Governor-General that the Master of the *Braunfels* had reported that three of his crew had been missing for a week. The Governor-General pointed out to Bremner that the German sailors had been confined within the limits of Goa for over three years and had little to keep them occupied. He also reminded him that the sole responsibility of the Goan authorities in this matter was to meet reasonable requests from the German and Italian captains and to provide services on repayment. Bremner later discovered that the three Germans had offered 500 rupees for a sailing boat, which had been turned down, but as the boat had then disappeared on the same day as the three sailors it seemed clear that it was they who had stolen it.[94] However, this particular incident closed with the news that the three Germans had been landed at Colombo by a British ship on 23 December 1942.[95] How far they had got before being rescued and where they were heading was never established.

The Governor-General made it clear to Bremner that the four ships were a problem for him but that he could do little about them for so long as Portugal remained neutral. Should, however, his country join the Allies (as privately he hoped it would) then he had plans to seize the ships and to intern their crews at the earliest opportunity.

The Goan Garrison

The Portuguese military strength in Goa was negligible. The permanent garrison comprised one company of light infantry, one mortar company and one battery of artillery – about 500 men in all. There was no coastal defence, although one gun was believed to be in the process of being installed, and there was no anti-aircraft defence whatsoever.

By chance, a reinforcement force *en route* from Lourenço Marques to Portuguese Timor had been diverted to Goa, arriving in early February 1942. This comprised some 550 men, Africans with Portuguese officers in nine light infantry platoons; two light artillery batteries; a support company and some further small detachments.[96] A small warship called from time-to-time and there was no air force.

In total, the Portuguese garrison comprised two small battalions, with limited artillery support, which could have been brushed aside in a major British invasion, although they could be expected to provide resistance to small-scale raiding parties.

The Ships

There had been a number of Axis merchant ships in Asian waters when war broke out in September 1939 and all were in obvious danger of being rounded up by the British. As described in the previous chapter, some made for Italian ports in Eritrea and Somaliland, but others headed for neutral ports, some in Arab countries and Iran, while three reached Mormugao Harbour in the Portuguese enclave of Goa. These were the *Braunfels*, *Ehrenfels* and *Drachenfels* of the *Deutsche Dampfschiffahrts-Gesellschaft Hansa* (German Steamship Company – Hansa) usually known simply as 'DDG-Hansa'. The Italian ship, SS *Anfora* of the Italian Lloyd-Triestino Line, arrived on 10 July 1940.

Table 3: The Four Axis Merchant Ships

	MV *Ehrenfels*	SS *Drachenfels*	MV *Braunfels*	SS *Anfora*
Flag	Germany	Germany	Germany	Italy
Owner	Hansa	Hansa	Hansa	Lloyd-Triestino
Builder	DeSchiMag	Howaldtswerke	DeSchiMag	San Rocco
In Service	1935	1921	1927	1922
Length	506.6ft (154.4m)	439.5ft (133.95m)	488.2ft (148.8m)	404.3ft
Beam	61.3ft (18.68m)	56.5ft (17.21m)	60.4ft (18.4m)	54.0ft
Draught (full load)	27.1ft (8.27m)	30.4ft (9.26m)	27.2ft (8.3m)	25.3ft
Displacement	7,752 grt	6,342 grt	7,844 grt	8,504grt
Propulsion	Diesel	Steam	Diesel	Steam
Cruising (full load)	16 knots	12 knots	12 knots	10kt
Crew	44	33 European 39 Indian	45	50
Passenger capacity*	12	4	7	10

*None were aboard on 8/9 March 1943.

Three of the ships were only on the sidelines in the forthcoming British operation, so can be quickly dismissed. These were two of the Hansa ships, *Braunfels* and *Drachenfels*, and the Italian *Anfora*, all of which were elderly and slow – in fact, typical 1920s tramps.

The fourth ship was in a different category altogether, being not only newer but also considerably faster. The Hansa Line had been experimenting with advanced propulsion systems (engines, gearboxes and propellers) for some years, concentrating on development of the marine diesel. *Ehrenfels* was one of a class of nine constructed for the line in the late 1930s. These vessels were fitted with twin diesels driving a single propeller, which was intended to give them long endurance on one engine and high speed on two, a combination which was simply not required in a conventional merchant ship. In addition, the second diesel could be brought on line very quickly, enabling the ship to accelerate rapidly – a valuable capability for a commerce raider closing on a potential victim. Such power also required the hull to be of significantly stronger construction than in a conventional merchant ship. All this made these ships highly suitable for wartime conversion to commerce raiders: long range, high speed, rapid acceleration and a reinforced steel deck. They also had built-in bases for gun mounts and collapsible bulwarks which would hide the guns until required.

Ehrenfels first came to the notice of the authorities in British India in 1939. The ship had visited Batavia in the Dutch East Indies where the Dutch Intelligence Service identified one of the passengers as a known *Abwehr* (German military intelligence) agent named Robert Koch (codenamed Trompeta). The Dutch alerted the British intelligence services so that when *Ehrenfels* arrived in Calcutta roads in mid-August the latter were ready.[97] The ship anchored in the Hooghly River and was subjected to a 24-hour watch, with arrangements in place to detain Koch should he venture ashore, although, wisely in the circumstances, he did not do so. Plain clothes policemen were sent aboard on a clandestine reconnaissance, and the movement of all crew and passengers who went ashore was carefully monitored.

After only two days in port *Ehrenfels*' captain suddenly requested tugs to move his ship down-river to the anchorage off Sagar Island where he would await a pilot to take her to the open sea. That was duly done, but, under cover of darkness and against port regulations, her captain raised anchor and made his own way down the Hooghly without waiting for a pilot and disappeared into the Bay of Bengal. The next the British knew was a report that *Ehrenfels* had entered Mormugao Harbour in the neutral enclave of Portuguese Goa on the west coast of India and it became clear that the ship's captain had been alerted to the imminent declaration of war, either by radio from Germany or from the German consulate in Calcutta.

Once in Mormugao Harbour, *Ehrenfels* was joined two other German ships, *Braunfels* and *Drachenfels*, also of the Hansa Line, while an Italian ship, the Lloyd-Triestino tramp SS *Anfora*, joined them on 10 July 1940. The four ships were legally 'taking shelter' and not officially interned, which meant that the crews were entitled to come and go as they pleased. All four were required by the Portuguese port authority to give up their ship's wirelesses and a few antiquated weapons. They carried a range of cargo, including electric batteries, electric wiring, a large car destined for an Indian prince, mining explosives, drums of kerosene and many other articles, which were left undisturbed by the Portuguese.

The Threat Posed by *Ehrenfels*
By late 1942 the British knew that seven of the ships in this nine-strong class had been requisitioned by the *Kriegsmarine*, the exceptions being *Ehrenfels* and *Hohenfels*. *Moltkefels* and *Neidenfels* had been due to be converted to commerce raiders, but this was cancelled and they were employed as fast transports in the Baltic and North Sea.[98] Two more were in the Mediterranean on the outbreak of war and were subsequently employed as fast transports between Italy and North Africa, where both were sunk: *Kybfels* on 22 May 1941 and *Reichenfels* on 21 June 1942. On the outbreak of war *Hohenfels* was trapped in the Persian port of Bandar Shahpur and was severely damaged during the Anglo-Soviet invasion in August 1941 (Operation Countenance) but was later repaired and pressed into Allied service.

On the outbreak of war, *Tannenfels* was trapped in Kismayu in Italian Somaliland, but after careful preparation sailed on 31 January 1940 and reached Germany. She sailed from Bordeaux on 2 February 1942, reached Yokohama, Japan, on 12 May 42 and left again on 8 August 1942, arriving in Bordeaux on 2 November.[99]

Two of the class were converted into very successful commerce raiders in 1939/40: *Goldenfels* was renamed *Atlantis* and *Kandelfels* was renamed *Pinguin* (see Chapter 17 for details of their careers).

Thus, by 1942 the British had more than sufficient evidence of the effectiveness of these nine ships and if *Ehrenfels* managed to escape she would undoubtedly make for Singapore where she could easily be outfitted with guns and ammunition from Japanese or captured British stocks. Table 4 shows the armament for *Atlantis* and *Pinguin*, which differed slightly but not significantly from each other. There were Japanese equivalents to all of these weapons, which could have been mounted in *Ehrenfels* without any problems. The Japanese could also have supplied one or two aircraft and another raider, *Orion*, operated a borrowed Nakajima E8N ('Dave') floatplane for many months.

Table 4: Armament of *Atlantis* and *Pinguin*

	Pinguin	Atlantis
15cm (5.9in) SK L/45 guns	6 x 1	6 x 1
75mm (3in) gun	1 x 1	1 x 1
3.7cm SK C/30 anti-aircraft guns (twin)	2 x 2	2 x 2
Torpedo tubes 533mm (21in)	2	4
Mines	300	92
Aircraft (floatplanes)	2	2

Atlantis and *Pinguin* were both fitted with a fire-control system which, while not as sophisticated as that of a warship, nevertheless meant that the fire of the various weapons could be controlled and coordinated. There was no catapult so that the aircraft had to be lowered into the water for take-off. The second aircraft was stored in crates and much work was required to make it fit for use. These commerce raiders were equivalent to light cruisers in many respects.

The Crews
The four ships sheltering in Goa had approximately 200 crewmen aboard – 122 Germans, fifty Italians and thirty-nine Indians – and not surprisingly, they became increasingly bored and fractious as time went by. There were still routine shipboard duties, of course, and the engineers, cooks and supply personnel would have had plenty to do, but for the rest there was a limit to how much maintenance and painting could be done.

Because the ships were legally taking refuge and not interned, the crewmen were refugees not internees and thus allowed ashore and once there to roam anywhere within Portuguese territory, without obstruction or interference. They prowled around the town, sailed in the harbour, canoed up rivers, took the train to the last station before the border, and some even rented accommodation ashore. Several attempts were made to sail small boats away from Goa, although quite where they hoped to go is unclear. Some were intercepted by the Portuguese, and one boat was rescued in international waters by a passing British steamer and the three men dropped off at Colombo, where they became prisoners-of-war.

All these activities were closely watched by the British Consul, Lieutenant-Colonel Bremner, who was extremely suspicious, sending regular reports to the government in New Delhi and periodically making informal – sometimes even formal – complaints to the governor-general – Colonel Cabral. The latter had to walk a delicate line, his main aim being not to make a difficult situation worse. In mid-November 1942 Bremner reported that:

> The Governor-General expressed it as his opinion that Axis personnel were experiencing very hard conditions having been confined within Goan limits for over three years and with no prospects of getting away for some considerable time. He pointed out that both officers and men had little or nothing to do and that little excursions etc., provided practically the sole amenity accessible to them.[100]

The Government of India did not agree with such a relaxed attitude and reminded Bremner that:

> . . . It is a principle of International Law that neutral territory should not become a base of activities by any one belligerent connected with war operations; and a neutral can be made responsible for such activities favouring or damaging a belligerent as he could be due diligence have prevented. Goa is surrounded on three sides by British territory and is the point of refuge of as number of Axis ships well conversant with the terrain owing to a prolonged residence therein.

Conclusion

In December 1942 SOE(India) decided that it should reconsider the possibility of either extracting *Ehrenfels* from Mormugao, or destroying all the Axis shipping there. The reasons for this conclusion centred on the possibility that there was an illicit wireless transmitter aboard *Ehrenfels*, which was being used to pass information from Indian nationalists, but, more importantly, to pass information on shipping movements to Axis submarines operating in the Indian Ocean.

Chapter 21

SOE (India)

The SOE's India Mission was established in May 1941 and was originally given the cover designation of GSI(k) (i.e., branch 'k' of the Intelligence Division of the General Staff) at GHQ India.[101] This was a suitably vague title, although it did have the unfortunate effect of making people think that it was an intelligence as opposed to an operational organisation. It was headed by Colin Mackenzie with Major Gavin Burton Stewart as his deputy and their aim was deliberately rather nebulous, but in essence it was to carry out clandestine tasks outside the scope of other overt or covert organisations.

Colin Mackenzie had served in the Scots Guards in the First World War, but was badly wounded in 1918, lost a leg and was invalided out. He then went to Cambridge and on graduating joined J&P Coates, the cotton firm, where he rapidly worked his way up to director. He was appointed the head of the Indian Mission of SOE and arrived in New Delhi in mid-1941; he remained a civilian and had no military rank. He was ideal for the task, being very efficient and an imaginative thinker, and was also a personal friend of the then viceroy, Lord Linlithgow,[102] and had many contacts in the Far East and the Diplomatic Service. His deputy was Major Gavin Burton Stewart, a member of the Stewart & Lloyd engineering group, who ran the Indian Mission's main outstation in Calcutta.

The HQ of the India Mission was at Meerut, some 40 miles north-east of New Delhi and a number of officers stationed there are relevant to this story. Lieutenant-Colonel Billy Beyts, 6th Rajputana Rifles, was Mackenzie's operational chief-of-staff. Prior to returning to India in 1941 he had been a key figure in setting up the clandestine 'Auxiliary Units' in the UK, which were intended to conduct armed resistance after a German invasion. In SOE(India) he was responsible for schools and training, but also included contacting prominent potential agents and then mounting joint operations with the Royal Navy to bring them to India for training before returning them to their native countries.

Lieutenant-Colonel Lewis Pugh, Royal Artillery, was Director of Country Sections, whose responsibilities were to decide and recommend to Mackenzie those countries which he deemed to be ripe for setting up clandestine operations. Pugh was a career soldier, who had spent most of his service to date in India, which had included being seconded to the Indian Police Special Branch in Bengal from 1936 to 1940. During this period he was based in Howrah, the industrial centre located on the west bank of the Hooghly River, opposite Calcutta. Thus, he knew Calcutta and the British community well and is known to have had many friends in the business community.

Mr Alex Peterson was Director of Psychological Warfare, who had been acting head of the Rumour and Propaganda Section of SOE in London, before being sent to establish a similar organisation in South East Asia Command. He arrived on 15 April 1942 and established his office at Howrah.

A more controversial officer at HQ was Mr Walter Fletcher, previously a London-based rubber broker, who was responsible at this time for Operation Mickleham, a plan which he had devised to smuggle rubber out of Japanese-occupied territories. A very colourful character, he was not directly involved in Longshanks/Creek, but sat in on the planning conferences.

The India Mission quickly established training centres, including the Guerrilla Training Unit at Kharakvasla, some 50 miles west of Poona, with water training, such as canoeing, being carried out on the nearby Lake Fife. There was also an amphibious warfare training centre near Trincomalee in Ceylon.

The Mission had its own large communications organisation, with radio transmitter and receiver sites, signals schools, and various outstations. There were four main radio stations, two at Calcutta and one each in Colombo and Chungking. Field operators communicated into one of these four stations, usually on laid-down schedules, but there were also elements in Calcutta and Ceylon which 'guarded' emergency frequencies on a 24-hour basis.

SOE(India)'s geographical area in August 1942 was vast, covering all of British India, Afghanistan, Burma, eastern Persia and Tibet, although its actual responsibilities in each varied, ranging from sabotage prior to a Japanese attack to post-occupational resistance. The Mission's task was made more difficult by resistance from elements and some individuals in both the army and navy, who were mistrustful of its large number of civilian staff and their possible interference in what were considered to be traditional military responsibilities.

One of SOE(India)'s early tasks was to prepare a number of installations in Calcutta for demolition, which would be activated in the event of an imminent Japanese attack. Among the targets were the power stations for which SOE(India) made the plans – designated Operation Dogleg – although their actual implementation was to be carried out by specially-trained members of the Calcutta Scottish, an Auxiliary Forces' infantry battalion. This established a link between SOE and this regiment, which would later be of value in Operation Longshanks/Creek.

By late 1942 SOE(India) had its main headquarters at Meerut, with three major subordinate elements. Group A, the largest at this time, was in Calcutta, which, among other responsibilities, included the country sections covering Burma, French Indochina and Siam. Group B was in Ceylon, covering the Federated Malay States, Straits Settlements, and Sumatra of the Dutch East Indies.[103]

There was, however, no doubt that in the early days of its existence SOE(India) did not win many supporters. So much so, that it was reminded by some in London and New Delhi that it was supposed to be organising *operations* against the enemy and not just gathering intelligence, as, indeed, seemed to be implied by its cover title of GSI(k). As a result SOE(India) felt under strong pressure to do something to justify its existence and the immediate outcome was Operation Longshanks in Portuguese Goa and Operation Bunkum (quickly renamed Operation Baldhead) in the Andaman Islands.

Codenames
The codenames used cause confusion to this day, so it is necessary to clarify them:

- Monsoon. This was the codename originally allocated by SOE(India) 'for the projected operation against enemy shipping in the Indian

Ocean . . .' Although used for planning, no actual operation ever took place under this codename.

- Longshanks. This was allocated by the Inter-Services Security Board (ISSB) in London and came into effect on 13 November 1941, replacing Monsoon.[104] This was the name used in London (e.g., between ministries) and between SOE(London) and SOE(India) when communicating with each other.
- Creek. Within India, the actual operation against Goa was always referred to as Creek, but this codename was never used when communicating with London.[105]
- Hotspur. This was used within India for the reconnaissance conducted by Pugh and Stewart on 17–19 December 1942, as will shortly be described. As far as is known neither the codename nor the details of the operation were made known to SOE(London).

Chapter 22

Operation Hotspur

Operation Hotspur was an SOE undertaking, involving the extraction of a German intelligence officer named Koch and his wife from Portuguese Goa to British India. It is certain that such an event took place, as it is reported in various documents, but there are several widely-contrasting versions of what actually happened.

First, the facts which are not in dispute.[106] Robert Koch first came to the notice of the intelligence services in British India before the war when they were notified by their opposite numbers in the Dutch East Indies that he was an officer in the *Abwehr*, the German military intelligence organisation. The Dutch warned that he was aboard the *Ehrenfels* when she sailed from Batavia in mid-1939 and a British agent in Tokyo, the ship's next port-of-call, confirmed that he was still aboard when the ship left that port. *Ehrenfels* then sailed on to Howrah, the port of Calcutta, which was reached in late August. Once there, the officer responsible for keeping Koch under surveillance was Captain Lewis Pugh, a regular officer of the Royal Artillery, then on secondment to the Bengal Police Intelligence Branch. Pugh organised a round-the-clock watch on the ship and hatched a plan that if Koch came ashore he would be detained as he crossed the Howrah Bridge to Calcutta. Pugh was not able to board *Ehrenfels* in person and had to be satisfied with sending agents aboard to assess her capabilities, nor, since Koch did not attempt to disembark, did he get an opportunity to meet him – that would come later.

Ehrenfels had only been in Howrah Roads for two days when her captain suddenly requested tugs, had them turn his ship around and then move her down the Hooghly River to Garden Reach. Once there he was supposed to anchor and await a pilot, but instead he proceeded to sea under his own power, which was against the regulations, but as war was declared two days later this became irrelevant.

A few days after leaving Calcutta *Ehrenfels* came to anchor in Mormugao Harbour and her captain and crew prepared for what they thought would be a stay of a few months at most, when, Germany having won the war, they would be able to sail on. Meanwhile, Koch transferred ashore and rented a bungalow, but was then unable to leave the colony, so he and his wife, like the men on the four Axis ships, appeared fated to remain in Goa until the end of the war.

This man is referred to in Pugh's memoirs, Leasor's book and the film as 'Trompeta', but Bremner and other contemporary official British papers name him as Robert Koch, and there can be no doubt that these are one and the same person, although why and by whom he was designated 'Trompeta' (the German word for 'trumpet') is not clear. Bremner was very suspicious of Koch and repeatedly informed New Delhi of the threat he posed, one example reading: '. . . Robert Koch, the directing brain of the Nazi refugees here is allowed full liberty of movement and from his residence in Nova Goa can (and does) proceed anywhere and everywhere at all times of the day and night. From the contacts he is known to have, it is unlikely that his activities are other than subversive.'[107]

In November 1942 SOE(India) sent Major Gavin Burton Stewart, the second-in-command of the mission, on a preliminary reconnaissance. When the results had been assessed, a second visit was made in December, but this time he was accompanied by Pugh and the undertaking had an official title – Operation Hotspur.

False identity documents were duly prepared for these two SOE operatives in the names of British merchants 'Adam Smith' (Pugh) and 'James Murray' (Stewart). Then, to add verisimilitude, Pugh asked a trusted friend in Calcutta, Bill Grice, a director of ICI India, to obtain a letter on Midnapur Zamindari[108] notepaper stating that these two men were representing that company and were visiting Goa to arrange a supply of groundnuts.[109] Pugh particularly asked for the letter to be signed by a genuine and readily identifiable officer of the company in case anyone checked back. Grice was happy to oblige on all counts.

Stewart and Pugh duly travelled to Bombay where they acquired a large Ford station wagon, had it repainted in a sandy colour to make it less conspicuous and also obtained false number plates to be fitted later. Finally, they hid a number of incendiary devices in the chassis, which they planned to use to burn down Koch's bungalow.

Pugh and Stewart set out from Bombay on 17 December accompanied by the Deputy Central Intelligence Officer, Bombay, and the three motored to Belgaum, the nearest town to the India/Goa border, where they spent the night in Green's Hotel. The next day they called on the local Superintendent of Police, who had been warned to expect them and presented them with no problems. They then called on the Garrison Commander, an elderly British lieutenant-colonel of the Mahratta Regiment, but he was not expecting their visit and became very suspicious. Indeed, he was so concerned that he ordered that the two SOE officers be arrested, but fortunately the police superintendent sent a messenger at midnight warning Pugh and Stewart that they were to be detained at 0230 hours. Collecting the Bombay intelligence officer, the three men hastily decamped, being led out of town and onto the road to Goa by a police car from the force that was about to visit their hotel to arrest them. They pulled up at a convenient place, fitted the false number plates, and then slept till dawn.

Refreshed, they drove on to the British Indian customs post at Anmode, where they dropped off the Intelligence officer to make all the necessary arrangements for their return journey. Pugh and Stewart then drove on to the Portuguese Customs post at Molem, produced their false documents and passed through without any problem. On arrival in Panjim the two officers booked in at the Palacio Royale Hotel and then went round to the British Consulate, where they had lunch with Lieutenant-Colonel Bremner and his wife Anne. According to Pugh they discussed the more general subjects of Portuguese-German relations in Goa, the morale of the crew of the four Axis ships, the extent to which the captains retained authority over their crews, and the financial situation of the Axis ships. They then got down to more detailed matters, including Robert Koch, and the activities and locations of other Germans living in Goa, at the end of which Pugh and Stewart returned to their hotel for the night.[110] There are four significantly different accounts of what happened the next day.

The Official Report
The official report written for Mackenzie on 15 March 1943 states that: '. . . After a brief discussion they [i.e., the Kochs] were persuaded to proceed to BRITISH INDIA by car. They were driven openly through

the streets of PANJIM and across the Portuguese and British frontier at about 1030 hours on 19 December without let or hindrance from the Customs posts, where normal formalities were observed.'[111]

Leasor's Account

According to Leasor's book and the film, the two British men left their hotel early the following morning and arrived at Koch's house at 0800 hours. When Koch answered the door they waved a piece of paper in his face saying that they needed to discuss urgent business with him. With that, they pushed their way inside and, drawing their pistols, told Koch that they were going to take him to India. At this point Koch's wife, Grethe, entered the room, which took the British men by surprise, as neither their various discussions about Koch nor Stewart's reconnaissance had revealed that he was married. If true this seems an astonishing oversight, although such things do happen, even in the best-planned military operations. They now had no choice but to take her with them and bundled their two prisoners into the Ford, either forgetting or, perhaps, deliberately deciding not to set fire to the house, as had originally been planned.

According to Leasor's account, shortly after they had left Panjim: 'Stewart opened the glove compartment and took out the hypodermic. Stewart jabbed Trompeta and his wife in their arms with the pentothal needle. Slowly, their eyelids drooped and they sagged back against the seat. Stewart pulled a blanket over them. . .'[112] The two Germans remained asleep during the passage through both sets of Customs, but had recovered by the time they reached Belgaum. On arrival at Green's Hotel, the Kochs promised to behave themselves and all four then entered the hotel where they had afternoon tea – how British! – and then drove on to Bombay.

Leasor only mentions Koch twice more. First, he suggests that Koch gave interrogators in Bombay a description of a clandestine courier and that the latter was duly arrested. Secondly, at the end of his book Leasor records that: 'Nothing has been heard of Trompeta and his wife. It is not known whether they returned to Germany after the war, or stayed in India. Some evidence points to this second possibility.' Leasor fails to say what that evidence might be.[113]

Anne Bremner's Account

There is, however, a substantially different version of events, recounted by Anne Bremner, who was not only the Consul's wife but also directly assisted her husband by encoding and decoding all classified correspondence. She was thus in a position to know what was going on.[114] According to her '. . . Koch's wife was unwell. He wrote to the Red Cross asking if he could take her to British India, to a prisoner-of-war camp. One day two men came and lunched with us. They said they were staying at a hotel in town. Next day the Kochs had gone, so had the two Englishmen. At the Frontier, the book was signed by "Mr and Mrs Cook. Journalist" [Cook is the English translation of Koch].'

An Indian Account

There is a suggestion on a modern Indian website that the two Kochs were shot in a wood on the day they were kidnapped. There is neither supporting evidence for this nor is it repeated elsewhere. It also seems somewhat improbable because even the most brutal intelligence service would not execute an enemy intelligence officer without first putting him or her through an extensive interrogation.

Comments

It is undisputed that Koch arrived in Goa in September 1939, although whether he was already married or married in Goa is not known, but he could not leave and settled down in a bungalow in Nova Goa. Pugh and Stewart arrived in Goa on 18 December 1942, had lunch with the Bremners and the following morning they called at the Koch's bungalow. The four of them subsequently drove across the border to Belgaum and thence to somewhere else in British India. The difference in the accounts centres upon whether the Kochs were taken by force, as suggested by Leasor and repeated in the film, or the whole thing was prearranged and they went willingly, as suggested by Anne Bremner.

Anne Bremner was present in Panjim throughout this affair and would have been privy to most, if not all, that went on. She clearly knew about the Kochs, husband and wife, and was aware that the former had written to the Red Cross. The British authorities would almost certainly have become aware of Koch's suggestion, either because they had intercepted and read the letter, or because the Red Cross discussed Koch's suggestion with them. It seems possible, if that was so, that SOE(India) decided to meet his wishes by sending suitable envoys to collect him and that the story of the kidnapping was concocted in order to cover the fact that he had defected.

What happened to the Kochs after that is another mystery, as they appear in no British official files that are open to the public. As they were not serving members of the German armed forces, neither husband nor wife would have been eligible for a prisoner-of-war camp, but they might have been sent to a civilian internment camp, of which there were two in India for Germans, at Dehradun and Deoli. However, if they had willingly defected, as indicated by Anne Bremner, then there would have been no need for them to be detained at all, other than for their own safety. The treatment of the three German seamen captured in the raid on Goa will be described in Chapter 28 and shows that SOE(India) was fully capable of hiding such people until the war's end and then helping them to rehabilitate themselves in the post-war world.

One of the surprising elements is that there do not seem to have been any repercussions in Goa. Koch was clearly well-known to the Portuguese administration and the German community, particularly the ships' captains, so it seems surprising that his disappearance (and that of his wife also) went officially unremarked. The Portuguese Governor might have been expected to comment on the sudden disappearance of a prominent German, while the three captains, who had regular dealings with Koch, could not have failed to notice his sudden departure. Unless there are files or individual folios not yet transferred to the National Archives, Bremner never mentions the subject in any of his letters or messages to New Delhi, although this may be because he had either firm knowledge or a strong suspicion as to what had happened and did not wish to repeat it, even in an official and highly classified letter.

The National Archive series HO 405 is a register of aliens who took British citizenship after the war. A number of those are in the name of Koch, some of which are then marked as being closed for 100 years as they 'contain sensitive personal information which would substantially distress a living person or his or her descendants'. The only details on public display are surname, initials, date of birth, and the date on which the files may be opened. There are at least four where the initials and dates of birth might include Robert or Grethe Koch, but the earliest any of these will be opened is 2056.[115]

There is no question that Robert and Grethe Koch departed neutral Goa on 19 December 1942 escorted by two British officers and were taken into British India. Although there is no absolute proof, it appears that they went of their own volition, but what happened to them after that remains unknown.

Chapter 23

The Plans

Both the British in SOE(India) and the Axis captains in their ships had their plans, based upon what they knew of their enemy, and incorporating lessons learned from previous operations during the war. In the event, neither plan worked the way its devisers had intended.

The British Plan

In late October 1942 Mackenzie called a conference attended by Beyts, Fletcher, Pearson, Pugh and Stewart which he opened by telling them that he had met the Viceroy to discuss the question of rapidly escalating shipping losses in the Indian Ocean. It had been alleged at that meeting that there was a German spy network in Goa, and that a wireless broadcast was being made every night at around midnight from a ship in the harbour. At this, Pugh said that in August 1939 he had carried out a close inspection of the *Ehrenfels* when it was lying in the Hooghly and had observed the proliferation of antennas which suggested that it had more than the normal merchant ship's wireless installation.

This meeting established that nothing must be done which might infringe Portuguese sovereignty and cause them to be less cooperative towards the Allies, particularly in Europe. It was also decided that attempts should be made to bribe the Master of the *Ehrenfels*, Captain Röfer, and carefully-selected members of his crew.

At the highest level in British India, neither the Viceroy nor any of his staff were ever given any information about the proposed operation. The flag officers commanding both the RN and RIN were adamant that they would dearly like to see the four Axis merchant ships, particularly the *Ehrenfels*, either taken into British possession or sunk. On the other hand, due to Portugal's neutral status, they were neither prepared to take part nor even to assist in such an operation. They considered that it was

SOE(India)'s mission to carry out unacknowledgeable activities of this nature, and, even then, only provided that it had been sanctioned by SOE's Head Office and the Foreign Office in London. It was, in effect, the Nelsonian blind-eye and as a result, there was no high-level naval input to either the planning or execution of the forthcoming operation. Fortunately for SOE(India), however, some subordinates, particularly the Naval Officers-in-Charge (NOIC) at Calcutta and Trincomalee were prepared to afford some minimal assistance, although neither of them seem to have been told what was really going on.

The Army's General Headquarters India took a similar line, although at a lower level, the Commander-in-Chief of the Indian Army's Eastern Army, Lieutenant-General N. M. S. Irwin, gave permission for elements of two Auxiliary Force units, the Calcutta Light Horse and Calcutta Scottish, to take part in a special operation, but without being told any of the details.

From December onwards there was a frequent exchange of signals between SOE(India) at Meerut and SOE Head Office in London, which was initiated on 3 December 1942 with a message from Mackenzie to London, stating that since the Allies had broken through in the Western Desert at Alamein and were now pursuing the Axis forces westwards, while another Allied force (Operation Torch) had landed in Algeria and Morocco and was pushing the Axis forces eastwards, the end of the Axis in North Africa was clearly in sight. So, he asked, were there were any remaining objections to the forceful removal of Axis ships from Goa?

Head Office replied on 15 December that the Foreign Office remained adamantly opposed to any action involving force, but was prepared to condone trickery. They even tried to appear helpful by suggesting three possibilities: inducing the ships to sail into a trap; bribery of the crew; or faking sailing orders.

As described in Chapter 22, Pugh and Stewart escorted the two Kochs from Goa on the morning of 19 December, reaching Bergaum by late morning, so they should have been able to question Koch and pass an initial debrief on their findings to Meerut by the afternoon of 20 December at the latest. As a result, Meerut signalled London on 21 December stating that they thought the psychological moment had arrived, at least for the most valuable target – *Ehrenfels* – and they had already made contact with disaffected members of the crew for this purpose. They therefore asked London to obtain Treasury sanction for £100,000,[116] which was duly done in a letter Head Office sent to the Foreign Office on 22 December. That agreement was given orally on 25 December and was confirmed by letter the following day: 'I write to confirm that the Foreign Office will raise no objection if this operation is carried out without violence or overt action within Portuguese territorial waters, and provided that the words "trickery" and "chicanery" in your letter mean "Bribery" pure and simple, and nothing else.'[117]

From this point on planning in India went ahead without interruption, as all reports from Goa indicated that there was serious deterioration in morale aboard *Ehrenfels* and that a significant element of the crew was anti-Nazi and would be only too willing to cooperate with Allies, preferring internment in India to continuing a pointless existence in Goa. SOE(India) was also confident that they had approval from London for an attempt based on bribery.

The Meerut plan, bearing in mind the lessons of previous operations elsewhere, comprised four elements. First, to bribe as many as possible of those in responsible positions aboard *Ehrenfels*, in compliance with the Foreign Office's direction. Secondly, to further reduce the effectiveness of the crew by luring as many as possible ashore on the night of the operation, as had been done in Operation Postmaster in Fernando Po. Then, having reduced the crew's numbers, seize the ship and steam it outside the three-mile limit. But, however much they hoped and expected a peaceful outcome, it was deemed militarily prudent to include an armed party to deal with unexpected contingencies, as otherwise just one or two members of the German crew with weapons could frustrate the entire plan.

In January SOE(India) continued to make contact through cut-outs with some members of *Ehrenfels'* crew, including the captain, with substantial sums of money being offered as bribes. Unfortunately, the British agents also learnt that there were at least two dedicated Nazis aboard who should not be approached: the chief officer and the head steward, named Marks. This meant that it would be impossible to bribe the whole crew.

Preparations were going ahead in India, but in early February they hit another snag, as outlined in a further signal to London:

A. Impossible move A [Ehrenfels] under own power despite assistance elements on board with whom we are arranging handing over on cash on safe delivery basis.

B. Propose therefore to assist removal of A surreptitiously at night by awaiting boat. Cooperation by B [i.e., the crew] assured. This will obviate S.O.E. agency becoming apparent.

C. We require authority now from Minister of War Transport for B [i.e., the proposal in Paragraph B] to place suitable ship at our disposal.[118]

SOE London responded on 6 February that it would be impossible to obtain any help from the Ministry of War Transport without prior agreement by the Foreign Office, and to that end London asked for more details of the plan.[119] However, seemingly anticipating refusal from London, SOE(India) had succeeded in obtaining a vessel in India and three days later replied to London 'Many thanks your warning. Please take no further action on my telegram 962 as have made satisfactory local arrangements.'[120]

There was no further response of any kind from London, so SOE(India) assumed that they now had tacit approval to the plan from both Head Office and, through them, of the Foreign Office. This plan was to send in a ship with SOE personnel into Goa harbour to take possession without violence of the *Ehrenfels* and tow it out. So SOE(India) planning went ahead, while SOE(London) seems to have simply put the matter to one side until 9 March when they received a signal from Meerut telling them that Operation Longshanks had already taken place.

While all these higher-level communications were passing to-and-fro a plan was being formulated. This was relatively straightforward:

- The first group, comprising the ship, *Phoebe*, and her crew would sail from Calcutta, via Ceylon, to the port of Cochin.
- A group of six SOE men, all full-time soldiers, would make their way by train from Calcutta and Kharaksavla to Cochin.
- The remaining eighteen, all part-time soldiers, fourteen of the Calcutta Light Horse and four of the Calcutta Scottish, would make their way in parties of three or four from Calcutta to Cochin, also by train.

- At Cochin the land groups would embark aboard *Phoebe* and then sail to Mormugao Harbour which would be entered under cover of darkness. *Phoebe* would then be secured alongside *Ehrenfels*, where members of the crew, having already been bribed, would hand over physical control of the ship to the British.
- The anchor chains having been blown, *Phoebe* would then propel the German ship to beyond the three-mile limit where the British would take formal control and sail *Ehrenfels* to Bombay.
- At no point was there ever any intention to board or attempt to take over any of the other three Axis ships.

Apart from the actual raid, other preliminary steps were also taken. Contacts were made with carefully selected members of the crew of *Ehrenfels*, including Captain Röfer, with a view to bribing them to ensure that they did not resist the raiders. This was conducted by 'cut-outs'. Discreet arrangements were made, again through agents, to organise Portuguese-hosted parties ashore on the night 8/9 March to attract as many members of the Axis ships' crews as possible. The British consul and his wife, Claude and Anne Bremner, received a summons to go to Bombay for a meeting, which was intended to ensure that the consul was away from Goa when the raid took place and thus could not be accused of complicity.

The German Plan
The British had a plan, but so, too, did the Axis captains. These men were well aware that their ships must be a potential target for some form of raid by British forces, and they would no doubt have picked up some information about the British raids on Bandar Shahpur and Fernando Po. They would also have been aware of the British/Australian occupation of Portuguese Timor in December 1941, which suggested the possibility of a land assault from British India (and which had, indeed, been seriously considered by General Wavell). Their main counter to this was a plan to scuttle their ships, and shore observers saw their crews conduct regular drills in which they practised opening the seacocks at very short notice.[121] They also placed explosives and combustible materials in the holds, engine rooms and intermediate decks. A system of alarms using repeated blasts on their ships' sirens was also agreed.

At some point in late 1942 the Portuguese became aware of these preparations and ordered the explosives removed, which was done. However, on 20 December 1942 Robert and Grethe Koch suddenly disappeared which, in view of the central role he had been playing in intelligence matters, must have caused some alarm in the German community. Then, in February 1943 Röfer was offered a substantial bribe, and which, it may be inferred, he had not the slightest intention of accepting. Others in the crews were offered similar, but probably smaller, bribes. Realising that something was in the offing, the explosives, which had earlier been removed, were now replaced and were regularly inspected, and Röfer aboard *Ehrenfels* is known to have carried out a detailed inspection on 7 March and the other captains may have done the same.

It is often said that military plans are good until the first shot is fired and that was certainly the case here, as will shortly be seen.

Chapter 24

The Units and the Men

Once the SOE had a plan it was necessary to find the men to accomplish it. As in Africa and their previous experience in Asia, it was clear that the regular Army commanders were unlikely to release anyone for such an operation, particularly against a neutral territory. But, as described earlier, Operation Postmaster had shown that enthusiastic volunteers with a short period of highly specific training could carry out a single operation very effectively. In the event, apart from a few SOE specialists, all the manpower needed for Operation Longshanks was found in Calcutta.

Special Operations Executive
Lieutenant-Colonel Pugh and Major Burton Stewart have already been covered in Chapter 21. Major James Hislop, a Scotsman, had been a rubber planter in Malaya before the war but joined the Johore Volunteer Force in 1941. He escaped from Singapore in early 1942, sailing to Sumatra with a friend in a Malay kolek, where they crossed the island and then went to Java and found a ship which took them to Ceylon. He was commissioned into 5th Royal Gurkha Rifles and then seconded to SOE. He had only one eye, but was an excellent shot. He was 31 years old.

Major John Francis Fieldon Crossley had served as a regular in the 9th Lancers from 1921 to 1935, when he resigned to work in the family firm in India. He rejoined the British Army in 1940 but transferred to the Indian Army in 1942, where he was seconded to SOE. One of life's true eccentrics, he was a firm believer in yoga and practised it on a daily basis, including long periods standing on his head, which proved somewhat disconcerting to those trying to conduct a conversation with him.

Captain Laurence White, Royal Engineers, was a local government officer who joined the Territorial Army in 1938, initially in the infantry but he then transferred to the Royal Engineers. He was called-up when war broke out and took part in the retreat to Dunkirk and the cross-Channel escape. He then attended a series of courses, one of which was on explosives, which he found most congenial and became his specialisation for the rest of his time in the Army. He went out to Malaya in 1941 as a sergeant to become a founder member of the famous 101 Special Training School (101STS) where he trained Chinese volunteers in sabotage with explosives. He was commissioned 'in the field' just before Singapore fell and then, with other members of 101STS, escaped in a coastal steamer and having coaled at Djakarta, reached Ceylon without major incident. White then undertook various instructional jobs before joining the newly-established SOE training camp at Kharaksavala. He then volunteered for this most secret operation (Operation Longshanks/Creek) as the explosives expert. He was 25 years old.

Captain Colin Mitchell McEwan was on the posted strength of the British Army Aid Group (BAAG) which was located in China where it conducted various operations including sending men into Hong Kong and helping prisoners and internees escape. As described in Part I, BAAG was developing a plan to rescue prisoners-of-war from Hong Kong, which would include attacks on shipping in the harbour – Operation Chopsticks. McEwan was sent to take part in Operation Longshanks/Creek in order to learn what was involved in such an enterprise. He was a gymnast and fitness expert and was 27 years old at the time of the attack.

The Calcutta Units
This huge commercial city offered a number of advantages. First, it was so far from Goa that any preparations or lapses in security were unlikely to be linked to an operation so far away. Secondly, there was a large SOE outstation there, which was where both Pugh and Stewart were based. Thirdly, there were a number of Auxiliary Force units who were likely to be able to produce sufficient volunteers for the mission. Finally, Pugh had worked in the city before the war, when he was seconded from the Army to the civil police, so, he was well acquainted with the city, its British community, and, in particular, the senior officers in the auxiliary units.

The British Indian Army recruited a large number of reserve units, spread across the entire sub-continent, and collectively designated the Auxiliary Forces India (AFI) and which approximated in organisation and commitment to the British Territorial Army and US National Guard. A number of such units were based in and around Calcutta, but only the Calcutta Light Horse (CLH) and the Calcutta Scottish (CS) regiments were involved in this episode.

In regular Indian Army infantry and cavalry units, the entire soldier strength and most of the officers were Indian, with just a few of the more senior officers British. In the CLH and CS, however, the entire strength was British, with Indians only employed in tasks such as clerks, mechanics, cooks and grooms (known in India as syces). Apart from their military utility, these units also had a social function, since they provided a focus within the expatriate communities and, in particular, gave young bachelors – of whom there were many – something to keep them occupied in their off-duty hours. It was also believed by the government and most commercial companies that these units instilled a feeling of discipline and 'strengthened characters'.

On the outbreak of war, the Government of India passed the National Service Act, which was, in effect, conscription for Europeans only, who had to be categorised for retention by their firms. Those in the lowest, Category C, could be easily released and most of those quickly joined the Armed Forces, almost always with a commission, but they went as individuals, not as formed units. Category A were deemed essential to the functioning of their companies and could not be released, while Category B fell somewhere in between.

The Calcutta Light Horse
The Calcutta Light Horse (CLH), raised in 1872, was one of a number of light horse regiments formed in the British Indian Empire in the latter half of the nineteenth century in large cities, such as Calcutta and Bombay, or states, such as Punjab and Bihar. Their purported role was the defence of their local area in the event of a foreign invasion, but it was clearly understood that their real mission was 'aid to the civil power' in quelling communal unrest, especially any recurrence of the never-to-be-forgotten Indian Mutiny. These units were essentially mounted infantry, using their horses for rapid movement, but fighting dismounted; as a result, although they carried swords, their main weapons were the

rifle and machine-gun. Some were also employed as couriers, carrying messages and dispatches between headquarters.

In the 1920s one of the squadrons was converted to armoured cars, although the other squadron retained its horses. In the late 1930s the CLH had an 'establishment' (i.e., an authorised ceiling) of 350, and, although actual strength fluctuated, this would typically be some 250 'active' (i.e., attended the full quota of drills plus annual camp), fifty as 'Reserve A' (committed to forty drills per year) and the remainder 'B Reservists' who had no commitment to drills. The regimental strength during the war years is not known and was probably not published for security reasons. However, it is known that there was a constant outflow of men to the British and Indian Armed Forces, almost all with commissions, but recruits continued to be taken on although they obviously required training. Uniform was provided free-of-charge and working dress comprised khaki jacket and shorts, ammunition boots, puttees, hose tops and a pith helmet, although most had their tunic and shorts tailored privately. There was also a grand formal uniform for officers and the men who provided a mounted guard-of-honour for the Viceroy and other notables. The cap-badge was an eight-pointed silver star, bearing the initials CLH, surmounted by the imperial crown, and the motto 'Defence Not Defiance'.

In the early 1940s the CLH had a regimental HQ comprising the commanding officer (a lieutenant-colonel), a second-in-command (major), an adjutant (captain) and a regimental sergeant-major, all of whom, except for the adjutant, were volunteers. There was also a small permanent staff of officers and NCOs on secondment from regular cavalry regiments, consisting of a major, who supervised the administration and training; a regimental quartermaster-sergeant, who looked after the stores and equipment; and two staff-sergeant instructors, one with each of the two squadrons. These two 'sabre' squadrons were each commanded by a captain, assisted by a squadron sergeant-major.

The Horsed Squadron comprised three troops, each commanded by a lieutenant or second lieutenant, with three sections, each of a sergeant, four to five junior NCOs and fifteen to twenty troopers. They rode horses, known as walers, which were imported from Australia and sold to them at a heavily subsidised 150 Rupees. These horses were stabled in the

Light Horse Club building and looked after by syces employed by the troopers. The troopers or their syces exercised their horses every morning before breakfast. In 1942 the Mechanised Squadron, which was also divided into three troops, was mounted in Ford Armoured Reconnaissance Vehicles, essentially a commercial truck with light armour protection, armed with a Vickers-Berthier light machine-gun and capable of limited off-road movement. The Mechanised Squadron also included a motorcycle despatch rider section of five men. Finally, there was a signal troop of a sergeant and eighteen men. It is extremely unlikely that they were equipped with wireless, but would have provided lines, telephones and heliographs to connect the various headquarters, and to provide a link into the civilian telephone system.

The personnel were Europeans, with Anglo-Indian mechanics and Indian syces. A major emphasis was placed on parades and the CLH provided a mounted bodyguard for the Viceroy during his regular visits to Calcutta. An unusual feature of the unit was that the officers were elected by the men, their commission then being confirmed by the Viceroy, but promotion thereafter followed the usual army practice. This meant that the Calcutta Light Horse Club was, in effect, an all-ranks mess, where Army rank was irrelevant, which sometimes perplexed visiting senior officers of the regular army.

The four permanent staff looked after the day-to-day administration and organised the training, which does not seem to have been too arduous. The horses had to be exercised daily for about an hour, regardless of the weather, and there were squadron parades on Friday mornings. There was also an annual camp at the start of the cold weather in October, usually held at Ranchi, some 50 miles from Calcutta. There were undoubtedly extensive plans for the local deployment of the CLH in war, but the only specific activity that was recalled in survivors' memoirs was the provision of an anti-aircraft machine-gun on the roof of the racecourse stand.

In early 1943 Lieutenant-Colonel Pugh of SOE India Mission approached his friend, Lieutenant-Colonel Grice, Commanding Officer of the CLH, with a request for help. These two men knew each other well as Pugh had been based in Calcutta in the late 1930s whilst seconded to the Bengal Police. Grice had also recently provided Pugh with the letters needed for Operation Hotspur (see Chapter 22). Thus, it was natural that

Pugh should contact him once again when he needed more active help.

The CLH's Commanding Officer, William (Bill) Grice, was born in Wantage in 1897 and on war being declared in 1914 immediately tried to enlist in the British Army, despite being underage. He was rejected but managed to join the RNVR in 1915 and in 1918 took part in the famous and hard-fought amphibious operation against Zeebrugge (22 April 1918), in which he was the Leading Mechanic aboard HM Motor Launch *283*, which was tasked to rescue the crews from HMS *Brilliant* and *Sirius* after they had blocked the entrance to the Bruges Canal. His commanding officer was awarded the DSO and Grice was 'Mentioned-in-Despatches'. Shortly afterwards *ML283*, again with Grice aboard, took part in a similar operation against Ostend (9 May 1918). He was commissioned as a Sub-Lieutenant RNVR shortly before returning to civilian life in 1919, and then joined ICI (Imperial Chemical Industries) in India. He enrolled in the CLH as a trooper in 1920, reached the rank of sergeant by 1924 and was elected an officer in 1927. Between 1930 and 1935 ICI sent him to the other side of India, where he served with the Punjab Light Horse but on his return to Calcutta he rejoined the CLH, where he was soon promoted to captain. He was promoted to lieutenant-colonel on taking command of the regiment in 1939. Grice was renowned as an aggressive horseman, always physically fit and a devoted – and very popular – member of the CLH. His period in command was particularly testing as large numbers of individuals left to join regular Army units and there was a constant need to train new recruits, while keeping the unit as a whole ready for anything higher command might ask of it.

The men of the CLH were generally found from managers, accountants and auditors in the large companies and institutions in and around Calcutta, as well as a number in the tea and jute industries. When Grice was asked to assemble a party of fourteen men for an undisclosed task at an unknown destination he set four basic criteria. First, that the participants should be volunteers, and this was easily met since every man who was asked to volunteer did so. The second was that they should be fit and suitable for this unspecified mission. Third, that they should be unmarried and fourth that they should, wherever possible, be under 35 years old. The men selected are shown in Table 5.

Table 5: Operation Longshanks/Creek, 8/9 March 1943:
Participants from the Calcutta Light Horse

Name	Rank	Age	Civil Employment
BRYDEN, William Donald	Trooper	29	Bengal Chamber of Commerce
CLARKE, Geoffrey Hayman John	Trooper	35	Imperial Tobacco Co of India
FARMER, Frank Darrell	Corporal	35	James Finlay & Co Ltd*
FERGIE, Kenneth Rishton	Lance-Corporal	32	George Henderson & Co Ltd*
GRICE, William Henry	Lieutenant-Colonel	45	I.C.I. (India) Ltd
LAW, Colin James Drummond	Lance-Corporal	37	Hongkong & Shanghai Bank
MACFARLANE, Alistair Forbes	Lance-Corporal	40	Jardine Skinner & Co
NOBLE, William Mathewson	Lance-Corporal	33	Commercial Union Assurance
SANDYS-LUMSDAINE, Colin Cren	Lieutenant	35	Williamson Magor & Co
STENHOUSE, Nicol	Lance-Corporal	31	Andrew Yule & Co Ltd*
TANNER, John Darley	Trooper	27	Lovelock & Lewes*
TURCAN, Charles Ian	Lance-Corporal	28	Andrew Yule & Co Ltd*
WATSON, Cecil Herbert	Lance-Corporal	32	Shaw Wallace & Co Ltd
WILSON, Ian Birrell	Trooper	32	Ford, Rhodes, Thornton & Co*

Notes: Ages and ranks shown are as on the date of the operation.
   * Denotes those with civil occupation of accountant

Grice himself broke both the unmarried and age rules, but he was the Commanding Officer, was determined to lead from the front, and was the only one with previous experience of such an amphibious assault. As shown in the table, the other thirteen men selected were, with two exceptions, under 35 years old, and, Sandys-Lumsdaine apart, were unmarried. The average age was 33.6 years. By employment there were: accountants – six; management – six; insurance – one; and banking – one.

Grice also had the difficult task of asking the volunteers' employers to release their men for at least two weeks for a task about which he could give them no information whatsoever. In his later report Grice says that 'Heads of Firms were duly consulted and with few exceptions were most helpful', and it seems that the 'few exceptions' denied permission for certain individuals on the grounds that their qualifications made them indispensable to their firms.

The Calcutta Scottish

The Calcutta Scottish was one of many Scottish corps raised around the British Empire in the nineteenth and early twentieth centuries. It was officially formed on 1 August 1914 as the Calcutta Scottish Volunteers, its recruits being mainly Scots in the East Bengal jute industry – the so-called *jutewallahs*. There were, however, also some members not of Scottish descent, who preferred the infantry environment to that of the quasi-cavalry CLH. Colour-Sergeant James Adams, for example, a water engineer, came from Cumberland, while Second-Lieutenant Charles Tindall, who had worked for a Calcutta bank since 1923, came from Lambeth in London.

As with other similar volunteer units the battalion was integrated into the AFI in 1920, but its title was shortened to the Calcutta Scottish. Although theoretically capable of deployment in general war, its primary role was in 'internal security' and it was called out on numerous occasions at times of communal riots, when its main role was to patrol the streets at night and to guard important buildings. All that were usually required were small parties, but the entire battalion was mobilised in 1919, 1926 and 1930, for two months at a time on each occasion.

The men of the Calcutta Scottish wore full Highland uniform, including kilt in Hunting Stewart tartan, sporran, cut-away doublet, and Glengarry bonnet. This was worn on all formal occasions, including the monthly church parade, which was followed by an all-ranks family curry lunch, an event much enjoyed by all. Working dress was the usual khaki uniform with a pith helmet. The cap-badge was a St Andrew's cross bearing the Calcutta city crest. The battalion was also awarded King's and Regimental Colours.

The possibility of a Japanese invasion caused the British Indian authorities to prepare measures to resist, which included plans to destroy the power stations in East Bengal – Operation Dogleg. The plan for this was made by the SOE India Mission, but the responsibility for carrying it out in the Calcutta area was passed to the Calcutta Scottish, which had teams specially trained for demolition work.

Command of the Calcutta Scottish changed during this period. Initially, the CO was Lieutenant-Colonel Thomas Bain Gunn, who had served with the Cheshire Regiment in the First World War, where he had won the MC, but he handed over to Lieutenant-Colonel Charles Randolph Bowles Woolford on an unknown date between January and April 1943. Woolford had also served in the Great War and had also won the Military Cross, in his case while serving with the Machine Gun Corps. The adjutant was Wavell Henry Dewis, a captain in late 1942 but promoted to major in early 1943, while retaining the post of adjutant.

It is assumed that Pugh would have approached the commanding officer in the same way that he had Colonel Grice of the CLH. Following that the CO and adjutant would have been involved in selecting the four men required and ensuring that they were properly trained and equipped for the mission.

Robert Hutton Duguid had been born in Inverurie in 1907 and completed his qualification as a chartered accountant in 1932. Apart from being successful academically he was also a noted front-row rugby player, turning out regularly for his local club and Aberdeenshire county team. He then sailed immediately for Calcutta to work for Duncan Brothers, tea and jute growers and traders. Like many bachelors, he joined the Calcutta Scottish and was dismayed when his post in Duncan Brothers was declared 'protected' thus preventing him from joining the Army. He remained an enthusiastic member of the Calcutta Scottish and in early 1943 he was approached by a senior officer and, having been sworn to secrecy, was asked if he would volunteer for a mission, for which he could be given no other information other than that the head of his firm would be informed, also on a secret basis, of his intended absence and the reason for it.

The other three were William Miller, the local manager for India Tyres; Jimmy Patterson, a Lloyd's surveyor and marine engineer; and Gilman Wylie, who worked for Norwich Union Insurance. According to his grandson, a fifth man, Colour Sergeant James Adams (b. Sep 1889), a water engineer and an excellent shot, was originally selected for the mission. He carried out most of the training, but was stood down at the last minute because, he was told, he was a widower with three dependent children. He was furious and inconsolable for weeks afterwards.[122]

As the Calcutta Light Horse had more than sufficient volunteers – and it would have proved even more secure to confine participation to one unit – it must be presumed that the Calcutta Scottish brought some special skill to the operation. This may have been weapon handling where, as infantrymen, their skills could have been greater than those of the CLH, or it might have been handling explosives, derived from their experience in Operation Dogleg. However, Pugh's pre-war experiences in Calcutta and the Calcutta Scottish's involvement in Dogleg would have meant that the SOE India would have been well acquainted with the regiment and its capabilities and so had good reason for its inclusion.

Chapter 25

Preparations Completed

The attack force for the operation in Goa was now complete and comprised twenty-four men: six from SOE, four from the Calcutta Scottish and fourteen from the Calcutta Light Horse. There was one professional soldier – Pugh – one who had been a professional – Crossley – four were wartime soldiers – Burton Stewart, Hislop, McEwan and White – and the remainder were part-timers from the two Calcutta volunteer units. The oldest was Grice at 45 and the youngest White at 25.

The SOE officers made their own preparations and moved to Cochin under their own arrangements. Meanwhile, in early February the commanding officers of the Calcutta Light Horse and Calcutta Scottish held separate assemblies for carefully selected members of their units and told them that their services were required for a military operation about which all they could be told at this stage was that they would be away for about ten days and there would be an element of danger. All those present immediately volunteered and the two COs then selected those who were sufficiently fit. These men were then instructed to approach their heads of firm and to request ten days leave of absence, starting in about two weeks' time. A very small number of these volunteers were denied such leave by their firms on the grounds that their qualifications were particularly valuable and their companies had already released as many as possible to join the regular forces. However, as there were more than enough volunteers, these were easily replaced.

Those that had been cleared by their heads of firm then started intensive training on 19 February. This took place every day for an hour before breakfast on the Ballygunge Maidan, a large open area, parts of which had been requisitioned for military training. The lessons were conducted by regular sergeants and covered such subjects as revolvers, Sten guns and unarmed combat. They were also instructed to keep the reason for their absence secret from their families. Robert Duguid of the Calcutta Scottish had to postpone his wedding without being able to give his fiancée any good reason for doing so, although fortunately for him she accepted this without serious questions. Ken Fergie of the CLH told his fiancée that he was going on a visit to the firm's tea gardens and then wrote her some spoof letters, as if from the gardens, which he then sent to the garden manager, a friend, with instruction to post one each day.

They were also given a list of personal kit they were to take with them. This included military field uniform; steel helmet; bedding roll; eating irons (knife, fork, spoon, plate, mug); washing items; and first field dressing. Every man also had to carry a Service revolver and eighteen rounds of ammunition.

They were assembled again on 26 February to be given their orders for the move. They were told that they were to travel by train in civilian clothes and would be divided into groups of two or three, each group keeping separate from the others. They were to report to the station at Calcutta at laid down times, where they would be given their tickets to Madras, and once there they would be given further tickets for the onward journey to Cochin. For the Calcutta Light Horse, the first group of two men left that very day, followed by five men in two groups on Saturday 27th and the remaining seven on Sunday 28th. The four men of the Calcutta Scottish travelled in one group. After endless games of cards, numerous cigarettes and a few nips from the single bottle each man was allowed to carry, the twenty-four reached Cochin safely and on schedule.

Chapter 26

The Voyage of the *Phoebe* (Hopper Barge Number 5)

The SOE planners had concluded early in their deliberations that that the only realistic method of approaching the enemy ships in Mormugao Harbour was from the sea. However, it soon became clear that no help would be forthcoming from either the Royal Navy or the Royal Indian Navy. Furthermore, merchant shipping was at a premium, due not only to the demands of the war and losses incurred due to enemy action, but also to the Bengal famine which was gathering momentum, so that ships were needed desperately to move food stocks.

Nevertheless, a ship had to be found and it was considered that if one was taken from a west-coast port, such as Bombay or Cochin, the unusual activity would almost certainly be observed, deductions made and information passed to the Germans in Goa. So, as most of the plans were being made and virtually all the manpower found in Calcutta, SOE(India) approached the Port Commissioners there and they proved more amenable. However, the only vessel in their fleet that they were prepared to offer was the antiquated Hopper Barge No. 5, affectionately known as *Phoebe*, together with its regular crew.

Powered hopper barges were to be found in many ports around the world, their sole task being to keep navigable channels clear by collecting silt removed from the seabed by a dredger and taking it out to sea where it was dumped. These were essentially daylight-only, fair-weather vessels and the design was reasonably standard. All had a small forecastle, a large open-topped hopper taking up the entire midships section, and a section aft containing the engine, propeller, steering and bridge. Other amenities such as accommodation, cooking and toilets were minimal. They also had a raised gangway running lengthways above the hopper, linking the forecastle and superstructure aft.

Loading such hopper barges was not a problem. A separate dredge barge equipped with a crane and bucket simply raised the silt from the bottom and deposited it in the hopper barge, which was secured alongside. When it was fully loaded the hopper barge cast off and went out to sea. Now came the more difficult task and various methods of off-loading were developed. The earliest used a crane and bucket, in the reverse of the loading process, but this was both slow and laborious. Later came barges with doors in the bottom which were opened to drop the silt, while in most modern barges the hold splits into two to drop the load even more rapidly. The two hopper barges for Calcutta, however, were of an interim type developed in the early 1900s in which large diameter pipes (trunks) ran along the floor of the hold. When in position out at sea, powerful motors sucked the silt into the trunks, which then conducted the silt to openings in the side of the ship, usually one on either side of the hull, from which it was ejected into the sea.

Phoebe was one of a pair of twin screw, side-discharging hopper barges built in Port Glasgow by Ferguson Brothers and launched in 1912.[123] She had a design displacement of 1,200 tons, with a length of 200ft between perpendiculars, a 38ft beam and draught of 16ft 3in. This meant that the vessel was not exactly small, being almost identical in size and displacement to a 'Flower' class corvette, which famously operated in all oceans and all weathers throughout the Second World War.[124] *Phoebe* was powered by two coal-fired steam engines driving two three-bladed propellers, which gave a maximum speed on builder's trials of 11.1 knots, although thirty years later this was probably no more than 8–9 knots at most, with a speed of advance of approximately 6–7 knots. Although built specifically for coastal and estuarine work, it is to their credit that in 1913 both vessels safely made the 8,000-nautical-mile delivery voyage from the Clyde to the Hooghly under their own steam.

In normal operation, *Phoebe* had a crew of three officers and about twenty-five sailors, who were a mixture of deckhands, stokers, engine room artificers and cooks, all of whom were well used to the daily round of loading and dumping silt in the Hooghly estuary. On this occasion, however, they were told that the vessel was going to take part in a military training exercise, which would involve several days' absence, although great care was taken not to mention their actual destination, nor the possibility of military action.

In command of *Phoebe* for this voyage was Commander (retired) Bernard Davies (b.1899), a former Royal Navy officer, who had recently commanded a destroyer in action, making him an ideal man for this job. He had joined the Royal Navy in 1917 and spent most of his career in destroyers, retiring on his fortieth birthday in 1939 to take up an appointment with the Port Commissioners of Calcutta as an Assistant Conservator. But he retained a residual reserve commitment for the Royal Navy and on the outbreak of war was recalled in his previous rank of Commander. After a period in Singapore, he took command of the Hong Kong-based destroyer HMS *Thanet*, which remained based on that colony until 9 December 1941 when Davies was ordered to take his ship to Singapore, which was reached on the thirteenth.

On 26 January 1942 the destroyers *Thanet* and HMAS *Vampire* were ordered to attack two Japanese troopships landing troops at Endau, a small port on the east coast of the Malayan peninsula, some 150 miles north of Singapore. As they approached their objective the two ships encountered an unexpected and powerful force of six Japanese destroyers and one cruiser, and in the ensuing night action, *Thanet,* was hit and sunk with heavy loss of life. *Vampire* tried to help but was driven off. A number of survivors from *Thanet* reached the shore, some of whom, Davies among them, made it back to Singapore.

By early 1943, Davies had been recalled to his civilian post in Calcutta but when asked had no hesitation in volunteering for Operation Creek. There was, however, a technical problem in that since *Phoebe* was British-registered and flew the Red Ensign, the legal requirement was that she had to be commanded by an officer possessing a civil Master's Certificate, which Davies did not have. As a result, another Calcutta-based officer, named Harrison, who did have the required certificate, went along too. This was, in effect, like Napoleonic times where an executive officer (Davies) was in command and fought the ship, while the sailing and manoeuvring was the responsibility of the master (Harrison).

No details of the loading of *Phoebe* for this voyage can be found. However, it is clear that her capacious hopper was used to carry a large amount of coal, sufficient for the entire voyage to Bombay, as well as water and rations for the crew and passengers. She also carried military stores, including Bren and Sten guns, rifles, ammunition, explosives and items needed for the attack such as bamboos, timber, railway sleepers, rope, grappling irons, fire extinguishers and bags of cement.

Phoebe's peacetime role in the Hooghly estuary did not require any wireless sets to be carried, but two were installed for this operation.[125] The main set was an SOE Wireless Set Type B which was required to enable the vessel to communicate with HQ SOE(India) at Meerut. This was the well-known 'suitcase set' and worked in the High Frequency band, using a Morse key. Also, as a British-registered ship, *Phoebe* was required by the Naval Control of Shipping organisation to have a wireless in order to report the approach of hostile ships, submarines or aircraft. A Type 1154 transmitter and Type 1155 receiver were therefore installed, sets which were normally installed in RAF air-sea rescue launches. This transmitter/receiver combination both met the naval requirement and also served as a stand-by to the Type B set. Strict wireless silence was imposed throughout the voyage, with just one exception on 9 March, when the success signal 'Longshanks' was transmitted. It was sent on both sets and was received in both cases.

In his book, Leasor claims that Davies had *Phoebe*'s funnel lengthened in order to confuse shore-based observers. Davies is, however, adamant that he actually wanted the funnel to be shortened, but did not have the time to do so, as a result of which the ship sailed with her usual funnel.[126]

The Voyage

Phoebe's known route was from Calcutta to Trincomalee where she spent a night, then south-about around Ceylon to Cochin, where all the passengers came aboard, and thence to Goa for the operation. That concluded, *Phoebe* steamed on to Bombay, disembarked the passengers and then returned to Calcutta. The logbook for this voyage cannot be found and only four times are known with any degree of certainty:

1623 hours 5th March. Sailed from Cochin.
2200 hours 8th March. Arrived off Mormugao Harbour.
0400 hours 9th March. Departed Mormugao Harbour.
1000 hours 10th March. Arrived Bombay

Using that data and assuming a speed of advance of 6 knots, the voyage can be reconstructed as shown in Table 6.

Table 6: The Voyage of the *Phoebe*.

Depart		Arrive		Distance (nm)
Calcutta	19 Feb	Trincomalee	27 Feb	1,091
Trincomalee	28 Feb	Cochin	5 Mar	780
Cochin	5 Mar	Mormugao	8 Mar	333
Mormugao	9 Mar	Bombay	10 Mar	278
Totals				2,482

The voyage from Calcutta to Trincomalee went well. Davies sailed just far enough off the coast to avoid alerting the Coast Guard, but not so far off as to offer a tempting target for marauding Japanese warships or aircraft. He had no option but to call in at Trincomalee since the pass issued to him by the Naval Control of Shipping Officer in Calcutta was only valid for the east coast and he needed a new pass for the west coast which could only be obtained in Trincomalee.[127] That done, they sailed on, going around the southern tip of Ceylon and then onwards up the west coast.[128]

This part of the voyage may not have been as simple as it sounds, since the Admiralty Sailing Directions caution that: 'Strong & variable currents are experienced around the southern Ceylon coast during both monsoons; and a wide berth should be given to it. A south-westerly set has sometimes been experienced, with a rate of 2 knots, towards Komariya Ridge; a dangerous off-lying shoal in latitude 7 degrees 02' North, 81 degrees 54' East and this should be guarded against.'

Leasor alleges that the crew attempted a mutiny on the grounds that some sort of armed action appeared imminent for which they had not contracted and that they had to be bought off by an increase in pay. This is vehemently denied by Davies, who marked the offending paragraph in Leasor's book with the single word 'Rubbish'.

On the morning of 5 March *Phoebe* steamed into Cochin harbour and dropped anchor. She had covered a little less than 2,000 nautical miles in fifteen days without major incident and as required by the Longshanks planners' timetable. She was now ready to embark her passengers and proceed on the next, and far more active, phase of Operation Longshanks. For an old ship designed for the mundane task of moving mud out of the Hooghly estuary and dropping it in the Bay of Bengal it was a major achievement, but even better was to come.

Chapter 27

The Raid

Phoebe steamed into Cochin Harbour on the morning of Friday 5 March 1943 and anchored a short distance offshore. First to board was the SOE party, comprising Lieutenant-Colonel Pugh, who was in overall command of the operation, Majors Stewart, Crossley and Hislop, and Captain White. Also in this group was Captain McEwan, attached from BAAG. The men from the Calcutta auxiliary units who wrote later accounts seemed vague about the names and units of the SOE party – perhaps they were either never told or were under some obligation to obfuscate – Davies later describing them as 'commandos' and Fergie as 'SAS-type people'.[129] In the early afternoon the party from the Calcutta Light Horse boarded, followed a short while later by the Calcutta Scottish.

As soon as all twenty-four were accounted for the anchor was raised and at 1623 hours precisely 'Creek Force' set sail. It was considered necessary to try to confuse watchers ashore, so, as soon as the ship was clear of the harbour – and despite some of the landsmen, particularly Duguid, being seasick as soon as they crossed the bar – Davies turned southwards and gradually headed out to sea until he was almost out of sight of land, when he turned through 180 degrees and headed north.

Once safely at sea the members of the Calcutta Light Horse and Calcutta Scottish were assembled and told for the first time what was planned. They discovered that their destination was, as some had already guessed, Mormugao Harbour in the Portuguese enclave of Goa, where three German merchant ships – *Braunfels*, *Drachenfels* and *Ehrenfels* – had been lying at anchor since 1939. However, they were told that this operation was intended to 'acquire' only the latter. *Braunfels* and *Drachenfels* were then dismissed and nobody who was there can remember the Italian ship, *Anfora*, being mentioned at all.

Ehrenfels, it was explained, posed a particular danger to the Allies, being of very recent construction and with two powerful diesel engines, identical in type to those used aboard the notorious 'pocket battleships'.[130] None of those at this briefing can recall any mention of any wireless sets aboard *Ehrenfels*, nor of alleged communications with submarines.

They were also told that British agents had encouraged some locals to organise parties which would be attended by at least some of the Axis ships' crews. Agents had also tried to bribe the captain and other members of his crew to cooperate in taking *Ehrenfels* out to sea. Thus, there was a significant degree of uncertainty about the scale of German resistance and they would only know if the measures had been successful when they boarded her. If, however, there was significant resistance, then it would be necessary to use force.

The plan was to enter the anchorage after dark, secure *Phoebe* to *Ehrenfels* and then board her, for which the party would be divided into groups, each with a specific task. The first would go straight to the bridge to deal with the captain and any other members of the crew there. Two groups would go to the bows and stern respectively and use explosives to cut the anchor chains both fore and aft. Another group was to head straight for the engine room to prevent any attempts by the Germans to sink the ship by blasting holes in the ship's bottom or opening the seacocks, or to disable the engines. Two more groups were to search the crew's accommodation and round-up any crew not ashore at the parties. Knowing that on the Persian attack, Operation Countenance, the Germans had set fire to their ships (see Chapter 19) another group was tasked with firefighting, for which there was a stock of fifteen portable fire extinguishers. The final group, which would not leave *Phoebe*, was to man a Bren gun on a sandbagged position on the bridge wing to give covering fire, should that be needed. They were also told that if *Ehrenfels*' engines could not be started, *Phoebe* would tow her out to sea until the pair were outside the three-mile limit, where the Royal Navy would take over.[131] Finally, if things went wrong a series of short blasts would be sounded on *Phoebe*'s siren, and on hearing that all were to return immediately, regardless of what they happened to be doing and without question.

The briefers explained that the reason for using members of the

Calcutta Light Horse, Calcutta Scottish, and a civilian ship and crew was so that, if captured, they could be disowned by the British as over-enthusiastic amateurs who had taken it upon themselves to undertake this raid. The meeting closed with them being issued with 30 Rupees each and told that if anything went wrong they were to get ashore as best they could and then make their way to the Burmah-Shell Refinery, whose manager had been warned of the possibility of 'visitors'.[132]

All members of the Calcutta Light Horse and Calcutta Scottish had brought their personal weapons including a revolver, knuckleduster and dagger. Once aboard *Phoebe* most were issued with Thompson or Sten submachine-guns, while one team was formed to man the Bren gun on the bridge. They were also issued with various items of equipment, including camouflage paint.

A varied training programme was begun on the afternoon of the 5th, which continued all day on the 6th and 7th and on the morning of 8 March. This training concentrated on weapons-handling, covering the revolver, Sten and Thompson submachine-guns, Bren guns and grenades. They were also given instruction on silent killing, self-protection and knife fighting by Captain McEwan, which Duguid described as 'training on murder with professional officers'.[133] Other instructors covered knotting, lashing, and securing prisoners. An assault course was devised, making as much use of *Phoebe*'s companionways, gangways and ladders as possible, which had to be performed in full kit by both day and night. The after dark training included jumping into the unlit hopper and making their way across the piles of coal lying there. They were also required to undertake night watches to improve their night vision.

A scale plan of *Ehrenfels* was drawn from photographs and other information, and all parties and every individual were given the exact routes they had to follow. Group leaders were required to prepare and brief their men on detailed plans, and rehearsals were carried out. Finally, a password was issued and everyone due to board *Ehrenfels* had to sew a large white cotton disc on the back of their shirts to prevent being killed by a friend.

The morning of the 8th was devoted to rigging *Phoebe* for the forthcoming action. Three bamboo ladders were assembled and one placed ready on the forecastle. The other two were placed amidships, ready to be mounted on either side, so that, once a decision had been made to tow *Ehrenfels* to sea, stores could be quickly transferred from *Phoebe*. Timber, including railway sleepers, three-quarter-filled sandbags and cement bags were brought up from the hold and also placed amidships. The conning position on the open bridge was given a protective surrounding of sandbags, and a sandbag-protected emplacement was also constructed on the bridge wing for the Bren gun. The firefighting appliances were made ready and all unwanted gear was stowed where it would not interfere with the activities on deck.

The afternoon was devoted to further weapon training and a final conference of party leaders was held at 1700 hours. Then at 2100 hours all members of the assault group blackened their faces and hands, donned their steel helmets, checked weapons and equipment, and then rested ready for action. There is no mention in any of the accounts of the weather, so it seems safe to assume that it was calm and visibility was good.

At 0100 hours everyone took up their positions. On the forecastle, and using such cover as was available, were the assault groups with the ladder and grappling irons ready, and an officer whose task was to answer challenges in either Portuguese or German. Amidships were the porter parties ready to launch their ladders and carry any stores requested, plus the firefighting party with their extinguishers.

At 0145 hours Phoebe approached the buoy marking the entrance to Mormugao Harbour, but several, including Davies and Duguid, noted that the expected red light was not lit. They also quickly observed that the Axis ships were totally blacked out, but Davies pressed on and steered unerringly towards them and after a few minutes the silhouettes came into view. As they approached Davies ordered members of the ship's crew to suspend ropes and fenders over the starboard side.

At about 0215 hours *Phoebe* passed unchallenged under the stern of *Braunfels* and set course for *Ehrenfels*. When they were very close to their target the men on the forecastle heard shouts of '*Achtung*! *Achtung*!' from the German ship which was now towering over them, followed by a challenge in English.[134] A searchlight was then aimed at *Phoebe*, but Burton Stewart shouted, somewhat melodramatically, 'Let them have it,' and a burst of automatic fire shot out the lights and forced the German afterguard to flee. Despite this distraction, *Phoebe* was placed with great skill alongside *Ehrenfels*, abreast the after well-deck and the grappling irons successfully thrown. There was a momentary hiatus as *Phoebe* still carried some way and the ladder tangled with the mainmast shrouds, but a touch of 'astern' brought her back to the correct position. As soon as the ladder was freed, by which time it was about 0225 hours, two men held the ladder while the designated men quickly swarmed up it and dispersed to their allotted tasks. At this point, according to the official report, the British came under fire from *Ehrenfels'* crew members located on the bridge and forrard on the port side.

Meanwhile, Captain Röfer had reached his ship's bridge and personally started to sound the agreed signal on the ship's siren to alert the other Axis ships. He had no sooner started than the first of the SOE party burst into the bridge, and when Röfer refused to stop, he was immediately shot and killed. There is no mention in any of the accounts of any of the men of the Calcutta Light Horse or Calcutta Scottish firing any shots at this point, so it appears probable that this must have been done by one of the SOE party.

Corporal Turcan of the Calcutta Light Horse and his group followed the SOE up the boarding ladder and after a brief pause to hold it steady for the next group followed the SOE party to the bridge where they saw the captain lying on the floor, already dead. In accordance with the plan, the bridge was cordoned off while the other attack groups fanned out around the ship to capture any crew and to assess the state of the engines.

However, *Ehrenfels'* Chief Engineer had reached the engine room, secured the steel doors behind him, blown the scuttling charges, ordered his men to open the seacocks and begun the planned sabotage of the engines. When the raiders reached the engine room, White, the explosives man, used his magnetic charge to blow the door off its hinges and then entered but it was immediately obvious to him and Patterson that they were too late, although the actual extent of the damage could not be ascertained in the time available.[135] The Chief Engineer also ignited the incendiary charges, starting the intense fires which eventually engulfed the whole ship, then jumped into the sea and swam ashore. All concerned, including his enemies, acknowledge that he was a brave man who did his duty with great efficiency.

Corporal Farmer, Lance-Corporal Fergie and Trooper Tanner made their way, as planned, to the stern to search the crew's quarters. They only found one person, a cabin boy, who, according to Fergie 'was more scared than we were'. They took him prisoner and when they subsequently heard the recall signal took him with them back to the *Phoebe*.

Meanwhile, Crossley and Duguid headed for the Chief Engineer's cabin, their orders being to demand that he power up the ship to take it to sea; if he refused, they were to shoot him on the spot. On the way to the cabin they bumped into a young German, wearing singlet and shorts, who told them that he was a steward. Duguid felt that he could not comply with the order to take no prisoners, ordered him to turn around and then frisked him for hidden weapons. Not being practised in such tasks, Duguid found a lump in his prisoner's trousers which turned out to be the latter's private parts and, despite the urgency and chaos, found time to apologise for such a personal intrusion. He then manacled the German to the ship's rail and hastened to catch up with Crossley.

Also at this stage the fifteen MiniMax fire extinguishers were carried aboard *Ehrenfels* and stacked on the after well-deck for use if the Germans set fire to the ship, but, when the fire did break out, it was so fierce and so widespread that they were of no use and had to be abandoned. Although the raiders had little time to spare for events outside the *Ehrenfels* several of them observed that the other two German ships, *Braunfels* and *Drachenfels*, were also alight.

Meanwhile, Crossley and Duguid tried to enter the engineer's cabin but found it ablaze and could just see a bottle of kerosene upended over a box of wood shavings. Duguid dashed off to get some extinguishers, which Crossley used until he could stand the heat no longer, when he staggered out and asked Duguid to finish off the job.

By 0235 hours (i.e., some 8 to 10 minutes after boarding) *Ehrenfels* had sunk some 12 feet and was sitting on the bottom and this, coupled with the ferocious fire, made it clear that there was no question of taking her out of the harbour, let alone reaching Bombay. So, the recall signal – repeated blasts on *Phoebe*'s siren – was sounded and all the British men returned at once to their own ship, many of them noting as they did so that there was no need for ladders as the two ships were now at the same level. They brought with them the prisoners, now numbering three, and the evacuation was completed by 0240 hours.

As soon as all men had been accounted for Davies gave the order to cast off. Several accounts suggest that it was realised that two men had been left aboard *Ehrenfels*, so that *Phoebe* had to return to collect them, but Davies vehemently denies this.[136] There was no pursuit and at 0315 hours *Phoebe* slipped out of the harbour, passed the outer buoy and set course for Bombay, leaving four ship ablaze from stem to stern and sitting firmly on the harbour bottom.

Once well on the way, the success signal was transmitted over both wireless links, the only known occasion on which silence was broken. In both cases the message was the same – the single word 'Longshanks'. Both messages were received at the SOE signal stations and passed to Meerut.

The British suffered no losses, although three were slightly wounded: Crossley with a burnt hand, Duguid with a singed face and one other with a minor bullet wound to the chin. According to the SOE report it was estimated that sixteen Germans had been killed, including the captain and the majority of the ship's officers.[137] Several reports refer to the captain being seen dead on the bridge. Duguid later wrote that he was told by 'one of the chaps' that the latter had seen a German sailor on the boatdeck 'filled with lead' by another of the raiders with a Thompson submachine-gun.[138] However, there was no direct proof of this.

When the fires had burnt themselves out the Portuguese authorities came aboard and found five bodies, all of them burned beyond recognition. One body was tentatively identified as that of Captain Röfer, who was missing and a gold tooth cap was thought to be his. There is no indication on the records as to the cause of death; Rofer was certainly shot, and the one referred to by Duguid may have been but the other three could have been shot or trapped by the very fierce fire.

Bremner, the British Consul, reporting some ten days after the attack wrote, '. . . several fairly large bore (9mm and over) pistol cartridge cases have been discovered.'[139] This suggests that they may have been 0.45in ACP (11.43mm) rounds, which could only have been fired by Thompson submachine-guns. Bremner also states elsewhere that 'short bursts of fire as from tommy guns' had been heard during the night (although he had not been there in person to hear them). As he was a former infantry officer it seems reasonable to suppose that he had a good knowledge of firearm, cartridges and their sounds.

Braunfels and *Drachenfels* had been seen to burst into flames very shortly after the alarm was sounded by *Ehrenfels'* siren, while the Italian ship, *Anfora*, did not start to burn until about an hour later. By midday on the 9th all four ships were firmly on the bottom, but continued to burn for several days. All 106 surviving Axis personnel were rounded up and arrested by the Portuguese and taken off to a camp.[140]

Chapter 28

Aftermath in Goa

For those ashore in Goa matters unfolded rapidly. The first sign that anything was amiss was a series of double hoots on ships' sirens and within minutes *Braunfels* was seen to be on fire, followed very quickly by *Drachenfels*, and some minutes after that by *Ehrenfels*. Perhaps because it was the first to show signs of a fire, the watchers assumed that *Braunfels* was the one to give the first of the hoots on the siren. Crewmen from the German ships were soon reaching the shore – in ship's boats, canoes, and, in several cases, by swimming. The *Anfora* was seen to start her fires about an hour after the Germans and soon her crew also arrived at the shore, to taunts from the Germans standing on the jetty that 'Italy was late, as usual'.

The Portuguese armed police were quickly on the scene, followed by a platoon of African troops, the latter proceeding to round up every non-Portuguese European at the point of the bayonet, including, for a short time, the British vice-consul. Neither the German nor Italian crews offered any resistance and all were taken to Nova Goa.

With daylight the Portuguese were faced with four burning, grounded ships, a number of crew who had been at parties ashore, and the balance of the crews who had been aboard the ships but had escaped by various means to the shore. It was soon established that all men from *Anfora*, *Braunfels* and *Drachenfels* could be accounted for, but there were five dead and unrecognisable bodies aboard *Ehrenfels* and three men missing. One of the bodies was identified as that of Captain Röfer, a second as that of 'Marks', who was said by Anne Bremner to have been the chief steward and 'Gestapo man', but quite what was made of the other three bodies and the fact that three men could not be found at all, is not known.

The Portuguese arrested all those who had been aboard the ships at the time of the attack and charged them with setting fire to and scuttling their ships. Those who had been ashore at parties at the time could obviously not be charged, and were simply interned. The hulks and their cargoes were sequestrated and became Portuguese property.

The Axis crews told differing stories. The Germans were unanimous in stating that all three of their ships had been boarded by armed and masked men from small boats carrying eight men each. They were quite convinced that these had all come from a British tanker, which happened to be in port delivering kerosene to the colony. On the other hand, the captain of the *Anfora* claimed that he had seen a small steamer draw up alongside first *Ehrenfels* and subsequently *Braunfels* and *Drachenfels* and then put to sea again. The much-derided Italian captain was very nearly correct, but his credibility was challenged when it was pointed out to him that the fires aboard his own ship had been started at least one hour after he alleged that the 'small steamer' had put to sea again.

Claude Bremner was not given any advance notice of the raid and someone, it is not known who, had ordered him and his wife to go to Bombay, which meant that they would be away from Goa during the operation and could justifiably plead ignorance when they returned. However, as so often happens, the best laid plans were thwarted by a chance meeting. On the day after the raid Anne Bremner was in the Bombay Yacht Club when she heard a group of men drinking, laughing and talking about Goa. She went up to them, introduced herself, and asked why they were discussing Goa. 'Oh,' they replied, 'We've just been there.' Anne explained that her husband was the consul there, whereupon they asked her to join them and told her about their unit, the Calcutta Light Horse, *Phoebe* and their involvement in the operation.[141] Fortunately, Anne Bremner was far more security-conscious than these men and passed this on to her husband who reported such a serious security lapse to the authorities in Bombay, who in turn had a sharp word with the men concerned. This meant that Bremner then had to play a double game in which he had no choice but to insist to the Portuguese that he had no knowledge of what had really happened.

On 17 March Governor-General Cabral discussed the affair with Bremner and said that he was well aware that the ships' captains had made preparations to fire and scuttle their ships in an emergency, but that nobody could explain to him precisely what emergency had arisen on the night of 8/9 March to cause the plan to be implemented. He was also aware that there had been unrest aboard *Ehrenfels*, whose captain was considered harsh towards his crew, while the chief officer and the chief steward, Marks, were well-known to be convinced Nazis. This led the Governor-General to conclude that there must have been an armed uprising aboard *Ehrenfels*, which explained the shots that had been heard, the death of the captain and the cartridge cases that had been found the following morning, although the discovery of a number of unused fire extinguishers remained puzzling. Bremner was, of course, more than happy to agree with the governor's analysis of what had happened.

The Portuguese judicial process dragged on for many months. The first interrogation by a judge did not start until July and took three months to complete, and it was not until March 1944 that the accused were told that they were to be charged under the Portuguese Criminal Code with incendiarism and scuttling their ships in Portuguese waters. The trial duly took place and all the accused were found guilty and sentenced to varying terms of imprisonment. There was then a series of appeals, which were transmitted to the Supreme Court in Lisbon. In 1946 all proceedings and sentences were quietly closed and the men sent home.

Since Portugal was not at war with either Germany or Italy, the former crews of the Axis ships became internees. Those that had been aboard ship at the time of the scuttling were all arrested and held in a fortress, while those had been ashore were given a degree of freedom within Goa. All were a distinct nuisance to the Portuguese authorities in that they had to be housed, fed and provided with medical treatment, while, although their expenses were in theory the responsibility of their parent countries, British controls meant that it was very difficult for the German government to get money through, while Italy was effectively bankrupt anyway.

In early 1944 the Portuguese Government proposed that six sick German seamen should be repatriated in exchange for a like number of British merchant seamen held in Germany. Then, since Italy had signed an armistice in September 1943, in April 1944 the British Ministry of Economic Warfare proposed that all the Italian seamen should be repatriated. These proposals were then discussed in a very desultory manner between various departments in London, the British Indian government in New Delhi, and the embassy in Portugal. It is clear from the correspondence that while no department had any serious objections, none of them were particularly enthusiastic, either, and in January 1945 the proposal simply petered out. With the end of the war, the majority of these internees were quietly sent home, although several are believed to have settled in Goa.

Although they had been ordered not to do so, when the raiders abandoned *Ehrenfels* they took with them three prisoners: deckhands Able Seamen Hans Borchers (30) and Anton Harmes (27), and Steward Heinz Bernadini (29), all unmarried. On arrival in Bombay they were handed over to the civil police, but they had committed no crime, so could not be held in a civil gaol, while since they were merchant seamen, they could not be placed in a normal prisoner-of-war camp either. Nor could they be held in a civilian internment camp, where they might tell the story of the British raid which might, somehow or other, be relayed back to Germany or Portugal, becoming an embarrassment for the British. So, the three men were handed back to SOE, who held them in various camps under their control in India until the end of the war. They were employed as gardeners and labourers, behaved impeccably and seem to have been content with their lot.

However, their position became a problem at the war's end and plans for their release were discussed at length between New Delhi and London. Not surprisingly, the British personnel in India wanted to go home as soon as possible and although the issue of the three men was initially raised in September 1945 it was given a very low priority and dragged on for many months. All three wanted to become British citizens and were vehement in their wish not to return to Germany and, of course, they knew a great deal about the raid on *Ehrenfels* and its participants, which was intended to remain a state secret for at least another thirty years.

The first suggestion was that they should be allowed to become crew members of a ship sailing from an Indian port would then be encouraged to desert and seek asylum in some suitable South American country. The next idea was to allow them to quietly settle in India, but as independence was approaching there was doubt that the new Indian government would want them. When these proposals had been rejected, the Home Office was approached but refused to consider granting them British citizenship. SOE in London then suggested that they might be employed by the British occupation forces in Germany, which would have been the worst of both worlds, so that, too was turned down. It would appear, however, that Home Office resistance was overcome in at least one case as Heinz Wilhelm Bernadini changed his name to Peter Shortland and was naturalised on 25 October 1948.[142] No trace can be found of the other two.

There was an unusual postscript which showed that the neutral status of Goa, and, in particular, of Mormugao Harbour, had not been irreparably compromised. This took place just six months after Operation Longshanks when there was a large-scale exchange of civilian internees between the United States and Japan, which was organised and supervised by the International Committee of the Red Cross, and hosted by the Portuguese authorities in Goa. The two liners involved – the Swedish *Gripsholm*, under charter to the US government, and the Japanese *Teia Maru* sailed under 'safe passage'. *Teia Maru* arrived on the 15th followed by *Gripsholm* the next day and the actual operation took place on the 19th with 1,513 Japanese being exchanged for 1,503 Americans.[143] The ships sailed from Mormugao on the 21st and 22nd and returned unmolested to their original ports.

Apart from these events in Goa, however, the most immediate outcome of the raid on the British side was that a tremendous row erupted between SOE(India) and its headquarters in London.

Chapter 29

Aftermath in London

News of the raid came as a great shock to London where the immediate reaction was that Mackenzie had acted in complete disregard of his orders to avoid any violence. Sensing that this might be the case, Mackenzie sent a signal just two days after the raid:[144]

- Will not know details until later tonight.
- No reason to suppose evidence left behind but statements of one crew will sound convincing if [Portuguese] want to be convinced. Consider you can justifiably disown all knowledge.
- Believe external affairs department [of the Government of India] will deny all knowledge unless this made impossible for them.
- [Viceroy] who was not previously informed for obvious reasons states I retain his full confidence and has offered to wire London but I thought it undesirable at this stage.
- Please consider my resignation in your hands. To use if best interests of organisation demand it.

The response of SOE Head Office was rapid and unequivocal: 'You have our fullest confidence and we would certainly not consider your resignation though we value your loyal offer.'[145]

Nevertheless, Head Office was understandably apprehensive about world reaction to the affair, but to their surprise and great relief there was almost none. The BBC included an item in the nine o'clock news on 9 March, quoting an agency despatch from Bombay, which stated that German cargo ships at Mormugao had been set on fire by their crews. The despatch explained that the crews were very anxious to end the discomfort of cramped quarters in hot weather, but that while some wanted to live on shore, others wanted to risk a dash to Singapore. A violent struggle then arose in one of the ships and the fire was the result.

On 11 March *The Times* of London included a brief report on an inside page.

AXIS SHIPS BURNT IN GOA. From Our Own Correspondent. Bombay, March 10. The German cargo ships *Braunfels, Drachenfels* and *Ehrenfels*, and the Italian cargo ship *Angora* [*sic*], which have taken refuge in Goa (Portuguese India) since the beginning of the war, have been set on fire by their crews and almost destroyed. The officers and men were taken ashore in charge of the Portuguese authorities.[146]

There was no protest either at the time or later from the German government, whose initial source of information would have been the BBC broadcast, but they may have had more from the Portuguese government or from the Swiss government whose consul in Bombay had forwarded occasional messages between Goa and Berlin (most of which seem to have been read by the British).

Head Office still needed to cover its tracks, however, so Colonel G. F. Taylor, the London-based head of SOE's overseas missions, was despatched to investigate. His task was to establish whether Operation Longshanks had been carried out in accordance with Mackenzie's instruction from London, and, secondly, whether it had been planned and executed with the approval of the high command in India. His report was sent from Meerut in July and sought, very successfully as it transpired, to pour oil on troubled waters.[147]

He dealt with the second part first and showed that neither the Army nor RN commanders-in-chief had been involved in the planning. They had known, in vague terms, that MacKenzie wanted to resolve the problem of the four Axis ships and had expressed guarded approval, but declined to play any part whatsoever in its implementation. The Viceroy was not informed at all. After the event both commanders-in-chief expressed themselves very satisfied with what had been achieved, as did the Viceroy, the latter again emphasising that Mackenzie retained his full confidence.

Taylor then turned to the London issue. He established that the intelligence available to SOE(India) was that there was a serious deterioration in the morale of *Ehrenfels'* crew, that a significant number of the crew was anti-Nazi, and that many would prefer internment in India to the conditions they were enduring aboard their ship. Conversely, there were two strong Nazi supporters among the officers, and there was no obvious leader to coordinate a surrender. SOE(India) therefore concluded that a three-pronged approach was necessary: to bribe certain individuals among the crew; to lure a number of the crew ashore for a party; and to send in a British ship to tow *Ehrenfels* out to sea. This, so SOE(India) thought, could all be achieved without any violence, as stipulated by SOE(London), the Foreign Office and the Ministry of War Transport. So, Taylor continued, SOE(India) devised a plan under which a British ship would enter Goa harbour to tow out the *Ehrenfels* and that sufficient Germans would cooperate to enable this to happen peacefully. However, it was clearly a sensible military precaution to have an armed party aboard the towing vessel in case matters did not work out as planned. Taylor considered that Mackenzie should have made London explicitly aware of the presence of the armed party and its possible use in an emergency, and that he had made an error of judgement in failing to do so. Conversely, London had been aware of the intention to take a ship into Goa harbour and had not only failed to appreciate the possible consequences but had also neglected to ask Meerut to elaborate on their plans.

Taylor concluded that despite everything, and bearing in mind that it was the Germans and Italians who had fired and sunk their own ships, the outcome was very satisfactory and the threat posed by the ships had been totally eliminated. He also drew attention to the courage and efficiency of those taking part, although he did not make any mention of the five dead Germans and the three prisoners.

When Bill Catto's regimental history of the Calcutta Light Horse was published in 1957 the chapter concerning the Second World War included: 'THE UNWRITTEN CHAPTER. This portion of the History is suppressed for reasons of security.'[148] This of course only made any sense to those already 'in the know'. Catto clearly knew the story but was unable to do anything about it until the thirtieth anniversary in 1972, when he contacted James Leasor, a well-known author of the day, which led to the book *Boarding Party* published in 1978.

Chapter 30

Analysis

Operation Longshanks/Creek cannot be considered in isolation as the Axis merchant ships in Goa had presented a long-running problem for the British. This had led to a succession of plans, varying from a 'cutting-out expedition' from the sea to General Wavell's 1941 proposal for an outright invasion by land. The original and continuing threat was that *Ehrenfels* would escape and be converted to an AMC. Later, however, as shown in Chapter 17, when the Allied shipping losses in the Indian Ocean in 1942 became serious it was inevitable that operational and intelligence staffs should cast around for possible explanations and seize on the possibility that there was a clandestine wireless transmitter aboard the German ship.

Operation Longshanks had three main aims, the first of which was to physically remove *Ehrenfels* from Goa. If this was achieved it would silence the alleged radio station aboard the ship and thus, it was hoped, reduce the effectiveness of German U-boats operating in the Indian Ocean. Also, this would neutralise the maritime threat posed by the *Ehrenfels* should it escape and be outfitted as an armed merchant cruiser. Finally, although perhaps of lesser importance, it would make a significant addition to the Allied merchant fleet. It is important to note, however, that at no stage was Longshanks concerned, in any way, with the other three Axis ships.

The numerous U-boat successes against Allied merchant ships in the Indian Ocean in 1942 and early 1943 were a matter of grave concern to Allied planners. One possibility, based on proven examples of U-boats entering Spanish ports to replenish from Axis merchant ships, was that the four ships in Goa might be supplying U-boats with fuel and other supplies. However, this author's detailed examination of all U-boat records for the Indian Ocean shows no evidence whatsoever of such visits to any Indian port. Further, in the case of Goa, it seems highly unlikely that a nocturnal visit by a U-boat would have escaped Consul Bremner's notice and there is nothing in his correspondence with New Delhi to indicate that he had even the vaguest of suspicions that such visits could be taking place.[149]

The second Allied suspicion was that information on sailings from Bombay was being collated by a spy and then taken by courier to Goa from where it was transmitted to waiting U-boats by a wireless hidden aboard the *Ehrenfels*. There was a known Portuguese government radio station in Goa, but this had been the subject of intense diplomatic pressure from the British earlier in the war and by mutual agreement was not being used for anything other than Portuguese government traffic. Again, numerous official archives and post-war books on the U-boat campaign in the Indian Ocean and on British wireless interception have been consulted and nowhere is there the slightest suggestion that the U-boats were receiving information from clandestine transmitters anywhere on the Indian sub-continent, let alone Goa.

Table 7: Allied Merchant Ship Losses in the Indian Ocean, March-December 1943

Month 1943	German	Japanese	Italian	TOTAL
March 1–9	10	0	0	10
9 March	OPERATION LONGSHANKS			
March 10–30	2	1	0	3
Apr	3	0	4	7
May	9	1	0	10
Jun	5	5	0	10
Jul	16	3	0	19
Aug	9	0	0	9
Sep	4	4	0	8
Oct	11	4	0	15
Nov	0	4	0	4
Dec	6	1	0	7
TOTALS	75	23	4	102

Table 2 in Chapter 17 showed Allied merchant ship sinkings up to February 1943, which peaked in the months of October and November 1942. Table 7 (above) shows the sinkings over the nine months following Operation Longshanks. There was, indeed, a distinct reduction in the rate in March, which undoubtedly gave some encouragement to the wireless transmitter theory. However, this fall in losses was simply due to a reduction in the number of U-boats actually in the Indian Ocean for other reasons, primarily because the original *Gruppe Eisbär* (Polar Bear Group) had run its course and returned to France, while its replacement, *Gruppe Monsun* (Monsoon Group), did not sail from France until May and when the latter did arrive in July merchant ship losses in the Indian Ocean were almost as bad as before.

In his book, Leasor describes a scene set on 10 March 1943 in which Lüth, captain of *U-181*, surfaces somewhere in the Indian Ocean in the expectation of receiving a wireless message from Goa, but there is none.[150] In reality, *U-181* had started its voyage home on 2 December 1942 and reached Bordeaux on 18 January 1943. The submarine then entered refit while her crew went on leave, and they did not sail again until 23 March 1943.[151] It was, therefore, impossible for *U-181* to have been in the Indian Ocean on 10 March 1943 and this scene was entirely a figment of the Leasor's imagination.

Leasor's book and the film *The Sea Wolves* gave rise to a perception that the men from these two auxiliary units were middle-aged amateurs who had somehow got themselves involved in a real-life drama. It is certainly true that they were older than might have been the case in a regular special forces unit, but the average age was 33. These men had all served in their units for some years, which had included basic military training, such as minor tactics, weapon handling and obedience to orders. Further, once selected, they were given very specific training for the proposed mission, both in Calcutta before departure and aboard the *Phoebe*. They were also carefully briefed and carried out some fairly realistic rehearsals aboard *Phoebe*. Thus, they were in many ways better prepared than the colonial government officers from Nigeria who took part in Operation Postmaster.

As with the allegedly amateur soldiers, the ship *Phoebe* has come in for adverse comment, due mainly to its age and antiquated appearance. It is, however, indisputable that it did all that was required of it, sailing a considerable distance, keeping to the schedule required in the operation order, delivering the raiders to precisely the spot required, taking them on to Bombay, and then returning to Calcutta 'job done'.

Davies and Harrison received some credit in Leasor's book, although Davies was omitted altogether in the film, where his role was conflated with that of Grice. But the Bengali crew are barely mentioned anywhere. Approximately twenty strong, they were hoodwinked into believing that they were going on a short-range military exercise but by the time they reached Trincomalee it must have dawned on them that not all was what it seemed, which was confirmed when they took a load of armed Europeans aboard at Cochin. There are some reports that they rebelled but were persuaded to continue by an increase in pay, although this was vehemently denied by Davies. Whatever the truth of that, the fact is that they did what was required, and moreover, not one word seems to have leaked out after their return – no rumours were reported from the Calcutta waterfront, no startling revelations in the local newspapers.

Albeit quite unintentionally, the Germans contributed significantly to the Allied success, as their arrangements for destroying their ships worked so well. The fires were started as soon as the warning siren sounded and spread so rapidly that there was no chance of extinguishing them. Further, the scuttling of *Ehrenfels* was achieved so quickly that there was no chance of stopping it and the raiders were left no choice but to withdraw after only about ten minutes aboard. The other three ships were not part of the SOE plan, but they, too, were set alight and scuttled.

There is no doubt that there was a large element of luck in the British success, as so much could have gone wrong, but did not. The resistance aboard *Ehrenfels* could have been stronger and better armed, or one or more of the British party could have been wounded, captured, killed or left behind, thus providing irrefutable evidence of British participation, which would have given rise to enormous diplomatic complications.

The situation ashore was confused by conflicting reports as to what had happened. Some reports stated that masked raiders had arrived in rowing boats from a British tanker which happened to be in port at the time of the raid and that they had boarded all three German ships. Others claimed that there had been a mutiny aboard the *Ehrenfels*, where many of the crew were known to be very discontented, and that Röfer (and perhaps others) had been killed by their own crew. The Italian captain, whose version of events was nearest the truth, was simply not believed.

The lack of response in Germany is unusual and nothing can be found in the archives, possibly because there were many far more important events much closer to home. German forces in North Africa were being squeezed towards defeat in Tunisia between the Anglo-US armies from the west and the British Eighth Army from the east, while in the Soviet Union the Germans had surrendered at Stalingrad on 2 February, although a counter-offensive by Manstein launched on 18 February was having some initial success. In the naval campaign Dönitz had just taken over from Raeder and his attention was on the Battle of the Atlantic where his U-boats were doing increasingly badly. It also seems possible that the pictures of the burning ships lying on the bottom of Mormugao Harbour might have brought back unwelcome memories of similar pictures of the High Seas Fleet being scuttled at Scapa Flow in 1919 and of the burning *Graf Spee* off Montevideo in 1939.

In any case, the German government would have had little information as to what had happened apart from the BBC broadcast and a few minor items in some newspapers. Röfer was dead, all the other crews of the three ships were in custody and Koch, who might have had some clandestine communication channel back to Germany, was missing.

In summary, Operation Longshanks had achieved the total elimination of the threat of any of the four ships escaping from Goa, which came as a great relief to the RN and RIN. All surviving Axis crew members had been rounded up by the Portuguese and either imprisoned or interned. There had been no losses among members of the raiding party nor among *Phoebe*'s crew, all of whom returned home safely. Finally, British involvement was never publicly suggested and if some of the Portuguese officials had any suspicions they kept them to themselves.

There were costs on the German side. Robert Koch, coordinator of intelligence activities in Goa, together with his wife, disappeared and neither of them were ever seen nor heard of again since departing Belgaum on 20 December 1942. In addition, five German lives were lost aboard *Ehrenfels*, the only three known with any degree of certainty being the captain, who was shot on the bridge after being ordered to stop sounding the siren. One German sailor was reportedly shot, as indicated by Duguid, although the latter was not himself an eyewitness. Mrs Bremner named one of the dead crew as Marks, and as she has proved to be a reliable witness in other areas, this seems very probable. How the other two died is not known; they may have been shot or they may have been trapped and killed by the fires.

In the final analysis, this operation was a tactical draw in that the British aim of removing *Ehrenfels* from Goa was prevented by rapid reaction from the German ships' crew, who burned and scuttled their ship. But it was a British strategic victory in that all four of the Axis ships were destroyed and rendered unusable, while their crews were interned for the rest of the war. The British responsibility was kept a well-guarded secret for thirty years and the book and film in the 1970s/80s have been shown to have been very misleading. Now, however, the truth is out.

PART IV

Envoi

Chapter 31

None of these special operations in remote areas has been properly recorded until now. Their effect on the overall conduct of the war was minimal, but those who took part were men of great courage, who knowingly put their lives at risk. Those who took part in Operation Minerva ventured into Japanese-occupied Sumatra, knowing that if anything went wrong there was no hope of rescue, as, indeed, turned out to be the case. The men of Operations Baldhead and Hatch, who spent so much time in the Andaman Islands, were also fully aware that they would be too far away for any meaningful support, but fortunately for them it was never needed, except in the case of Subedar Habib Shah, but for him death was virtually instantaneous and no outside rescuer could have saved his life. Then there were the men from the Calcutta Light Horse and Calcutta Scottish who did not know for what they were volunteering, except that it would be 'dangerous', until they were at sea aboard *Phoebe* and on the final leg towards the objective. They did not know what resistance the Germans might put up and also knew that they would be disowned by the British if it went wrong and would then most probably spend the remainder of the war in a not particularly pleasant Portuguese jail.

Minerva, Longshanks/Creek and the early Baldheads show that after the dismal defeats of 1941 and early 1942, the Allies were already showing a return to the offensive spirit. Not only that but the early Baldheads showed that British and Indian soldiers had already learnt to live, survive and fight in the jungle and that these skills were by no means confined to the Japanese.

These were not super men, but very ordinary, of the type that Shakespeare described as 'warriors for the working day'. But, on these operations they performed splendid deeds which have now, at long last, been properly recorded.

Appendix A

Glossary and Abbreviations

AB	Able Seaman (RN rank)
ABDA	American-British-Dutch-Australian (Command). Overall command for Allied forces in South-East Asia from 1 January to 23 February 1942.
AMC	Armed Merchant Cruiser (merchant ship outfitted with weapons such as guns and torpedoes to enable it to conduct offensive missions against enemy merchant ships).
BAAG	British Army Aid Group
BRE	Bureau of Record and Enquiry. Office run by prisoners-of-war in Changi jail to maintain records of British and Allied PWs
Capt	Captain (RN or Army)
CinC	Commander-in-Chief
DEI	Dutch East Indies
DMI	Director of Military Intelligence
GHQ	General Headquarters. (Army headquarters)
Gruppe	(Group) German term for an assembly of U-boats for a specific task
GS	General Staff. The operations element of the staff at an Army headquarters.
GSI(e)	General Staff Intelligence sub-section (e). Branch at GHQ India responsible for prisoners-of-war, Allied escapers and evaders. Also reported to MI9 (qv) in London.
HMS	His Majesty's Ship
HMAS	His Majesty's Australian Ship
HNethMS	Her Netherlands Majesty's Ship
INA	Indian National Army

ISLD	Inter-Services Liaison Department.
ITMA	*'It's That Man Again'*. British radio comedy show, very popular in the 1940s.
Lt	Lieutenant
LtCol	Lieutenant-Colonel
Maj	Major
MEW	Ministry of Economic Warfare
MiD	Mention in Despatches. British award for outstanding service.
MI9	Military Intelligence 9. Division in the War Office in London, responsible for prisoners-of-war, Allied escapers and evaders, etc.
MV	Motor Vessel. Prefix indicating a merchant ship is diesel-powered.
ORB	Operational Report Book. RAF war diary, maintained by all squadrons.
PBY-5	US Navy aircraft designation for flying boat known in RAF as 'Catalina.' (US Navy system: PB = Patrol Bomber; Y = company designation for Consolidated Aircraft; -5 = specific designation for Catalina flying boat.)
PW	Prisoner-of-war (also POW)
RA	Royal Artillery
RAFVR	Royal Air Force Volunteer Reserve
RAS	Replenishment-at-Sea
RCAF	Royal Canadian Air Force
RIN	Royal Indian Navy
RNethN	Royal Netherlands Navy
RNethNAS	Royal Netherlands Naval Air Service
S/Ldr	Squadron-Leader
SASO	Senior Air Staff Officer (chief-of-staff in an RAF headquarters)
SD	Staff Duties. General staff section at an Army headquarters responsible for organisation, control of manpower.
SEAC	South-East Asia Command
Sgt	Sergeant

SOE	Special Operations Executive
SOE(India)	Special Operations Executive (India), with headquarters in Meerut.
SS	Steam Ship. Prefix indicating a merchant ship is powered by steam engines.
TF	Task Force (group of warships assembled for a specific task)
TNA	The National Archives (Kew, England)

Appendix B

Dennis Whitehouse[152]

One of the most extraordinary individual stories to come out of the Andaman Islands was that of Royal Navy Able Seaman Dennis Whitehouse, who remained at relative liberty in Japanese-occupied Port Blair from 7 June 1942, having survived eighty-eight days in an open boat, to September 1945, when the British returned. Dennis was born in Canada on 18 May 1921, but he, his mother and brother returned to their original home in Bromley, England in 1926. On leaving school Dennis became a van driver, but as soon as war was declared he joined the Royal Navy, where he was trained as a gunner for employment aboard Defensively Equipped Merchant Ships (DEMS).[153] He was one of many thousands of individual reinforcements sent to Singapore in late 1941 but his troopship was diverted first to Batavia and then to Ceylon, where he disembarked.

After a week ashore Dennis was ordered to join SS *Woolgar*, a 3,000-ton Norwegian cargo ship, transporting ammunition to the Dutch East Indies. It had a 48-strong crew, comprising seven Norwegian officers, thirty-eight Chinese engineers, deckhands and stewards, and the three-man British gun crew. The ship sailed on 26 February 1942 and at midday on 7 March 1942 was some 150 miles off the coast of Java when it was attacked by nine Japanese aircraft; visibility was excellent, the sea like a millpond and the Japanese pilots had an easy target. One bomb hit amidships and Dennis, who was manning twin Lewis guns in an open mount, was blown overboard. Two boats got away – a motor launch and a lifeboat – and Dennis was pulled aboard the latter as *Woolgar* exploded and sank.

The lifeboat was equipped with a mast and sail, but no oars, and carried water, food (mainly biscuits, tinned fish and tinned meat), a Verey pistol and a small number of cartridges. The captain could not be found, so First Mate Olsson took command, and placed the surviving Chinese men in the motor launch (whose engine would not work as the fuel had been contaminated with seawater) and the remainder – five Norwegian officers plus Whitehouse – in the lifeboat.[154]

The lifeboat towed the immobilised launch for some days but then the rope parted (or was cut) and they drifted apart; the fate of the Chinese is not known. Aboard the lifeboat a tarpaulin offered some shelter from the sun and was also used to collect rainwater. Potable water was kept in a large galvanised tank and issued at a rate of about half a wineglass per man twice per day. At one point the mast broke but was repaired with boards and lashings. The boat itself was reasonably sound although there was some leakage and the on-duty watch had to keep pumping. The men caught a few fish on lines and occasionally flying fish hit the sail and fell into the boat. They also caught and ate some very large birds; first drinking the blood, then pulling the feathers off, before chewing the raw flesh. Mate Olsson tried to head for Australia but wind and current pushed them northwards and on 4 June, after a remarkable eighty-eight days at sea, they drifted towards land. Strange armed men arrived in a landing craft, took them in tow and brought them alongside a jetty. The survivors crawled up the steps – none of them was strong enough to walk – and discovered that their captors were Japanese – the very people they had struggled for so long to avoid.

The Japanese, while not actually cruel to the survivors, were not particularly helpful either, and Dennis's watch was taken from him. They were taken to a town – Dennis had no idea he was in the Andaman Islands, let alone Port Blair – where they were put in an empty house and then left to fend for themselves. One of the Norwegians died of dysentery and exhaustion after about four weeks, but, despite the lack of food and medical care, the others slowly recovered. Once the Japanese had established that the four officers were Norwegian they sent them to Singapore on 2 December 1942, where they were held in Changi jail until released in September 1945.

On an earlier occasion Dennis had seen some Japanese soldiers pushing a Chevrolet car, while an officer beat the Indian driver who could not start it. In order to stop the beating, Dennis went to the car, located the fault and started the engine, whereupon he was immediately given the job of mechanic/driver. When the Norwegians left Dennis was kept on as the Japanese valued his skills with vehicles. He had to make his own arrangements for accommodation, food and clothing, but provided he stayed within Port Blair he was not confined in any way; but there was, in any case, nowhere for him to go. There were no fellow prisoners with whom to plan an escape, he had virtually no contact with any of the local population as they were too frightened of the Japanese to be seen speaking to him, the jungle was dark and seemingly impenetrable, and, as he still had no real idea where he was, there was little point in trying to go to sea. He drove the Chevrolet as instructed by the Japanese, although since the roads on the Andamans were very limited, the longest of his journeys were to the sawmill on Chatham Island or to the airfield which was being built some miles to the south of Port Blair.

The Japanese were brutal. The officers and NCOs slapped their own soldiers, all the Japanese slapped the Koreans, and all of those treated Dennis equally brutally, although he seems to have accepted being 'beaten around the chops' with considerable equanimity. Nevertheless, he continued to do his job as driver, whilst being allowed to wander around Port Blair on foot, as the Japanese knew that he could not escape. The Japanese regularly carried out public executions, usually by shooting or beheading, and he once saw a Burmese beaten to death with a jack-rod for some minor misdemeanour. Despite all of that, Dennis said that he did not fear for his own life.

The Japanese seemed paranoid about British spies on the Andamans. There were numerous bombing raids by British and American aircraft and on at least one occasion a British submarine surfaced off Ross Island and bombarded the former governor's residence.[155] Dennis reported after the war that he knew that the Chiefs of Police and of the Fire Brigade were beheaded because they were suspected of passing information. Dennis remarked that 'the Japanese had a "bee in their bonnet" that someone was giving information to the British but did not know who.'

At some time, Dennis was not sure when, but probably in mid- or late-1944, he was moved to Ross Island, where the Japanese were building gun emplacements. He was employed as a truck driver and was also responsible for cutting grass to feed a mule, which, he recalled later, was a vicious beast. Here he found a bed in the old coolies' quarters and survived on scrounging, occasional fishing, and some clandestine thieving. He had nobody to talk to, and nothing to read apart from tombstones and a prayer book he found in the church.

He was still there in September 1945 when the British returned. He immediately made himself known to a Royal Marines officer and was placed under a degree of protection and then sent to India, where he spent a month in a military hospital before being returned to England in a French troopship. After the war he worked for thirty-three years for the Daily Mail Maintenance Department and then retired. He died in 2004.

As far as is known, this is a unique story and quite why the Japanese treated a British able seaman in this way is an enduring mystery. On 28 September 1945, very shortly after the reoccupation, a British officer interviewed the former Japanese governor, Vice-Admiral Teizo Hara,[156] during which the former admiral volunteered the information that:

> . . . I was ordered to send all English prisoners-of-war to Singapore and this was done except for Whitehouse who is here now.[157] He asked if he could stay here and I said yes. He was so young and simple he had become a sort of pet amongst the sailors. After the peace I asked him if he wanted to go back home but he said 'No!' – that he would like to stay on Ross Island.

This statement is very misleading. As far as is known, there were no other British prisoners to be sent to Singapore, and, in any case, the decision to allow Dennis to remain on the Andamans had been taken in December 1942, long before Teizo arrived. It also seems improbable that Dennis would have chosen to remain in the Andamans rather than return to his beloved Bromley.

Dennis cannot have been of any intelligence value to the Japanese – he held the most junior rank in the Royal Navy and his service had comprised gunnery training, a long voyage in a troopship and eighty-eight days in a lifeboat. Nor was he of any propaganda value. He spent most of his time as a driver which was unusual, but permitted employment for a prisoner-of-war.

The Japanese regime in the Andamans was particularly brutal. They executed a number of British when they took over and used torture and executions against the Andamanese on a regular basis. Thus, they could have turned on Dennis at any time and executed him within minutes, but he posed no threat to them, and despite their paranoia about messages being passed to the British they appear never to have accused him of being involved. It is possible, but unproven, that the Japanese, particularly the officers, may have derived satisfaction from having a European at their beck and call and driving them around as a chauffeur. On the other hand, there is no evidence that the British reconnaissances – Operations Baldhead and Hatch – ever got wind of a European in Port Blair and there is not a single mention of him in any of their extensive reports.

Sergeant Lau Teng Kee[158]

The only member of the Operation Minerva group for whom no records can be found and whose name is not on any known memorial is Lau Teng Kee. This annex records the attempts to trace him, and thanks are due to a number of very helpful people.[159]

The five men involved in Operation Minerva were:

Name	Rank	Service/Corps	Unit	Background/Role	Memorial
HUNTER, Alexander	Acting Captain	Royal Engineers	GSI(e) GHQ India	7 years in Sumatra	Singapore, Kranji
KEYT, Richard Antony	Lance Bombardier, Acting Sergeant	Royal Artillery	CSDIC(India)[160]	Singapore seamanship	Rangoon
LAU Teng Kee	Sergeant	Unknown	Unknown	Japanese experience/medic	None
RUSSELL, Basil Henry Sackville	Acting Squadron-Leader	RAFVR	GSI(e), GHQ India	In command and chief planner	Singapore, Kranji
SLADEN, Hugh Frederick Lampart	Captain	Bedfordshire & Hertfordshire Regiment	GSI(e), GHQ India	Second-in-Command/ communications	Singapore, Kranji

Lau Teng Kee was an ethnic Chinese, born in about 1920, who is believed to have come from Batu Pahat in the State of Johore, which was at that time one of the Unfederated Malay States. The first firm documentary evidence of his existence that can be found is when he joined the Hong Kong University Medical College in 1938 and he is known to have just completed the first term of his fourth and final year when the Japanese invaded in December 1941.[161]

He escaped to Free China in early 1942, where he joined the British Army Advisory Group (BAAG) as a civilian auxiliary, designated 'Agent 36'. He then carried out two daring and dangerous missions into

Japanese-occupied Hong Kong. In the first of these he made contact with R. C. Robertson, professor of pathology at the Medical College, in order to recover the great seal of the university and take it to Free China for safekeeping. During this mission he also sought and obtained the help of one of the local Triads (Chinese secret society), in itself a matter of some personal risk. Lau returned to BAAG, but when it transpired that the seal had not been sent out of Hong Kong as had been promised, he went back, this time with a comrade, Raymond Chang. They succeeded and Chang returned to China with the seal.[162] Meanwhile Lau guided a group of twenty-three university graduates and students to freedom in a sampan, reaching Waichow on 11 August 1942.[163] This party comprised three graduates of Hong Kong University, nineteen undergraduates and three who were not directly associated with the university.

Squadron-Leader Basil Russell, RAFVR, a staff officer at GHQ India in New Delhi, visited the BAAG from 7 to 17 July 1942 at a time when Lau was in Hong Kong, so it must be presumed that Ride briefed Russell on Lau's background and skills. Russell was clearly impressed with the description because he invited Lau to volunteer to join the Minerva mission. There is irrefutable proof that Lau flew from China to Ceylon in November 1942 as he wrote to Ride from Chungking. The original letter, in Lau's own hand, is now in the Ride Archive and a transcription is below (p.198).

In his diary entry for 22 November 1942 Russell recorded: 'I will just write a few lines on each . . . The fourth is 36 [i.e., Agent 36 in BAAG] a Lau Teng Kee, a Malayan Chinese who has been working for Ride and has done very well. He has had to come from Kweilin and so far has not turned up. He should arrive in a week, possibly with Sladen.'

There are three official documents that show conclusively that Lau Teng Kee took part in Operation Minerva, and it seems impossible that such official documents would have referred to him as a sergeant unless he was properly authorised to hold such rank. The first is a letter from the Netherlands Institute of Military History that the passenger manifest for the flying boat that flew the five men from Ceylon to Sumatra included a 'Sergeant Lau Teng Kee' (pp.198–9). The second is the post-war report on the activities of GSI(e) 1942–45, which also includes his name in the section on Operation Minerva (p.200). Thirdly, is a letter from No 7 War Crimes Investigation Team to Searcher Organisation Clearing House Ref 49/22 dated 2 March 1946 (not copied).

It thus appears that at some point between arriving in Ceylon in late November 1942 and departing for Sumatra on 20 December Lau was enlisted into the British Army. It is presumed that this was done because he was due to take part in an active operation behind enemy lines in the company of commissioned/enlisted men and needed proper military status, for which being a civilian auxiliary with BAAG was inappropriate. It further appears that he was then quickly promoted to the rank of sergeant.

It is evident from his diaries that Russell considered himself to be a man-of-action and was impatient with Service, and particularly the Army's, administrative procedures. It seems possible, therefore, that he may have made arrangements to enlist Lau into the British Army, but left some of the details to be tied up when they both returned from Operation Minerva – which neither ever did. On the other hand, Sladen was a regular officer, who had served for over a year as Adjutant of a TA battalion, and would have been very well acquainted with British Army administrative procedures, including attestation, maintenance of individual records, pay, and so on.

The normal method of enlisting a soldier into the British Army was that he/she would undergo a medical examination, fill in a number of forms and swear an oath of loyalty to the King. He/she would then become a member of a specific regiment (i.e., infantry or cavalry) or corps (e.g., Royal Engineers, Royal Army Ordnance Corps, etc). Each of these bodies had a Records Office, where every soldier's documents were not only maintained throughout his/her service but also retained permanently thereafter.[164]

Extensive enquiries have failed to locate any record of a Sergeant Lau Teng Kee. This included the Army Personnel Centre Support Division, where all soldiers' documents are retained after their discharge, but a careful search failed to locate anyone of that rank/name (replied 23 April 2012). It was thought possible that S/Ldr Russell might have used his RAF contacts to enlist Lau into the RAF, so RAF Disclosures, ACOS (Manning) HQ Air Command was contacted, but they found no trace (replied 8 October 2012). The National Army Museum holds a collection known as the 'Soldier Effects Records' a huge index concerning the disposal of deceased soldiers' effects, including pay owed to the next-of-kin, etc. There is no record of a Lau Teng Kee, but it should be noted that it does hold a record for Sgt Keyt, the other NCO on Operation Minerva (replied 12 March 2013). It should be mentioned that all three departments clearly conducted thorough and enthusiastic searches.

The General Registration Office holds death certificates for Hunter, Keyt, Russell and Sladen. Again, a full search failed to find one for Lau.

The General Service Corps (GSC) was formed in wartime mainly to serve as a holding unit and provide a 'cap badge' for recruits until they had been allocated to a regiment or corps. However, it is known from other research that the GSC was also used to commission/enlist special agents in Europe and may have been used for the same purpose in SEAC. The records of the GSC cannot be found in any of the known archives, so the possibility that Lau served in it cannot be pursued.

Most Hong Kong Chinese who escaped from the colony enlisted in or were employed by the BAAG in China. However, there were a number who were in India and who wished to enlist in the Army. It appears that the 'rules' prevented them from enlisting in the Indian Army, whose members had to be either citizens of British India or Nepal, or British (officers). Further, there did not seem to be any means of enlisting them into an existing British (i.e., UK-based) unit. To overcome this the 'British Chinese Unit' was formed, as described in a letter GSI(e) File 43-A signed by Basil Russell who was the secretary of a meeting held in early October 1942.[165] It was agreed that the 'British Chinese Unit' (BCU) would be formed in India, and would embody all former Hong Kong Volunteers of whatever nationality, under the command of an experienced officer, Lt Col H Owen-Hughes. A depot would be established so that all Chinese volunteer personnel, as well as regular British Chinese troops, could be posted there immediately on arrival in India. It is known that elements of the BCU took part in the Chindit operation in Burma, where it appears to have been known as 142 Commando Company, Hong Kong Volunteers. It seems possible, therefore, that Russell, who had been involved in forming the BCU and needing to find a unit for Lau, may have had him enlisted into that unit, but no documentary evidence can be found.

Turning now to post-war events, the Army had proper records for

Sladen, Hunter and Keyt, and the RAF for Russell, so that after the war the fact that they were 'missing' and then presumed dead was properly recorded, their next-of-kin informed, medals issued, accounts settled and their names subsequently included on the Singapore and Rangoon war memorials. But if Lau's next-of-kin were informed no trace can be found. The only known evidence of a search for him is a private notice posted in the *Straits Times* on 18 May 1946: 'Will Mr Lau Teng Kee please contact Francis Chong, 2237 Bukit Rabit Road, Teluk Anson.' This town, now renamed Teluk Intan is in the state of Perak, approximately half-way between Kuala Lumpur and Penang. Recent research, including a visit to Teluk Intan by Dr Patrick Tan, has failed to locate Mr Chong or any relatives. Thus, it has proved impossible to establish the link between Lau Teng Kee and Francis Chong. They may have been friends from school in Malaya; friends from Hong Kong; colleagues from BAAG – nobody knows.

A 200-word article was published in the *New Straits Times* on 8 August 2012 outlining the story and asking for any information on Lau Teng Kee or his family. As a result this author was able to establish contact with Captain Ho Wing Tho and also with Dr Patrick Tan, son of Dr Eleanor Tan (née Eu) Gaik Choo. Captain Ho and Dr Eu were both among those who took part in the escape to China in July-August 1942. Dr Patrick Tan has carried out extensive and thorough research in Malaysia and Singapore, including many personal visits and meetings, but could find no trace of Lau Teng Kee.

It is therefore concluded that Lau Teng Kee came from Johore, spent three-and-a-half years at Hong Kong University Medical School, escaped to Free China and was recruited for Operation Minerva. He travelled to Ceylon, arriving in November 1942, where he joined the Minerva team. Official references to him as a sergeant indicate that he was enlisted into the British Army, although no documentary proof can be found. He then deployed with the rest of the Minerva team to Sumatra on 20 December 1942. Extensive research in Hong Kong. Malaysia, Singapore and the UK has failed to discover any more information on him.

Lau was never seen again, his death has never been recorded and is not on any known war memorial, so this is his memorial.

Letter Lau Teng Kee to Colonel Ride; Chungking, 11 November 1942
(Transcribed from handwritten original in possession of Elizabeth Ride.)

c/o Military Attaché,
HBM Embassy,
Chungking.
10/XI/42

Dear Col Ride,
Arrive(d) here safely on the 8th at 9.30 a.m. and I found my way to town only on the next day. It was a problem trying to get a transport. However, the A.V.G. were decent because they gave me a place to stay for the night and they tried their best to send me to town at the first available opportunity. I could not prove my identity because I did not possess proper credentials when the American colonel asked who I was. He had to know my position before allowing me to travel on their truck. I satisfied his curiosity by showing him the sealed envelope for the Military Attaché.

I saw Major Mears & he is arranging for a seat in a CNAC plane which leaves here on Saturday. The application for an accommodation in the plane has already been signed & sent in and I will be inoculated against Cholera tomorrow to complete the necessary preparation for the trip.

I will write again when I reach Calcutta. With best regards,
Yours Sincerely,

Lau Teng Kee.

**Letter to D Miller from: Netherlands Ministry of Defence;
Netherlands Institute of Military History**
Reference; NIMH 2009 23184 dated September 15th, 2009

Subject: Captain Sladen/Sumatra/PBY Catalina 321 Squadron

Dear Mr. Miller,
Concerning the flight of captain Sladen to Sumatra with the PBY Catalina in World War II I herewith inform you:

December 20th 1942 *Operation Minerva I*
PBY-5 Y-57, 321 Squadron China Bay
Crew: Lt. Cdr G.F. Rijnders (Royal Netherlands Navy)
Sgt. pilot B.J. de Jager
Observer Lt. Polderman
Sgt. mec. Fitter De Vos
A/C Fitter Heijligers
Cpl. WT De Bruin
S/L Russell
Capt. Sladen
Capt. Hunter
Sgt Keith
Sgt Lau ten Kee

Flying time: 21 hrs 30 min.
Source: Flying Book of Lt.Cdr. G.F. Rijnders (R. Neth. N.A.S. / No. 321 Squadron – Ceylon)

March 3, 1943 *Operation Minerva II*
PBY-5 Y-57, 321 Squadron China Bay
Crew: Lt. Cdr G.F. Rijnders (Royal Netherlands Navy)
Sgt. pilot Kemper
Observer Lt. Polderman
Sgt. mec. Fitter De Vos
Cpl mec. Fitter Dijkema
A/C Fitter Heijligers
Cpl W/T Noothout
Cpl W/T Vlielander Hein

Total flying time: 19 hrs 15 min

Y-57 had to pick up British S.O. officers & Sgts from pre-arranged meeting point somewhere on Sumatran coastline. No sign of British party was received/observed when Dutch Catalina crew arrived at location.

Further searching for the party was abandoned and Catalina Y-57 returned to their base at China Bay/Ceylon.

Unfortunately no further details about orders given to Lt. Cdr.

Rijnders (Incl. origin of/for carrying out to this special trip to Japanese occupied territory on Sumatra) are unknown to our Institute.

Operation Minerva was a secret transport by air of a British intelligence party from Ceylon to enemy-held territory on West-Coast of Sumatra (near Padang). The party would be flown on a pre-arranged date and location, but did not turn back.

The reason why a Dutch Catalina with crew was involved in this operation was acquaintance/familiarity with local geography and circumstances.

With kind regards,

(Signed)

Head, Public Information and Collections Division

For Director Netherlands Institute of Military History

Dr A.P. van Vliet

EXTRACT FROM '*Summary of MI9 Activities in India and SEAC*' (TNA WO 208/3251)

'G. OPERATIONS IN SUMATRA.

49. Oddly enough it was in what was to prove the most difficult country, in which to operate from a clandestine point-of-view, that the first MI9 operation was mounted.

50. The plan was conceived and executed by S/Ldr RUSSELL, while on the staff of GSI(e), in December 1942. The object was to land a party in SUMATRA to contact evaders who had reached SUMATRA after the fall of SINGAPORE, and later to attempt to contact the PW Camps on SINGAPORE ISLAND itself.

51. S/Ldr RUSSEL got together a party consisting of himself, Capt SLADEN, Capt HUNTER, Sgt KEYTE and Sgt LAU TENG KEE and after spending some time undergoing training in Ceylon they were put ashore from a Catalina flying boat on the night of 20/21 December in the vicinity of PANDJANG ISLAND (98° 15'E 20° 06' N). A diversionary raid was carried out by the RAF on SABANG at the Northern end of SUMATRA.

52. In spite of the fact that this party was equipped with W/T no news was received from them and it was not until 1944 when a Japanese Intelligence summary was picked up that it was learned that two of the survivors of an air crash off the WEST coast of SUMATRA were S/Ldr RUSSELL and Capt HUNTER.'

Notes

1. *Summary of MI9 Activities in India and SEAC*. TNA WO 208/3251 paragraphs 49–52.
2. Hembry, *Malayan Spymaster*, pp. 217–18.
3. As far as can be established, this operation had no codename, and is referred to in some sources as Operation Padang, after its destination, and in others as Operation Wijnmalen, after its sole participant.
4. His body was buried in the local cemetery and in 1945 his grave was found to be properly marked, which was rather unusual by Japanese standards. De Man, *Opdracht Sumatra*, p. 21.
5. The National Archives, Kew: Patrol Report CSP17, Colombo, 24 December 1942 in TNA ADM 199/1879. This document is in two parts: the main body, which is classified SECRET, and an annex which deals with the special forces aspect and is classified MOST SECRET.
6. Hembry, *Malayan Spymaster*, p. 220.
7. Some post-war accounts suggest that this was a 'spur of the moment' decision, but it is clear from Hembry's account that this kidnapping was part of the plan.
8. Charles McCormac DCM, *You'll Die in Singapore*, Robert Hale, London, 1954.
9. Russell's detailed movements are reconstructed from his unpublished diaries now in the possession of B. Peek, Esq, and made available to this author.
10. Kukong (now known as Shaoguan) is in northern Guandong province, some 180 miles from Hong Kong.
11. Russell, Diary No. 1, p. 32. Sladen was Russell's deputy and had escaped from Singapore just prior to the surrender.
12. The Director of Military Intelligence (DMI) was Brigadier Cawthorn, an Australian who had spent his military career in the Indian Army.

13. Colin McKenzie, head of SOE (India).
14. Letter DMI to DSASO 8 Oct 42, via Elizabeth Ride.
15. TNA WO 208/3251.
16. *London Gazette* 23 February 1940.
17. Ironically for the French, it was Bastille Day.
18. He was posted to Air HQ India but was actually employed in the Army's General Headquarters (India). This was normal administrative practice when an officer of one Service worked in an HQ or unit of another Service.
19. He attended Number 2 Post-Mobilisation Regimental Signalling Instructors Course at the School of Signals from 14 October to12 November 1939.
20. This order emanated from General Wavell and was intended to provide experienced men to train the battalions in India and Burma in how to fight the Japanese. The Beds and Herts party comprised five officers, one sergeant-major, one sergeant, one corporal, one lance-corporal and three privates.
21. By now the party comprised eight from the Beds and Herts, but with four from the Foresters.
22. Russell, Diary No. 3, p. 2.
23. Ibid.
24. His name is spelt as Keyte, Keyt and Keith in various documents; I have standardised on Keyt, which is the spelling he used on his enlistment form.
25. Affidavit sworn by Keyt in Sydney, 19 May 1942. Keyt documents.
26. Bombardier is a rank in the Royal Artillery, equivalent to a Corporal in the infantry; Lance-Bombardier is equivalent to Lance-Corporal.
27. Johor was at that time one of the Unfederated Malay States; in effect a British protectorate.
28. Extensive and thorough searches for Lau's family have been carried out in Malaysia in 2012–14 by Captain Ho Wing To, one of the group of twenty-three, and Professor Patrick Seow Koon Tan, the son of another of those rescued by Lau. Advertisements have also been placed in Singaporean and Malaysian newspapers. Despite their best efforts no trace of the Lau family can be found.
29. Letter Lau to Ride, Chunking, 10 November 1942, via Elizabeth Ride.

30. The Catalina was technically an amphibian, i.e., it could operate from land or water. In all the operations described here it was used only in the waterborne role and will be referred to as a flying boat.
31. It was a Catalina of this squadron, piloted by Squadron Leader Leonard Birchall, RCAF, who detected the Japanese task force and transmitted the warning which enabled the Royal Navy to avoid what could have been a devastating attack
32. Some never reached the National Archives due to enemy action, loss in transit, fire, etc. A few others are missing having been removed by unscrupulous researchers.
33. This section is based on an unpublished memoir written just after the war by Gerhard Rijnders for his family and sent to me by his son.
34. These dates were later amended to 21 and 25 February, while 21 March remained unchanged,
35. Russell, Diary No. 3, p. 10.
36. Russell, Diary No. 3, pp. 9–10. There is no mention of the identity of the wireless, nor of the exact nature of the problem.
37. RAF aircraft were allotted 'squadron codes' which were painted in large letters on either side of the fuselage. The first two letters indicated the squadron; which were followed by a dash and then a letter identifying the individual aircraft.
38. Sources, ORB books for relevant squadrons
39. Farquharson, *For your Tomorrow: Canadians and the Burma Campaign, 1941-1945*, p. 57.
40. As far as is known, it was unusual for the pilot to include the names of men involved in clandestine operations in their log books; it is fortunate that in this case he did.
41. Pulau Pandjang is a tiny island, only shown on the largest-scale maps.
42. Netherlands Military History Institute; extract from the Flying Log Book of Lt-Cdr G. F. Rijnders. It can be considered 100 per cent reliable.
43. Nelson, *The Story of Changi: Singapore*.
44. TNA WO 208/2351. The GSI(e)/E Group final report states that: '53. At the time of writing this report (i.e., early 1946) there are indications that RUSSELL and Sergeant KEYTE were held in a jail on SINGAPORE ISLAND until May 1943 when they were reputed to have been shipped to JAPAN.'

204 Special Forces Operations in South-East Asia 1941–1945

45. Nelson, *The Story of Changi*, pp. 204–5.
46. War Office letter MOS/5-620/H dated 27 February 1946.
47. Mrs Hunter's letter from the War Office is MOS/1198/S dated 29 April 1947.
48. The fates of Hunter, Keyt, Russell and Sladen were originally reported as 'missing; 21 March 1943; Burma'. It is suspected that after the war those responsible for officers' records amended the details for Hunter, Russell and Sladen to read 'Sumatra, 20 December 1942' and transferred this information for recording on the Singapore War Memorial. However, this information appears not to have been passed to the office responsible for Royal Artillery soldiers' records, with the result that Keyt's name remained with the original detail (i.e., 'Burma, 21 March 1943') and his name is, therefore, on the Rangoon War Memorial. This suggests that the fault lay with military bureaucracy and failure to communicate, rather than any deliberate intent to treat officers and soldiers differently.
49. Letter from Major Stanley Duncan to Mrs Jocelyn Russell dated 8 June 1985, via W. H. C. Hoare, Esq.
50. Hembrey, *Malayan Spymaster*, p. 189.
51. C. Cruikshank, *SOE in the Far East*; R. Gough, *SOE Singapore 1941-1942*; I. Trenowden, *Operation Most Secret, SOE, The Malayan Theatre*. See Bibliography for details.
52. There is some evidence that a battery (approximately 150–200 men) of the Singapore Royal Artillery, who were prisoners-of-war in Singapore, were shipped to the Andamans to construct the airfield.
53. Beyts, *The King's Salt*, p. 23.
54. Letter Beyts to MacKenzie dated 2 April 1943 in HS 1
55. Churchill laid down in 1943 that military operations in which large numbers of men might lose their lives ought not to be described by codenames which implied a boastful or overconfident sentiment, nor should they be names of a frivolous character.
56. Bunkum. Operation Order No 1, dated 9 December 1942 classified MOST SECRET.
57. SOE's first Far Eastern training centre was set up in Singapore, but had closed on the British surrender in February 1942. The staff then moved to India where the new GTU was opened in July 1942. It was later redesignated the Eastern Warfare School (India).

58. Whitehouse's amazing story is told in Appendix B.
59. Montague Algernon Neville Rodulfo, born 21 December 1913. Commissioned into the Royal Tank Regiment, 29 April 1939. He was usually known as 'Monty'.
60. Francis Stanley Manford, born 22 December 1921. Commissioned into the Durham Light Infantry 22 December 1939.
61. Bill Beyts was commissioned into the 6th Rajputana Rifles in 1928. After an adventurous career in Burma and India for which he was awarded the MC, he was involved in setting up the Auxiliary Units in the UK in 1940–41 which would have formed stay-behind parties in the event of an invasion. For this service he was awarded the MBE. In 1942 he returned to India where he became chief-of-staff to Colin Mackenzie at SOE (India).
62. Station C signal 4 March 1943 in TNA HS 1/465.
63. The stores recovered included wireless sets, an electrical generator and clothing, weighing, according to the ever-precise Rodulfo, 1,512lb.
64. Both in the *London Gazette*, 16 December 1943.
65. *London Gazette*, 8 December 1944.
66. Major Charles Greig, DSO, MC, Royal Artillery.
67. Captain Keith Inglis Falconar, 4th/10th Gurkha Rifles. Killed Burma 25 February 1945.
68. Major T. V. (Terence) Croley, Skinner's Horse.
69. Major R. G. H. (Richard) Duncan, 8th Royal Garwhal Rifles
70. SOE (India) document X.903 dated 22 December 1943 in TNA HS 1/46.
71. This would appear to have been the Andaman Water Monitor (*Veranus salvator Andamanensis*) which can grow up to 9 feet in length.
72. These two prisoners are mentioned in White's memoirs. He does not specify their race, but it seems more likely that they were members of the INA, since if two Japanese soldiers had been lost, it seems probable that the whole garrison would have been turned out to look for them.
73. There would almost certainly have been one or two trained 'first-aiders' but, as with previous Andaman operations, there were certainly no professional medical officers or NCOs.

74. *Clyde* sailed from Trincomalee on 25 March 1945 and surfaced at 1900 hours on 28 March at 12.07N 92.36E. The final troops came aboard at 2047 hours. *Clyde* immediately sailed for Ceylon, arriving at Trincomalee at 1100 hours on 31 March.
75. Cabinet Conclusion: Minutes and Papers: CAB 65/40/15.
76. *Clyde* Log. ADM 173.
77. 240 Squadron ORB.
78. TNA ADM 1/19341.
79. No mention is made of either leeches or snakes and Croley's report is so detailed that had they been encountered he surely would have mentioned them.
80. Hudson, SOE (India)'s chief in Ceylon, had specifically advised that there was no need for a medical officer to accompany the group. TNA HS 1/45 BB450 to BB126 dated 3 December 1943.
81. Roychowdury, *Black Days in Andaman and Nicobar Islands*, p.184.
82. The insignia of the KBE was presented by the Viceroy of India in New Delhi on 12 February 1941 – letter to the author, Central Chancery of the Orders of Knighthood, 19/1/13 dated 24 July 2013.
83. Bremner papers.
84. *Seeadler*, a three-master windjammer of 1,571grt, was one of the last ever sailing ships to be used as a warship, sinking fifteen enemy vessels in some 225 days. Her captain, von Luckner, was greatly respected by all who knew him.
85. *Uckermark* was originally named *Altmark*, and served as the tanker/support ship for the *Admiral Graf Spee*.
86. Röhwer, *Axis Submarine Successes 1939-1945*.
87. TNA FO 371/31149.
88. Bandar Shahpur was renamed Bandar Khomeini after the Iranian revolution.
89. *Duchess d'Aosta* was sailed to the UK, arriving in Greenock on 13 July 1942. Unfortunately, she caught fire while unloading and sank but was soon refloated and repaired. She was taken over by the Ministry of War Transport and served out the war as the *Empire Yukon*.
90. Operation Postmaster also saw the emergence of a remarkable Danish soldier, Anders Lassen, then serving as a private in the

SSRF. For his role in Postmaster he was given an immediate commission in the field, and subsequently reached the rank of major and was awarded the VC and MC with two bars. He died in action in April 1945.

91. Letter AD/DL/104 dated Meerut, 14 July 1943 in HS 1/230.
92. The distribution was remarkably wide and included: Secretary of State, Chief of Naval Staff, Chief of Air Staff, Foreign Office, India Office, et al.
93. War Office signal 67347 1000 26/12/41.
94. The three escapees were all very young: Alfred Martins, 19; Gerhard Neef, 19; Walter Schonian, 21. British Consul, letter, 5 December 1942
95. India Government letter dated 23 December 1942.
96. Portugal and Portuguese Overseas Possessions Order of Battle (M.I.3/6911 dated 29 July 1942).
97. Pugh MS.
98. *Moltkefels* was sunk on 11 April 1945, but *Neidenfels* survived the war.
99. *Tannenfels* was still in Bordeaux on 8 December 1942 and was severely damaged by British commandos (Operation Frankton, i.e. the 'Cockleshell Heroes'). The vessel never returned to service and was sunk as a blockship in 1944.
100. Letter Consul Goa to External Affairs Department, New Delhi, No IB/1/SR-217 dated 27 November 1942.
101. Despite many assertions to the contrary, it was not redesignated Force 136 until the move to Ceylon in December 1944.
102. Lord Linlithgow was viceroy from 18 April 1936 to 1 October 1943.
103. Group C covering China came later.
104. Letter DCE2/KV/342 dated 13 November 1941. In HS 1/230.
105. All members of the Calcutta Light Horse and Calcutta Scottish refer to the raid on Goa as Operation Creek, never as Longshanks.
106. The following nine paragraphs are based on Lewis Pugh's unpublished memoir, forwarded to this author by his family, but this ends abruptly on the night of 18 December.
107. Bremner signal to New Delhi 19 Nov 1942, para 2(k).
108. Midnapur Zamindari was a large and well-respected commercial company.

109. Grice was also a lieutenant-colonel, commanding the Calcutta Light Horse. We will meet him again in Chapter 24.
110. Lewis Pugh's memoir simply stops at this point.
111. Document 'S.O.E. (INDIA) OPERATIONS' classified MOST SECRET dated 15 March 1943 signed by 'B/B 128 for B/B 100' in TNA HS 1/230. (B/B 100 was Colin McKenzie, head of SOE Indian Mission.)
112. Leasor, *Boarding Party*, 1978, p. 56.
113. Ibid, p. 196.
114. I am obliged to Tessa and Dr Ian Bremner-Macdonald, Anne Bremner's daughter and son-in-law, for drawing this to my attention.
115. For example, Koch. R., born 1 March 1902; closed until 1 January 2063 (TNA HO 405/27883)
116. SOE(India) message N0. 640 dated 21 December 1942.
117. FO letter 12906/1859/G dated 26 December 1942.
118. SOE(India) signal No 962 3 February 1943. This message is confusing as letters are used both to designate paragraphs, but also to denote *Ehrenfels* (A) and its crew (B). Nevertheless, in Para C the reference to 'B' seems to be to the previous paragraph and not to the crew. Perhaps the fact that the signal was drafted at about 11 p.m. might explain the drafter's confusion.
119. Foreign Office signal No 041 dated 6 February 1942.
120. SOE(India) signal No993 dated 9 February 1943.
121. TNA WO208/760 BIS Survey No 7/42 dated 14 February 1942.
122. Information from his grandson, Brigadier Simon Knapper.
123. They were Yard Numbers 207 and 208, respectively.
124. 'Flower' class corvette. Displacement 1,036 tons; length 205ft; beam 33ft; draught 11ft.
125. Davies, in the notes on his copy of *The Sea Wolves* is adamant that there were no wirelesses aboard. The SOE report is equally adamant that there were, and it seems that this was more likely to be correct.
126. MS note in Davies' copy of *The Sea Wolves*.
127. Leasor claims that Davies considered and rejected calling in at Colombo (p. 140.). Davies notes: 'Colombo was never considered. I went right into Trincomalee harbour and visited RN HQ who gave me clearance.' (Davies MS note)

128. Leasor's map shows *Phoebe* sailing through the straits between India and Ceylon. Davies has amended this to show that they sailed south about.

129. Fergie claims that there were a 'number of naval people aboard, whose mission was to start *Ehrenfels*' engines, cut the anchor chains, etc.' This is the only mention of naval people being involved (apart from the ex-RN Davies) and Fergie may well have been confusing them with the 'SAS types'.

130. These were *Deutschland* (renamed *Lützow* in 1940), *Admiral Scheer* and *Admiral Graf Spee*.

131. At least one memoir mentions this, but in view of the known attitude of the RN and RIN this seems unlikely and no warships are known to have been waiting offshore on the morning of 9 March.

132. The manager of the Burmah-Shell refinery was also the British vice-consul.

133. Duguid MS.

134. '*Achtung*!' (= attention/beware!) is the standard German shout to alert others in a group of impending danger, in this case, the sentry's shipmates. That the approaching *Phoebe* was then challenged in English should have caused no surprise, since it was highly unlikely that any seafarer in those waters would have spoken German and most, both Portuguese and Goan, would have understood at least basic English.

135. Leasor suggests that the injectors had been removed, but this cannot be confirmed.

136. Leasor, *Boarding Party*, 1978, p. 223, MS note by Davies.

137. SOE India Report dated 15 March 43, para 21.

138. Letter Duguid to Catto, 20 April 1976.

139. His WA/1/ES-125 dated 18 March 1943, paragraph 12.

140. This suggests that the total Axis personnel in all four ships on 8 March 1943 was: 106 arrested, five killed in the attack, plus three removed by British as prisoners, for a total of 114.

141. Anne Bremner, Narrative.

142. TNA HO 334/222/48070. He married Angela Ford in Uckfield, Sussex in 1952 and died in July 1998.

143. *Teia Maru* also brought thirteen people not of US nationality as normal civilian passengers.

144. SOE(India) signal No 216 dated 2125 11 March 1943.
145. SOE(London) signal No 315 dated 12 March 1943.
146. *The Times*, 11 March 1943, page 3, col 2.
147. Express Letter from A.D. (Fraser) to C.D. (Gubbins) AD/DL/104, Meerut 14 July 1943.
148. W. Catto, *Calcutta Light Horse AF(I) 1759-1947*, p. 90.
149. A German U-boat base was later established at Penang in Malaya, but that did not come into use until October 1943.
150. Leasor, *Boarding Party*, 1978, p. 188.
151. Wynn, *U-Boat Operations of the Second World War*, Volume 1, p. 136. See also Vause, *U-boat Ace, the story of Wolfgang Lüth*, pp. 145–51.
152. In later life Dennis recorded a long interview with a friend. Dennis died in 2004 and I am indebted to Mrs Pearl Metcalfe for making a copy available to me which forms the basis of what follows.
153. DEMS were merchant ships armed with low-angle guns for use against surfaced submarines and high-angle guns or machine-guns for use against aircraft. These were manned by soldiers of the Royal Artillery Maritime Regiment or, as in *Woolgar*, by Royal Navy gunners.
154. Captain Iversen was unintentionally left behind aboard his ship, but found a deserted lifeboat and after eighteen days alone reached Sumatra on 25 March. He managed to evade the Japanese for a while, but was captured in September and held in various camps in Sumatra until being freed in September 1945
155. It is known that HM Submarine *Taurus* bombarded Ross Island on the morning of 13 March 1944 and this may have been the occasion Dennis was reporting.
156. TNA ADM 1/19341
157. The second prisoner was Sergeant Harold Wynne, RAF, the sole survivor of Liberator KH250 shot down over Port Blair on 17 May 1945, who was held until 17 August 1945, when he was murdered by lethal injection. This was properly investigated after the war but was never brought to trial as there was considered to be insufficient evidence. However, the chief suspect, Lieutenant Toyosima Taneji, was tried for other war crimes and executed on 28 May 1946 (Air Historical Branch D/AHB(RAF)8/27 dated 10 January 2013).

158. As with many Chinese names Lau's name is transliterated into English with a variety of spellings. However, in a letter he sent to Ride he clearly signs himself as 'Lau Teng Kee' so that is the spelling I will use.
159. Elizabeth Ride, Dr Patrick Tan, Prof Peter Cunich, Captain Ho Weng Tho, Iris Chan, Barry Peek.
160. Keyt was posted to Combined Services Detailed Interrogation Centre (India (CSDIC(I)) which was controlled by GSI(e).
161. E-mail Prof Peter Cannich, Hong Kong University, 27 Sep 2012.
162. Information from Prof Cunich.
163. This is described by Dr Eleanora Tan Gaik Choo in the book co-authored with her husband, Dr Peter Tan Ewe Aik, *Prescriptions of Faith*.
164. For example, Keyt's records were held by the Royal Artillery Records Office until well after the war and then transferred to the Army Personnel Centre, where they remain.
165. Copy supplied to DMOM by Elizabeth Ride.

Select Bibliography

Books
General
Nelson, David, Captain, Singapore Volunteer Corps, *The Story of Changi, Singapore*, Changi Museum Private Ltd, Singapore, 2001.
Ride, Edwin, *BAAG Hong Kong Resistance 1942-1945*, Oxford University Press, Hong Kong, 1971.

Operation Minerva
De Man, J. Th. A., *Opdracht Sumatra, Het Korps insulinde*, Uitgeverij Uniebook bv, Houten Netherlands, 1987.
Farquarson, R., *For Your Tomorrow. Canadians and the Burma Campaign 1941-1945*, Trafford Publishing, Bloomington, IN USA, 2004.
Hembry, Boris, *Malayan Spymaster*, Monsoon Books, Singapore, 2013.
Tan Gaik Choo, Dr Eleanora and Tan Ewe Aik, Dr Peter, *Prescriptions of Faith*, Areca Books, Malaysia, 2011.

Operation Longshanks/Creek
Catto, W., *Calcutta Light Horse AF(I) 1759-1947*, Gale & Polden, Aldershot, 1957.
Leasor, J., *Boarding Party*, Heinemann, London, 1978.
Leasor, J., *The Sea Wolves* Corgi edition, London, 1980 (*Boarding Party* in paperback and retitled).

Operation Baldhead
Beyts, G. H. B., *The King's Salt*, privately published, 1996.
Bickersteth, A. C. *O.D.T.A.A.*, Aberdeen University Press, Aberdeen, 1953.
Roychowdhury, R., *Black Days in Andaman and Nicobar Islands*, Manas Publications, New Delhi, 2004.

SOE
Beevor, J. G., *SOE Recollections and Reflections 1940-45*, Bodley Head, London, 1981.
Cruikshank, C., *SOE in the Far East*, Oxford University Press, Oxford, 1983.
Gough, R. *SOE Singapore 1941-1942*, William Kimber, London, 1985.
Hembry, B., *Malayan Spymaster*, Monsoon Books, Singapore, 2011.
Trenowden, I., *Operations Most Secret, SOE The Malayan Theatre*, Crecy Books, Manchester, 1994.

MI9
Foot, M. R. D., and Langley, J. M., *MI9, the British secret service that fostered escape and evasion 1939-1945 and its American counterpart*, Book Club Associates, London, 1971.

Naval
Hermon Gill, G., *Royal Australian Navy 1942-45*, Australian War Memorial, Canberra, 1968.
Jordan, Roger, *The World's Merchant Fleets, 1939*, Chatham Publishing, London, 1999.
Rohwer, Jürgen, *Axis Submarine Successes 1939-1945*, Naval Institute Press, Annapolis, 1983.
Roskill, S. W., *The War at Sea*, Volume I and Volume III Part I, HMSO, London, 1954.
Vause, Jordan, *U-Boat Ace, the Story of Wolfgang Lüth*, Airlife, Shrewsbury, 1992.
Wynn, Kenneth, *U-Boat Operations of the Second World War*, Volumes 1 and 2, Chatham Publishing, London, 1997.

Documents/Interviews
Colbert, Company Sergeant Major, Bedfordshire & Hertfordshire Regiment; Diary 10 February – 9 March 1942; document; via RHQ, The Royal Anglian Regiment.
Deakes, Mrs Millicent D.; *I Was There*; typescript; via www.jenny familyhistorian.wordpess.com
Fergie, Kenneth R., Trooper, Calcutta Light Horse; Interview; tape; National Army Museum 33913 (1991-02-103)

Haid, Stanley S., Sergeant, Australian Army; 'My Escape from Singapore'; transcript of radio talk; via National Archives of Australia (SP300/3; 3252316).

Jacups, Howard, Lieutenant, Australian Army; *Escape from Singapore; Singapore to Sydney in 43 days*; manuscript; via Australian War Memorial (AWM/MSS1633).

Keyt, Richard Anthony, Sergeant, Royal Artillery; Affidavit sworn at Sydney, 19 May 1942; document; in personal documents from Army Personnel Centre, Glasgow

MacKenzie, Colin M; Interview; tape; Imperial War Museum (Cat No 9471).

McCarthy, Denis A. MacK., Major; *Andaman Interlude*; document; British Library (Mss Eur F161/27).

Thompson, R. G. B., Major, Bedfordshire & Hertfordshire Regiment; Letter to his family, 7 March 1942; document; via RHQ, The Royal Anglian Regiment.

Turcan, Charles I., Trooper, Calcutta Light Horse; Interview; tape; National Army Museum (1991-02-300).

Whitehouse, D.; Interview; tape; via Pearl Metcalfe.

Index

205 Squadron RAF 25, 29
222 Group RAF 15, 25
240 Squadron RAF 65
26th Indian Div 33
321 Squadron RAF 1, 25, 26, 29–31
4/10 Gurkha Rifles 49
413 Squadron, RAF 25, 29, 43
7 War Crimes Investigation Team 195

ABDACOM 4
Abwehr 131
Aceh 5
Adams, JA, C/Sgt 151–2
Admiral Scheer, 'pocket battleship' 85, 106
Africa Shell, tanker 95
Agent 36 (Lau Teng Kee) 193–4
Allen, F., Sgt R Signals 74
Allied ship losses 178
Allied ships sunk 101
Andaman islands 37, 46–90
Anfora 169–70
Anfora, freighter 122, 161, 168
Asama Maru, liner 93
Atlantis, raider 96, 125

BAAG 11, 13, 41, 145, 193
Bacon, Op 86
Bakla, Joseph 57, 60–69
Bakla, Peter 57
Baldhead I, Op 40, 55–69, 70–3, 184
Baldhead II, Op 58, 70–3

Baldhead III, Op 74
Baldhead IV, Op 76–84
Baldhead V, Op 80–1
Baldhead VI, Op 82
Baldhead VII, Op 82
Baldhead VIII, Op 82
Ballygunge Maidan 153
Balmoral, Op 87
Baratang Island 62
Barbara, Italian freighter 110
Bedfordshire & Hertfordshire Regiment 19
Bernardini, Heinz 172–3
Beyts, G. H. B., LtCol 55, 70–3, 127, 138
Bibundi, tug 112
Bird, Mr 50, 64
Bissell, C. L., Maj-Gen 14
Bluff island 80
BOAC 93
Boarding Party (book) 92, 176
Bogota, freighter 105–6
Bombay 155, 178
Borchers, Hans 172
Braunfels, freighter 120, 120, 161, 166, 168, 169–70
Breakfast Bay 74
Bremner, LtCol Claude 94, 120–1, 126, 132, 142, 167, 170
Bremner, Mrs Anne 133, 135, 142, 170, 181
Brereton, L.H., Maj-Gen 53
bribery 140
British Chinese Unit 196
Brontë, Italian freighter 110

Bryden, W. D., Tpr, 150
Buccaneer, Op 85
Bull, R. H., Lt RN 82–3
Bunkum, Op 56
Burton Stewart, Maj 14, 132–9,
  144, 153, 161

Caboto, freighter 110
Cabral, Col. José 93, 120–1, 128,
  170
Calcutta Light Horse 141, 146–50,
  184
Calcutta Scottish 141, 146–8, 150–
  3, 184
Calcutta 131
Car Nicobar 86
Catalina, flying boat 3, 15, 25, 26,
  28–9, 200
Catto, W., Maj 176
Cawthorn, W. J., Brigadier 15, 28,
  42
Ceylon 3, 5
Chatham Island 54
Chiang Kai Shek 14, 85
China Bay 25
Chopsticks, Op 13, 32–3, 41, 145
Churchill, Winston 6
Clarke, G. H. J., Tpr 150
Clearing House 33
Clyde, HMS (submarine) 82, 84–7
Cochin 141–2, 153, 155
Conte Verde, liner 93
Countenance, Op 110–11, 162
Creek Force 161
Creek, Op (*see also* Longshanks) 130
Croley, Terence, Maj 48, 76–81,
  88–90
Crossley 144, 153, 161, 166
CSDIC(I) 11, 21

Culverin, Op 6
Dakar 18
Darvall, L., Air Cdre 15
Davies, B., Cdr RN 157–9, 180
De Gaulle, Gen 18
De Vries 8, 10, 58, 70–3
Deakes family 50
Detachment 404 (OSS) 86
Dewis, W. H., Maj 151
Dickins, Sgt, RSignals 57, 59, 66,
  69, 74
Dogleg, Op 151–2
Drachenfels, freighter 122, 161,
  166, 168–70
Dresden, freighter 105
Duchessa d'Aosta, liner 112
Duguid, R. H., Capt 152, 154, 161,
  166, 181
Duncan, R. G. H., Maj 76

E Group 33
Eagle Claw, Op 44
Ehrenfels, freighter 92, 118, 122–6,
  131, 138–9, 141, 161–8, 169–70,
  176–8, 180, 182
Elsa Essberger, supply ship 106
Emden, cruiser 95
'Emily', flying boat 51
Emmy Friedrich, tanker 107
'*Essberger*' (codeword) 103, 105
Ettapendienst 104
Exporter, Op 18

Falconar, K. J., Capt 74–81
Farmer, F. D., Cpl 150, 166
Fergie K. R., LCpl, 150, 154, 161, 166
Ferrarganj 89
Flipper, Op 44
Folboats 77, 82

Fort de Kock 33
General Service Corps 196
GHQ India 2, 14, 17, 37, 41, 56, 127
Graf Spee, 'pocket battleship' 95, 105, 181
Great Andamanese 47
Greig, CL, Maj 74–82
Grice, W, Lt Col 132, 148–50, 153, 180
Gripsholm, liner 93, 173
GSI(e) 11, 13, 18, 37, 194
Gunn, T. B., LtCol 151
Gyan Singh 57

Habib Shah 57, 60–69, (death) 65
Harmes, Anton 172
Harrison (skipper) 180
Hartley, A., General Sir 14
Hatch I, Op 82
Hatch II, Op 84
Hatch III, Op 84
Head Office (HQ SOE) 139, 174–5
health 88
Heath, Lt Col 6
Helfrich, C. E. L., Adm 4
Hembry, Boris 6, 40,
Hislop, J., Maj 5RGR 144, 153, 161,
Ho Wing Tho, Capt, SAL 197
Hohenfels, freighter 110
Hong Kong 12
Hooghly river 55
Hopper Barge No 5 *see Phoebe*
Hotspur, Op 130–7, 148
Hudson, C., Lt Col RASC 7, 9, 35
Hunter, Alex, Capt RE 15, 20–1, 23, 28, 34–5, 39, 193, 197, 199

ICRC 12

Indian National Army (INA) 46, 89
Indraghiri, river 5, 19
Irwin, N. M. S., LtGen 139
ISLD 6, 7
Ivory Coast, Op 44

Jackman, R., Col 34
Jarawa, the 47–8, 61, 66, 90

Kanhoji Angre 48
Kawasaki Harumi, Capt 50
Kempetei, the 7, 33
Keyt(e), R., L/Bdr 15, 21–3, 34–5, 39, 193, 196–200
Kharaksavala 58, 141, 145
Koch, Mrs G. 134–7, 143
Koch, R. (aka Trompeta) 131–7, 143
Koggala 25
Königsberg, cruiser 95
Kormoran, raider 96
Korps Insulinde 7
Kota Raja 2, 36
K-XV, HNethMS, submarine 7, 8, 10

Lane, F/Lt 29
Lau Teng Kee, Sgt 22–4, 28, 32, 35, 39, 198–200
Laurenço Marques 93, 121
Laversuch, V., Maj, Int Corps 113
Law, C. J. D., LCpl 150
Leasor, James 92, 134, 158–9, 176, 179
Lees, A., AVM, RAF 25
Leyton, G., Adml, RN 14
Likomba, tug 112
Longshanks, Op 56, 83, 129–130, 141, 144, 173, 177, 181
LRDG 41

Lüth, W, Korvettenkapitän 179
Macfarlane, A. F., LCpl 150
Mackenzie, C. H., SOE(India) 127,
  133, 138, 174
Maid Honor, trawler 112
Manford, F. L., Capt DLI 72
March-Phillips, Gus, Capt 113
Marienfels, freighter 110
Marks (Nazi crewman *Ehrenfels*)
  140, 171, 181
Matriarch/Valour, Op 9, 40
'Mavis', flying boat 51
Maxwell-Hudson, Flt/Lt 29
Mayo, Earl of 48
McCarthy, D., Maj 36, 56–73, 88
McCormac, Cpl 12
McEwan, C. M. M., Capt 145, 153,
  161, 163
Medan 1, 2, 5, 33
Meerut 127, 139, 140
MI9 11, 13, 200
Michel, raider 97
Mickleham, Op 6
Military Police Battalion 49, 56
Miller, W., 152
Minerva I, Op 1–44, 184, 193, 200
Minerva II, Op 31
Ministry of Economic Warfare 171
Ministry of War Transport 141
Molesworth, G. N., LtGen 14
Monsoon, Op 129
Monte Pascoal, liner 105
Mormugao harbour 92, 94, 132,
  142, 155

Narbada, HMIS, frigate 87
Nelson, D., Capt, SVC 32
Netherlands Institute of Military
  History 198

Nias, island 39
Noble, W.M., LCpl, 150
North Staffordshire Regiment 49
Nuneaton, launch 113

O-24, HNethMS (submarine) 8, 10,
  58, 67, 70–3
Oesthaven 5
Omar Khayyam 84
Ongi 47
Operational Report Book (ORB)
  26, 43
Orion, raider 95
OSS 86
Outram Road gaol 33

Padang 3, 5, 7, 8, 19,
Palembang 3, 5
PanAm 93
Panjim 133
Patterson, J 152
PBY, *see* Catalina
Pearson, A. (SOE) 128, 138
Pedal, Op 54
Pel, H. G. C., Maj 4, 7, 8,
Peterson, Alex, SOE 128
Phoebe, hopper barge 141, 155–61,
  179, 181
Pinguin, raider 97, 125
Pocock Island 86
Popcorn, Op 87
Popski's Private Army 41
Port Blair 48, 53, 85, 87
Port Campbell 75
Port Glasgow 156
Portland, freighter 106
Portugal 93
Postmaster, Op 112–14, 140,
  144

Prince Henry, HMCS, armed merchant cruiser 108
Pugh, L., Lt Col RA 128, 131–8, 144, 148, 153, 161
Pulau Pandjang 31
Pulau Weh 2, 8

Ramification, Operation 114–15
Recce boats, description 77
Replenishment at sea, German 97–8
Ride, L., LtCol, BAAG 13, 14. 198
Ridgway, W. R., LtCol 11, 34
Rijnders, G., LtCdr, RNethN 27, 30–1, 38–9, 199
Rodolfo, M., Maj RTR 70–3
Röfer, Captain 142, 165, 169
Roosevelt, President 85
Ross Island 50, 190
Royal Signals 83, 89
Russell, B., S/Ldr RFAFVR 1, 13, 17, 20, 23, 27–8, 32, 37, 39, 42, 193–7, 199–200
Russell, Jocelyn 34

Sabang 2, 29, 36
Sandys-Lumsdaine, C., Lt 150
SAS 41
Scheepens, Capt 4, 9
Schomberg, R. C. F., LtCol 117
Scott, WgCdr, RCAF 29–30
The Sea Wolves (film) 92, 179
Seeadler, raider 95
Shakespeare, William 84, 184
Shalimar, HMS, submarine 54
Shaw, A., Capt 82
Shortland, Peter 173
Simaleur island 16, 27, 31
Singapore 1, 2
Sladen, Capt F 5, 13, 18, 19–20,

28, 34–5, 38, 39,193–4, 197, 199–200
SOE(India) 7, 36, 56, 117, 127–30, 132, 176
Sophie Marie, HMIS 49
Spears, General 18
Spike Island 60
Sten gun 30, 40, 65, 69, 163
Stenhouse, N., LCpl 150
Stilwell, Gen 14
Sturmfels, freighter 110
Subhas Chandra Bhose 51
submarines, Japanese 99–100
Sumatra 1, 2, 36

Tan Gaik Choo, Dr Eleanor 197
Tan, Dr Patrick 197
Tannenfels, freighter 107
Tanner, J. D.,Tpr 150, 166
Taurus, HMS, submarine 73
Taylor, G. F., Col 175
Teizo, Adml 88, 191
Teia Maru, liner 173
The Times newspaper 175
Thomas, D., Sgt, RSignals 76
Thompson sub-machinegun 96, 163
Thor, raider 96
transmitter, Goa 118
Treasury, the 140
Trincomalee 158
Troemon 8
Trompeta *see* Koch
Turcan, C. I., LCpl 15, 165

U-181 (German submarine) 179
U-boat successes 177–8
U-boats, 100–1
Uckermark, freighter 107

Ussukuma, liner 105

Viceroy, the 138
Vulcan, tug 113

Wagongo, German freighter 114
Wameru, German freighter 114
War Memorial Rangoon 1
War Memorial Singapore 1
Warren, A. Lt Col RM 5
Watson, C. H., LCpl 150
Wavell 4, 13, 55, 118, 142
Wavell ,A. Gen 177
Weißenfels, freighter 110
White, L., Capt, RE 82, 88, 144–5, 153, 161

Whitehouse, Dennis 52, 64
Wijnmalen, H. E. 1stLt 7, 10
Wildenfels, freighter 110
Wilson, I. B., Tpr 150
Windhuk, liner 105
Wingfield, Lt Cdr 74
wireless 158
Whitehouse, D. A. B., RN 188–92
Wolf, raider 95
Woodford, C. R. B., LtCol 151
Wooldridge, R. H., Sgt, RSignals 76
Woolgar, freighter 52
Wylie, G. 152